FOREWORD BY PATRICK RICARD
CEO, PERNOD RICARD

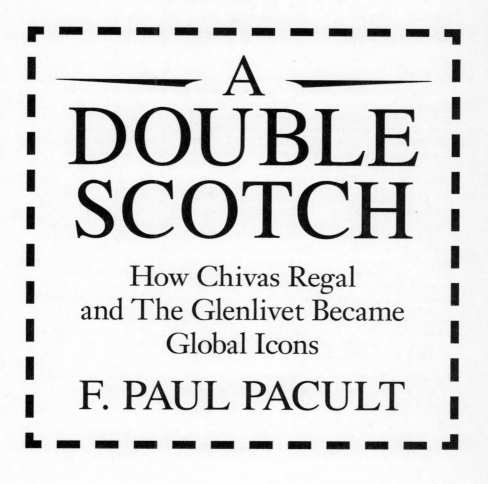

A

DOUBLE SCOTCH

How Chivas Regal
and The Glenlivet Became
Global Icons

F. PAUL PACULT

WILEY

JOHN WILEY & SONS, INC.

For Sue
The way you changed my life

Published by John Wiley & Sons, Inc., Hoboken, New Jersey.

Published simultaneously in Canada.

For general information on our other products and services please contact our Customer Care Department within the United States at (800) 762-2974, outside the United States at (317) 572-3993 or fax (317) 572-4002.

Wiley also publishes its books in a variety of electronic formats. Some content that appears in print may not be available in electronic books. For more information about Wiley products, visit our web site at www.wiley.com.

Library of Congress Cataloging-in-Publication Data:

Pacult, F. Paul, 1949–
    A double scotch : how Chivas Regal and The Glenlivet became global icons / by F. Paul Pacult.
        p.   cm.
    Includes bibliographical references.
    ISBN 0-471-66271-2 (cloth)
    1. Whiskey industry—Scotland—History.   2. Glenlivet Distillery—History.
    3. Chivas Brothers Limited—History.   4. Seagram Company.   I. Title.
HD9395.G73S366   2005
338.7′66352′09411—dc22

                                                                2004021372

Printed in the United States of America.

10   9   8   7   6   5   4   3   2   1

Contents

Foreword

IT IS WITH great pride and more than a touch of humility that I have the honour to be the current custodian of Chivas Regal and The Glenlivet. Pernod Ricard bought these two brands in 2002. Such is their international significance that we are now the largest Malt Whisky company, and the third largest Scotch Whisky company, in the world today.

As spirits journalist F. Paul Pacult depicts in *A Double Scotch,* the Speyside region in the North East of Scotland is the heart of the Scotch Whisky region, with its distinctive style and origins running back to the days of illicit distilling in its remote glens. Two whiskies typify this region in their own authoritative way. Chivas Regal, renowned and admired for its easy, smooth fruity style owes its character to the great single malt distilleries of Speyside including The Glenlivet, Glen Grant, Longmorn, and of course Strathisla. At the same time, The Glenlivet can rightly claim to be the single malt that started it all—even the Speyside region itself was originally called Glenlivet. Above all, the histories of Chivas Regal and The Glenlivet stem from the fascinating and visionary character of their founders—Scotsmen whose perseverance and determination to achieve the highest quality is a legacy that Pernod Ricard is proud to inherit and adhere to.

Chivas Regal's first real claim to fame came when Queen Victoria bestowed a royal warrant on the brand in 1843. Immediately it became fashionable among her loyal local aristocracy. But such a level of interest turned out to be only a ripple in comparison with the lucky break it subsequently enjoyed on the international stage. Reacting to the austerity of the war years, America took the brand to its heart. The era was confident and optimistic, and the people were generous and passionate about sharing good times together. Making the most of life was what mattered. Pretty soon Chivas became a firm favourite with celebrities like Frank Sinatra and the Rat Pack. Thus, the drink that was born in the magical highlands of Scotland truly came of age in boom-time America.

But it hasn't stopped there. Chivas Regal is now in demand in over 150 markets around the world—indeed, it is probably the most famous whisky in the world.

Such was the reputation of illegal whisky from the Glenlivet area that King George IV would drink nothing else during his visit to Edinburgh in 1822. Then, in 1823, the Excise Act was issued to encourage legal distilling. One man seized this opportunity to achieve his vision of perfect whisky. George Smith took the first legal distilling license in the parish of Glenlivet in 1824. While his legal distillery drew many threats from rival (still illegal) distillers, by 1844 *The Real Glenlivet Whisky* was being offered as far away as London. Soon the name *Glenlivet* became synonymous with quality.

What made The Glenlivet the definitive single malt as early as the 1840s is still true today: mineral-rich water; taller, wider stills; careful, slower, more gradual maturation; and a perfect location. These particularities have made it the benchmark by which all other single malts are judged. It is the definitive single malt that is still often imitated . . . but never equaled. I highly recommend it to you!

For me, Chivas Regal and The Glenlivet represent Scotch Whisky at its best—legends in their own right, with their distinctive taste and fascinating histories. As you will soon see, F. Paul Pacult has done an excellent job in telling their stories.

So—pour yourself a glass of Chivas Regal or The Glenlivet, sit back, and enjoy *A Double Scotch!*

PATRICK RICARD
Chairman and Chief Executive Officer,
Pernod Ricard

Preface

Sparks and
Bonfires in Whiskyland

I STARTED WRITING about Scotch whisky in 1989. Rich Colandrea of the *New York Times* asked me to write a story about Scotch whisky for a special advertising section in the *Times* Sunday magazine. The projected publication date was the first Sunday in December of that year. A month after signing the contract, I traveled to Scotland in May to conduct my research. Considering that I'm notorious for having less than brilliant memory skills, I recall that inaugural trip extraordinarily well. Something deep within me started to stir the day I was driven deep into the misty, green, and desolate Scottish Highlands on the winding A9, the main road that stretches from Scotland's Midlands all the way north to the town of Wick in the northern Highlands.

Though it wasn't raining, brooding clouds hung over the Highlands like a dark gray umbrella. Past the towns of Pitlochry and Blair Atholl, the snow-capped Cairngorm Mountains towered to the right of the A9 and the Monadhliath range rose like a monolithic giant to the left. *No wonder the Highlanders made whisky*, I wrote in my journal, my hand shaking from the chill, as the rugged, lonely, and dank but somehow beautiful landscape flashed by the passenger-side car window. Leaving the A9 at the exit marked "Boat-of-Garten/A95," I was unaware at the time that I would travel this route at least a dozen more times over the ensuing years as my fascination with Scotland and its whiskies grew from a flickering spark to a blazing bonfire.

Though I was an admitted whisky neophyte, the name of the first malt whisky distillery that I visited had a recognizable ring to it: The Glenlivet. The name was familiar because The Glenlivet was the best-selling single malt Scotch whisky in the United States. Still is. Vibrant impressions about my first stop at The Glenlivet included the sweet, beery, malted barley smells that permeated the atmosphere of the entire distillery complex, the spotless, shining, almost noble images of the tall copper pot stills, and the serene, rolling countryside that surrounded the distillery property. Fast-running streams and grazing sheep seemed to be present everywhere. When the sun emerged from the clouds in narrow golden bands, the color contrast from the ashy gray stone buildings to the intensely verdant hillsides to the cobalt blue patches of sky forced me to stop and gaze. The pastoral, narrow trough-like location is known as Glenlivet, the river valley in which Scotland's finest malt whisky has been made, legally and illegally, for centuries. As it turns out, Glenlivet is the setting for much of the first two parts of A Double Scotch.

Since that initial foray in 1989, Scotland and its whiskies have become integral parts of my being as a writer and as a person. On my third trip to Scotland in 1991, Logan Air, an internal carrier, lost every piece of my luggage, and consequently, I quickly became acquainted with Marks & Spencer, the U.K. department store chain. Three months after Logan Air sent me a compensation check for $1,700, my luggage with no prior warning turned up at my New York office. In 1993, I traveled the length and breadth of Scotland writing a New York Times story on the intertwined histories of golf and Scotch whisky. At the Brora Golf Course, I found myself reluctantly, and awkwardly, pitching short iron shots over the sheep that were grazing around nearly every green. Brora's greens were actually ringed with electric shock wires to protect them from the sheep. I played so poorly that day, though, it is the only time I've ever heard sheep boo.

In 1995 for another Times story, I performed a different job in a different distillery each day over the course of 12 extremely long and

The Glenlivet distillery in Banffshire.

arduous days. During that dreamlike period, I cut peat in peat fields in Speyside. I worked in a distillery mash tun room (Glengoyne Distillery), a stillroom (Cragganmore), and a warehouse (Longmorn). I filled casks with new whisky off the still at Macallan. I turned barley at Benriach. Imitating a famous assembly line skit from *I Love Lucy*, I did an action-filled stint on the Glenfiddich bottling line. I even constructed, or "raised," an oak barrel from nothing more than a bunch of staves and metal hoops at Speyside Cooperage and lived to tell about it. I sat in on blending sessions at Invergordon and created my own blend, deemed "Glen Horrible" for its ferocious nature. At times, my mind entered another dimension as I was introduced to yet another distillery worker with the first name of Ian. How many Ians could there be?

Two years later in 1997 for my monthly column in *Sky*, the Delta Air Lines in-flight magazine, I spent the night locked in the spooky aging warehouse of Highland Park Distillery in the Orkney Islands, attempting to catch a glimpse of the ghost of Eunson Magnus, the long-deceased Orkney man believed to haunt the building. Though I came away thinking that I hadn't bumped into Eunson, the warehouseman who unlocked the door at dawn assured me that though I might not have seen Eunson, Eunson doubtless saw me. The next year, 1998, I was inducted into the Keepers of the Quaich, the world's most exclusive Scotch whisky society, at Blair Castle in Perthshire. It was a rousing night of humorous speeches, singing, bagpipes, and ribald toasts recited while standing on chairs and tables, eating haggis, and drinking whisky. In other words, just a typical Thursday night in the Scottish Highlands.

And, Now, A *Double Scotch*

I conceived A *Double Scotch* knowing that a host of fine books on Scotch whisky by other writers had already been published. I wanted to explore the subject matter, however, by walking a different path. The other books have been written from the viewpoint of wide-angle examination of the distilleries, the whiskies, the whisky makers, or the industry as a whole unit.

By contrast, A *Double Scotch* maintains a keen focus on Scotch whisky's business, history, and marketing spanning more than five centuries, as viewed through the unique prisms provided by Scotland's two most illustrious brands, Chivas Regal Blended Scotch Whisky and The Glenlivet Single Malt Whisky. Among the scores of Scotch whiskies, these two brands especially, one the ultimate luxury blend, the other the quintessential single malt, have come to symbolize for whisky drinkers around the world what Scotch whisky is and should be.

A *Double Scotch* focuses largely on three enterprising, if idiosyncratic, families—the Chivas clan of Chivas Regal, the Smiths of The Glenlivet, and the Bronfmans of Joseph E. Seagram—who were alternately haunted, wounded by calamities, and rewarded for the success that befell the two brands. Intertwined with the families' compelling journeys are accounts of the continual excessive governmental taxation and ill-advised legislative interference imposed on whisky, which gave birth to an infamous era of widespread skulduggery, illicit distilling, rioting, smuggling, and even murder. Don't despair, though. For amid all the familial drama, industry intrigue, and occasional bloody mayhem thrive the inherent dry humor and survival sense of the Scots, who have always held that making whisky is an inalienable right.

Though *A Double Scotch* chronicles how a modest avocation fostered by resourceful Scottish Highlanders in the fifteenth and sixteenth centuries blossomed into a modern industry that wields enormous global influence, this is a contemporary tale. *A Double Scotch* is timely reading both for seasoned Scotch mavens and for wide-eyed beginners because Scotch whisky is more than the world's most popular and admired distilled spirit. It is *the* foremost prestige spirit of the early third millennium.

This is due, first, to Scotch whisky's immediate and irrefutable association with Scotland, throughout history a place of mythical, romantic, and mystical proportions; and, second, to Scotch whisky's aura of genuineness. Amid the present-day consumer clamor for product authenticity and impeccable credentials, Scotch whisky epitomizes the soul of its country of origin more accurately than any other fermented or distilled alcoholic beverage. Blended Scotch whiskies like Chivas Regal reflect Scotland's bold, hearty national character, whereas the single malt whiskies such as The Glenlivet identify and evoke specific Scottish Highland, Lowland, and island locations. No other distilled spirit offers such a broad array of virtues, tastes, and personalities. Scotch whisky, it can be said, is a nation, a nationality, and a notion captured in a glass bottle.

René Descartes, the seventeenth-century French mathematician and philosopher, wrote in 1637, *Cogito, ergo sum* (I think, therefore I am). My own altered version of Descartes' famous aphorism has guided the majority of my adult life and, more importantly, my career choice—*I drink, therefore I am*. That said, I recommend that you savor a dram of Chivas Regal or of The Glenlivet when you settle in to begin *A Double Scotch*. It is only natural that you, too, experience the feel, smell, and taste of the best of Scotland.

Here's to personal bonfires, sheep that boo, elusive distillery ghosts, and the scores of Scottish guys I know named Ian.

F. PAUL PACULT
Life Member, The Keepers of the Quaich

Wallkill, New York
September 2004

Map of Great Britian.

Acknowledgments

A *DOUBLE SCOTCH* became a living, breathing entity because of the following people, companies, and organizations without whose help I never could have completed the manuscript:

- Sue Woodley is my wife and business partner. Like everything we do, we researched this book together in Scotland and the United States.
- At John Wiley & Sons, Inc.: Matt Holt, Michelle Patterson, and Tamara Hummel.
- Iain Russell, the archivist from Glasgow University who was hired by Seagram in the 1990s to conduct in-depth research on the origins of both Chivas Regal and The Glenlivet. I have no doubt that Iain's generosity and painstaking research precision made *A Double Scotch* possible and accurate.
- At Chivas Brothers in Scotland: Yvonne Thackeray, Linda Brown, Alan Greig, Colin Scott, and Jim Cryle.
- At Chivas Brothers in London: Jim Long, Paul Scanlon, Robert Holmes, Christian Porta, and Martin Riley.
- At Pernod Ricard USA: Kevin Fennessey, Chris Willis, Rick Tapia, and Sandrine Ricard.
- At Pernod Ricard S.A. in France: Patrick Ricard.
- At Hunter Public Relations (USA): Joe Moscone, Amy Felmeister, and Claire Burke.

- At the Hagley Museum and Library—Soda House, Marge McNinch.
- Former House of Seagram USA marketing managers, Arthur Shapiro, Robert Dubin, and Ralph Pagan.
- Special thanks to Edgar Bronfman Sr.

PART ONE

Rascally Liquor

Prologue

The Guid Auld Drink

SCOTCH WHISKY IS the amber-hued liquid soul, the lifeblood of its nation of origin, Scotland. As an embodiment of much that makes Scotland fabled, Scotch whisky is an authentic, unique libation of place. It is the most elemental and reflective of alcoholic drinks created through two sequential biochemical transformational processes: fermentation and distillation. One Scotch whisky might smell of the damp earth after a rainfall; another of the briny maritime wind. To the delight of many of the world's imbibers, a few take on the character of ash and smoke from a smoldering fire while others evoke the delicate heather through which their water flowed. More than all other varieties of distilled spirits, Scotch whisky's faces, phases, and moods are too numerous to catalog. That is the seduction of Scotch whisky. The challenge. The surprise promised by the next sip. Scotch whisky is the ultimate distilled spirit adventure.

Whereas the lore of Scotland is largely what advances whisky's tradition, it is the business of Scotch whisky that underpins its international success. As with all consumer goods, the minds and palates of the public are nourished by the laws of commerce but steered by the stimulus of marketing. Within this upper echelon of the beverage alcohol industry, the competition is brutal and the stakes are staggeringly high. For all the romantic notions about Scotch whisky, on its business plane Darwinian rules apply.

Describing how Chivas Regal Blended Scotch Whisky and The Glenlivet Single Malt Scotch Whisky became legendary Scotch whisky brands demands chronicling their story within the greater context of the evolution of Scotland's native drink. The sagas of the Scotch whisky spirits category and its two superstars are inextricably linked. Though hundreds of Scotch whisky brands, blends, and single malts have existed over the generations of whisky production, no brands are as revered or as easily identified around the world as Chivas Regal and The Glenlivet. Chivas Regal debuted as the world's first luxury brand of blended Scotch whisky before World War I and remains the acknowledged gold standard to this day. The Glenlivet is the prototypical single malt whisky born in Scotland's most renowned Highlands river valley, Glenlivet. Through the beaconlike wattage of its reputation, The Glenlivet by the mid-nineteenth century made Scotland's malt whiskies the most prized whiskeys of all.

The founding families behind the brands, the Chivas clan of Aberdeenshire, who developed Chivas Regal, and the Smiths of Banffshire, who founded The Glenlivet Distillery, took distinctly different routes to achieve their family business objectives. The Chivas brothers, James and John, were proprietors of a highly successful grocery, wine, and spirits shop in Aberdeen, Scotland, that catered to the affluent sector of Aberdeenshire's population. Britain's Queen Victoria was so taken with their victuals and their first-class service that she granted them a Royal Warrant in 1843 to supply provisions whenever she occupied her beloved Balmoral estate, which lay west of Aberdeen. James and John Chivas did not own a distillery nor did they distill whisky. They purchased aged whiskies in barrels and then mixed them together to create blended whisky brands, the eventual crown jewel of which was Chivas Regal.

On the other hand, the father-and-son team of Smiths—George and John Gordon—were Highlands farmers by trade in the bucolic Banffshire district called Glenlivet. As their fledgling malt whisky business grew in fame, they turned to malt whisky distilling as a primary source of income. As described in upcoming chapters, the Smiths' The Glenlivet became so lionized in Britain by the 1860s and 1870s that other distillers in the district started using the word *Glenlivet* to identify their own whiskies. They took this action, not in tribute to the Smiths, but to brazenly cash in on the celebrity of the Smiths' *The* Glenlivet.

The Smiths and the Chivas brothers did share one characteristic in their approach to doing business. Each family operated under the guiding principles that product quality and authenticity and customer service must prevail above all else. Riding those codes through the harrowing peaks and valleys of Scotland's turbulent whisky industry in the nineteenth century, they adeptly conquered both regional and national marketplaces. They secured these triumphs, however, only at the cost of severe personal and professional tolls.

From the last half of the twentieth century up to the present day, succeeding families, specifically the Bronfmans of Canada and the Ricards of France, have confronted the world's increasingly complex commercial arena by continuing the founding families' quests and legacies. In the process, these groundbreaking brands have come to define in the minds of millions of global consumers what blended and single malt Scotch whisky should be.

To fully comprehend the remarkable accomplishments of the Smiths and the Chivas brothers requires laying a wide-ranging historical and terrestrial foundation that reaches much farther into the past than simply time-warping back to the late eighteenth and nineteenth centuries. The nineteenth-century world, and the centuries that preceded and critically influenced it, differed radically from our everyday life in the third millennium. The first leg in the journey of coming to know Chivas Regal and The Glenlivet is gaining a clear understanding of Scotland and of distillation, for without Scotland's idiosyncrasies and distillation's historical record, there would be no drink such as Scotch whisky. From that promontory of perspective, the tales of the founding families can be seen for what they are: stirring stories of personal courage, commitment to excellence, and commercial vision.

Put up your tray tables and make sure you have fastened your seat belts. Except for Scotch whisky, naturally, pass all drinks to the center aisle. The captain has started our initial descent into prehistoric Caledonia, the enigmatic, primitive, hostile, bone-chilling yet wonderful land we now call Scotland.

Scotland's Highlands are home to many malt distilleries.

A Magic of Locality

SCOTCH WHISKY IS and has been the quintessential people's potion. The great and the notorious, the privileged and the common alike have distilled and drunk Scotch whisky both legally and illegally for over six centuries. Novelists and poets, most notably Scotsmen Sir Walter Scott and Robert Burns, have through their words passionately celebrated Scotch whisky's comforting warmth in the breast and its stimulating effects on the mind. Robert Burns, Scotland's bard, in his late eighteenth-century poem *Scotch Drink*, called the native whisky of Scotland ". . . my Muse! guid auld Scotch Drink . . ."

Writers, though, have not been the only keen observers when it comes to Scotch whisky. Actor Humphrey Bogart commented during a slump in his film career, "I never should have switched from Scotch to martinis." Entertainer and famed Scotch admirer Joe E. Lewis quipped, "Whenever someone asks me if I want water with my Scotch, I say 'I'm thirsty, not dirty.'" But perhaps Ivor Brown, the renowned twentieth-century British drama critic, essayist, and novelist, captured Scotch whisky's essence best when he said, "Scotch Whisky is a mystery, a magic of locality. The foreigner may import not only Scottish barley but Scottish water, Scottish distilling apparatus, and set a Scot to work on them, but the glory evaporates: it will not travel" (H. Charles Craig, *The Scotch Whisky Industry Record*, 1994, p. 524).

While the legend of Scotch whisky may be exhilarating and singular, the saga of its rise first in Scotland's then in Great Britain's commercial environments has at times been more blood-soaked and chaotic than either benign or orderly. In eras past, ordinary Highland Scots who distilled whisky were arbitrarily jailed, unfairly taxed, and relentlessly hunted down by government excise agents. Many courageous Highland Scots, in the face of the unjust legislation by Parliament, sacrificed livelihoods and homes in the turmoil. A few even perished defending the right to make it. Nonetheless, Scotch whisky, both as a local libation and a national industry, flourished inside and outside the law. Because of Scotch whisky's astounding international market success against the seemingly insurmountable odds of overtaxation, wars, Prohibition, fierce whiskey industry competition, and temperance, Scotland has more than survived. It has prevailed while somehow miraculously retaining its special, innate national aura.

Scotland is a compact, pocket-size country of a mere 30,414 square miles whose remarkably enterprising inhabitants and ex-patriots have given the world such modern wonders as the telephone, the steam engine, penicillin, color photography, refrigeration, the telescope, and television. But even after all these landmark achievements and inventions that have advanced the cause of an entire civilization from the time of the Industrial Revolution forward, Scotch whisky remains Scotland's most recognized historical and commercial contribution. No other type of alcoholic beverage—wine, beer, or distilled spirit—is as closely and immediately identified with its homeland as Scotch whisky. Since genuine Scotch whisky can be produced only in Scotland, it indelibly mirrors all that is Scotland: its water and earth, its geological composition, its climate, the Scots who for generations have made it, even the nation's air.

Since the first half of the nineteenth century, the Scotch whisky industry has been a vigorous business with global ambitions. To accomplish this goal, the industry's visionary, if pragmatic, captains piggybacked its exportation onto a never-before-seen juggernaut, the rapidly expanding British Empire. By the last quarter of the 1800s, Scotch whisky was available in most ports of call around the world. Today, Scotch whisky can be found in over 200 nations.

Comprehending the purpose of Scotch whisky and, subsequently, the story of Chivas Regal and The Glenlivet means probing the nebulous mysteries and stark natural realities that compose Scotland, the landmass. Fertile, wet yet often still frightfully remote, Scotland is the world's most exotic and famous location for converting the dirty brown mash of water, grain, and yeast into the crisp, fresh-tasting, crystalline spirit that, in time, will be legally known as whisky. As part of an unforgiving North Atlantic island, coastal Scotland is sculpted by the blustery maritime influences of sea and wind. Lofty mountain peaks, deep valleys, and rolling pastures highlight inland stretches of pastoral splendor that have been shaped by rainfall, streams and rivers, and wind erosion.

Sharing the island of Britain with England and Wales, Scotland boasts a population of just over five million inhabitants. Greater Scotland includes the 787 islands of the Inner Hebrides, Outer Hebrides, the Orkneys, and the Shetlands. Of these rugged and windswept islands, 130 are inhabited. Six of the inhabited islands—Arran, Islay, Skye, Mull, Orkney, and Jura—currently produce single malt whisky.

First-time visitors to the Scottish Highlands, especially the Grampians in the heart of mainland Scotland, are typically struck by Scotland's vivid floral color displays from late April through August. The deep blue of Scottish bluebells and the golden yellow of gorse in spring; the dusty yellow of yarrow in early to midsummer; and the purple and rose-pink heather in August annually saturate the landscape in bright shades that contrast with the gray mountains, the deep green meadows, and the henna moors. Scotland is a feast for the eyes at any time of year.

Twelve millennia before the emergence of Scotch whisky and brands like Chivas Regal and The Glenlivet, the last Ice Age shaped Scotland's topography. As the massive receding glacial shelves scraped and clawed their way back to the Arctic Circle, they carved out many of the lochs (lakes) that today enhance the Scottish landscape. Loch Ness, Loch Lomond, and Loch Lochy, to cite only three, are all renowned defining aspects of Scotland's topographical personality. Interior Scotland is a land of free-flowing fresh water burns (streams) and rivers originating from the various mountain chains that dominate the central part of the nation. Central Scotland is predominantly a vertical landscape, featuring over three hundred mountain peaks that rise over 900 meters (roughly 2,950 feet). Ben Nevis in the western Highlands is Scotland's highest peak at 1,344 meters. The blue network of mountain-fed rivers and burns, along with ancient aquifers located deep within Scotland's bedrock base, provides the pure water necessary for distilling. It is no mystery why many of Scotland's malt and grain distilleries are perched next to long-established rivers and burns. Distilleries use copious amounts of water at almost every stage of whisky production.

Historians and archeologists calculate that, due to the forbidding presence of the glacial cap, the initial human presence in Scotland dawned no sooner than 10,000 to 9000 B.C. To date, the earliest known evidence of human hunter-gatherer habitation appears at Cramond, northwest of Edinburgh on the Firth of Forth, circa 8500 B.C. This nomadic group's high mobility, however, canceled any chance of unearthing a significant site. The initial Scots probably were women and children of the hunter-gatherers left behind by the ceaselessly roving bands who chased herds of game across the bleak tundra of northern Europe and the British Isles.

Agriculture, most likely in the fundamental forms of cereal grain cultivation and livestock farming, was introduced to Scotland by the early fourth millennium B.C. Tiny, primitive farms were established first in low-lying coastal pastures, then in the elevated glens and meadows that dotted the interior. At this embryonic stage, virtually everyone farmed the land as well as hunted. Scotland's damp, dank climate proved more suitable for growing hearty grains such as oats, wheat, and barley than for cultivating the fruits that were prevalent in the balmier climes of southern Europe. This environmentally influenced development in agriculture proved to be a significant step for the earliest beverage alcohol producers who, five millennia later, used malted barley initially as the key ingredient for brewing strong ale and later for distilling malt whisky from ale.

Also at this temporal point, deforestation began in earnest as Bronze Age agrarian communities cleared tracts of land to plant grains, graze livestock, and found settlements. Wood was needed for the construction of houses; for fuel to heat the crude, drafty domiciles; and for pens to protect livestock. Proving that point is an extraordinary excavation, dated at roughly 3600 B.C., of a farming community near Balbridie in Aberdeenshire. It includes a wooden structure that is approximately 26 yards long and 11 yards wide. Huge for its era, the Highlands lodge was a domicile, possibly for both families and their livestock. By the time the Romans invaded the island of Britain in 55 B.C., most of Scotland's original forests were leveled and cleared. Today, sadly, only one percent of Scotland's primeval forest remains.

Deforestation likewise indirectly affected the Scotch industry, in that, with the forests gone, the main source of fuel in prehistoric Scotland became peat. As any avid gardener knows, peat is tightly packed, decomposed vegetation (e.g., heather, gorse, grasses, weeds, and low shrubs) that has been compressed over time by layers of succeeding growth. Another loose definition bandied about in the Highlands is that peat is decomposing organic matter at about the halfway mark to becoming coal. The tradition of using peat as a primary source of fuel eventually turned into a key element of Scotland's whisky industry because peat became the customary fuel used to dry barley before it became part of the mash. Fortunately, Scotland has no shortage of peat since peat bogs still cover an estimated 810,000 hectares (over 2 million acres) of the nation's surface.

Well before Julius Caesar first set foot on Britain, or Britannia as the Romans called it, in the middle of the first century B.C., the growing of grain had been established in Scotland for more than three thousand years and peat was the leading source of fuel. Both the proliferation of grain growing, especially of barley, and the widespread harvesting and employment of peat proved three millennia later to be crucial building blocks in the formation of the fledgling whisky distilling industry.

An Awful Silence

Although the landscape of Scotland features scores of Stone, Bronze, and Iron Age ceremonial standing stones; massive burial mounds composed of grass, stone, and mud; stone watchtowers; and entire excavated villages such as Skara Brae (3100 B.C., on the main island of the Orkney Islands, no written historical account exists that we know of, prior to the recorded observations made by a Roman scribe of the first century A.D. According to historian Fitzroy Maclean in his book *A Concise History of Scotland*, second revised edition 2000, p. 6), that first recorder of Scotland's everyday doings was Tacitus, who accompanied the Ninth Legion into what is now southern Scotland from A.D. 81 to 84.

Tacitus told future generations, frequently in vivid detail, that his father-in-law, Gnaeus Julius Agricola, the Governor of the Roman Province of Britannia, rumbled north into southern Scotland with a well-oiled machine of 20,000 soldiers, including the Ninth Legion, and a fleet of ships off Scotland's east coast. Agricola's force represented approximately one-tenth of the total Roman Army. When marching, the army's ranks stretched to the horizon for about 20 miles. Having subdued most of Britannia (England), the conquering Romans yearned to gain control of the feisty and ferocious Caledonians, the name that the Romans bestowed on the various tribes of Picts who resided north of England. The dominant Pict tribe was called the Calidonii. The Romans considered the Caledonians to be dangerous and unpredictable savages. Tacitus described them as having "fair or reddish hair" and "large limbs." They were fearless combatants who regularly and with gusto took the fight to the Romans. Wrote Tacitus, "The native tribes assailed the forts; and spread terror by acting on the offensive."

At the time, Caledonia was anything but a unified nation. It could more accurately be described as a ragged, tenuously connected confederation of Pict tribes, who often fought among themselves. The common menace of the advancing Romans, however, compelled the fractious tribes to temporarily band together into a single fighting force of approximately 30,000 in late A.D. 83. Underestimating their opponent, the tribal chief Calgacus and his lieutenants decided that their course of action should be direct confrontation. In early A.D. 84, the unskilled Caledonian army, made up of farmers, hunters, and tradesmen, waged an ill-fated, hand-to-hand battle at Mons Graupius. Though they were fighting on their home turf and had a numerical advantage, the Caledonians were no match for the organized, disciplined, and relentless Roman brigades. Ten thousand Caledonians were slaughtered in a single disastrous bloodbath. The Caledonians who survived the rout retreated further into the Highlands, taking with them their women, children, and meager belongings. "An awful silence reigned on every hand; the hills were deserted, houses smoking in the distance, and our scouts did not meet a soul," reported Tacitus the day after the battle.

Just as Agricola's land and sea offensive was succeeding in bringing Caledonia under heel after Mons Graupius, orders arrived from Rome directing him to return to Britannia to regroup and refortify. With so many far-flung outposts from Britannia to Egypt to Germany to Mesopotamia, the Empire's overworked heart was deemed vulnerable to attack by marauding barbarians from the steppes of Asia. The critical middle, the solar plexus of the Empire, needed protection. Therefore, trusted, hardcore legions like those under Agricola needed to be drawn closer. As reported by Maclean in *A Concise History of Scotland* (p. 10), Tacitus bitterly wrote of this decision to withdraw from Caledonia, complaining, "Britain conquered and then at once thrown away."

Four decades later, the Roman Emperor Hadrian toured Britain. Tiring of the audacious Caledonians' pesky guerrilla-like strikes against his soldiers and encampments along the present-day border between Scotland and England, Hadrian ordered the construction of a wall, discreetly named Hadrian's Wall, which he hoped would discourage the Caledonians from future sorties. His stone wall was four meters high and two and a half meters thick; it marked the topography from Carlisle to Newcastle in what is now northern England as well as the northernmost reaches of the Roman Empire in the early second century A.D. Built between A.D. 122 and 128, the wall stands, relatively intact, to this day.

Realizing the expense in resources and troops of dealing with unruly indigenous tribes like the Caledonians, Hadrian instituted Rome's initial anti-expansion policy to firm up the Empire's center. Hadrian's stay-at-home strategy collapsed, however, when Antoninus Pius succeeded him and had Roman troops redeployed to southern Scotland to build the 37-mile-long Antonine Wall in the middle second century A.D. This stone line of defense against the dreaded Caledonians ran from the Firth of Forth to the Firth of Clyde just north of what are now Glasgow and Edinburgh.

Emperor Severus, Rome's next leader, conducted a hit-and-miss military campaign in A.D. 208 that the Caledonians fought off over the course of three years. Memories of the blood that Calgacus and his renegade force had spilled a century and a quarter earlier sharpened the tactical sense of the third-century Caledonians. Severus discovered that the Caledonians' past battlefield miscalculations had taught them never to fight the Roman legions head-on. Instead, they ceaselessly harassed them in lightning quick, hard-hitting raids. The small, mobile fighting units were difficult to capture. After invading Caledonia three times, after building 60 camps and forts, and after erecting two defensive walls, the Romans said "Enough." By the fifth century, the last remaining Roman outposts in southern Scotland and northern England were abandoned. In the end and at great cost, the Caledonian/Picts had rebuffed the world's mightiest and best-equipped army, the best strategically trained generals, and the overwhelming strength of the Roman Empire.

On such hearty disposition, love of the homeland, and single-minded determination was the fundamental character of the modern Scots built. But the invasions were just beginning.

The Four Tribes

Just who were the Pictish tribes of Caledonia that the Romans feared and respected? From what gene pools did the present-day Scots evolve to produce an elixir like Scotch whisky?

The majority of historical evidence identifies the Picts as the group that formed the core of the Caledonians. The Picts were a tribe of Celts who had arrived in Britain from continental Europe sometime in the Bronze Age (3500 to 1500 B.C.). The Celts were of Indo-European origins and dwelled first in central-western Europe during the Neolithic Age (8000 to 5000 B.C.). They were driven westward to the British Isles first by the Germanic Angles and Saxons, who invaded western Europe from the Baltic region, and then later by the Romans.

An artistic and imaginative people, the Celts constructed a vivid mythology and an earthbound philosophy that still are more than faintly evident in Ireland and Scotland. Both nations, although Christian, quietly tolerate the supposed ethereal presence of faeries, ghosts, elves, and pixies as well as the discreet practice of elemental rites and ceremonies based largely in Celtic beliefs that are thousands of years old. More than a few whisky distillers in Scotland, in fact, report "strange happenings" in warehouses and distillery buildings by unseen forces that have their basis in ancient Celtic legends. Scotland's distilleries are famous for three things: the world's best whisky, distillery ghosts, and celebrated cats who stalk the distilleries at night.

By the mid-fifth century A.D., the Romans departed from Britannia for good, leaving four main tribal groups in control of Scotland. Three of Scotland's four central societies were of Celtic lineage and communicated in similar though not identical languages. The Picts held firm mastery over the north and east of Scotland (today, the Caithness, Ross and Cromarty, Aberdeen, and Angus regions). The Britons, who also were Celts, resided mostly in Scotland's southwestern region known as Strathclyde (present-day Ayr, Kirkcudbright, and Wigtown). The Teutonic, or Germanic, tribes of Angles and Saxons moved into Scotland from northeast England and subsequently ruled the central southern Lowlands (modern-day Roxburgh, Berwick, and Selkirk). The Scots or Scoti, yet another branch springing from the thick trunk of the Celtic tree, lorded over western Scotland (Argyll and Kintyre) and the western islands (Arran, Islay, Jura). In fact, the Scots were the Gaels of Ireland, who crossed the Irish Sea and landed most likely on the long crooked finger of the Kintyre Peninsula. The Scots-Gaels introduced the Gaelic tongue to western Scotland, which about 80,000 people still speak in the western islands and Highlands. Their kingdom was called Dalriada.

During the two and a half centuries that immediately followed the final Roman evacuation, circa A.D. 430, the Irish Sea, the slender but turbulent body of water that separates extreme southwestern Scotland from the north of Ireland, was a remarkably busy corridor of salt water. According to historians Thomas Owen Clancy and Barbara E. Crawford writing in *The New Penguin History of Scotland: From the Earliest Times to the Present Day* (2001, p. 29), "Throughout the sixth and seventh centuries, the Irish Sea was abuzz with material and intellectual exchange, from Gaul to Britain and Ireland and around the points of this open saltwater loch."

This advancement of ideas, cultures, technology, and languages relates directly to two pivotal events in early Scottish history: the creation of Scotch whisky and the social impact of the spread of Christianity.

The Origin of Scotch Whisky

The Irish were acknowledged to be skilled barley farmers and brewers of strong ales, the forerunners of stout, possibly as early as 2500 to 2000 B.C. They advanced to become avid distillers at the latest by the eleventh or twelfth centuries A.D. Was it the Irish who introduced to Scotland the secrets, first, of fermenting grain into ale and then, later, distilling ale into whisky?

Though hard evidence does not yet exist, it falls within the realm of high likelihood—and deductive reasoning—that the Irish introduced and pioneered the distillation process in Scotland. Not so with brewing ale, however. Ale brewed from barley or wheat appears to have already existed in the regions of Scotland controlled by the Picts. Northern and eastern Scotland were especially good areas for grain cultivation. In his book *The Ale Trail* (1995, p. 159), British beer authority Roger Protz writes, "The earliest brewers in Scotland were . . . the Picts. . . . The Picts brewed a heather ale, the fame of which spread far beyond the borders of the remote, mountainous country. The navigator Pytheas, when he visited Scotland, recorded that the Picts brewed a potent drink."

Pytheas was the Greek geographer and adventurer who circumnavigated Britain around 325 to 320 B.C. Indeed, it was Pytheas who named the North Sea islands. He referred to them in Greek as the Pritanic Islands after a tribe called the Pritani. The Romans altered that moniker to *Britannia*, and they referred to the people as the *Britons*.

If the making of beer was already well established in Scotland, when did the art of *boiling* beer, or distillation, to make potent spirit first arrive? As detailed in Chapter 2, the first indisputable record of distilling in Scotland occurred in the late fifteenth century. Distilling knowledge itself arrived on the European continent no sooner than A.D. 800 to 900 So, the actual transfer from Ireland to Scotland of salient technological information on distilling could not have realistically happened before A.D. 1100. No one is certain. We may never know. By piecing together circumstantial evidence and conjecture, many contemporary whisky experts and distilled spirit historians estimate that widespread distillation most likely didn't have firm footing in Scotland until the fourteenth century. Chances are that the majority of early distilling in Scotland occurred in the cellars of Christian monasteries. The monks were proficient brewers at the minimum and quite possibly serviceable distillers as well.

The Impact of Christianity

From across the Irish Sea, Christian missionaries journeyed to Scotland around A.D. 560. Their "divine mission" was to convert the pagan tribes to the cause of Christ and, thereby, bring order and cohesion to wild and woolly Scotland. Stepping ashore on Scotland from Ireland in A.D. 563 was Columba, a charismatic monk and politically savvy and motivated orator. Born of aristocratic lineage, he was a favorite of the Scots-Gaels. Headquartered on the western island of Iona, Columba established a succession of monastic communities deep into Argyll to serve the local Scots-Gaels populations, who had reverted back to their pagan roots following their colonization of western Scotland. Before the Scots had migrated to Scotland, they had been northern Ireland Christians. The embracing of Christianity over traditional, environmentally infused Celtic pagan beliefs gradually altered the social and political fabric of southwestern Scotland.

Moving further north from Argyll, the energetic Columba pushed into the regions ruled by the Picts. J. D. Mackie reports in *A History of Scotland* (1964, p. 25) on Columba's zeal, "Armed with prestige, great gifts, unshrinking faith, and high oratory, Columba not only reawakened the dormant Christianity of the Scots but penetrated into Pictland . . ."

After Columba's death in 597, more missionaries fanned out across Scotland. By A.D. 750 to 800, most of the primary tribes had converted to the faith, at least outwardly. Paganism had a strong hold, however, and continued to be a quiet force for another two centuries. Over a little more than two centuries, Christianity brought, if not peace and cooperation, a fragile, nervous acknowledgment to the four groups—the Picts, Scots-Gaels, Britons, and Angles and Saxons—of medieval Scotland, whose uncharted territories overlapped. The Christian monks likewise established brewing as a commonplace activity wherever they founded outposts. Brewing eventually led to distilling. The four tribes clung to both strong ale and religion in the next three centuries, A.D. 780 to 1050, as another onslaught brought by a foreign enemy commenced.

Though Christianity dominated most regions of the four kingdoms of Scotland, long-standing loathing continued to separate the tribes. Then in the 780s, a vicious new adversary threatened Scotland's coastlines and islands. Stealthily approaching from northern Europe in sleek, oceangoing wood vessels named longships, these seafaring, fair-skinned Dane and Norwegian warriors were known as the Vikings. They swept westward across the British Isles, Greenland, and Iceland like locusts. For three hundred years beginning in the late eighth century and ending in the mid-eleventh century, all of maritime Scotland and much of the Highland interior came under attack by the swift-moving Vikings.

The impact on the destinies of the four groups was immediate and irreversible. Indeed, the regular assaults and subsequent devastation wreaked on the areas ruled by the Picts contributed to their race's decline, dilution, and eventual disappearance. Even though the heretofore politically and militarily robust Picts valiantly battled the Vikings—in many cases, triumphantly so—the defense of its islands and northern heartland, proved too much for the Pictish kingdom. Decay began to erode its core.

The vacuum created by the Picts' degeneration allowed the Gaelic-speaking Scots-Gaels of Dalriada to fill the void as they assumed control of vast areas to the north and east that the Picts had lorded over. In 843, the Scots-Gaels king, Kenneth MacAlpin who had Pictish ties, crowned himself king of both Dalriada and the Pictish kingdom, effectively becoming the first unifying monarch in Scottish history. The new realm, spanning most of what is present-day Scotland, was known as the King-dom of Alba. Over time, the Scots-Gaels' political dominance led to the renaming of Alba as *Scotia*, the forerunner of *Scotland*. By then, there was no stopping the Gaelic influence.

In the tenth century, the Scots reached out to the English to help stem the tide of the Norsemen, who were of equal threat to England. The English were far more powerful than the still, by comparison, disorga-nized Scottish monarchies. By the middle of the eleventh century, the Viking aggression in large measure abated. The extended influence of the Norsemen was evident culturally and biologically, particularly in the north of Scotland and the far northern Orkney and Shetland island chains, where intermarriage had become widespread. Scotland contin-ued, if painfully through bloodshed and social upheaval, to take shape as we know it.

In 1034, Duncan I the Gracious, seven generations removed from Kenneth MacAlpin, became the first Scotsman to ascend to a bona fide Scottish throne, with influence in all parts of Scotland and, as a bonus, northern England. Though a weak and inept leader, Duncan I's line would nonetheless, for more than 650 years, spawn generations of suc-ceeding monarchs of historical significance: Malcolm Ceann Mor; David I; Robert the Bruce; James I; Mary Queen of Scots; Charles I; James VI, who was also James I of England; and Charles Edward, who was called Bonnie Prince Charlie.

Historians David Ditchburn and Alastair J. MacDonald, in *The New Penguin History of Scotland: From the Earliest Times to the Present Day* (2001, p. 156), address the difficulties that the peoples of different races, tongues, and traditions in Scotland had in constructively coming together during the medieval era: "The Scottish realm was . . . by no means an eas-ily unified entity; it was of large extent and difficult terrain in much of its area; and the peoples of the kingdom were a very diverse assembly, emerg-ing from the early medieval groupings of Picts, Scots, Britons, Angles and Norwegians, and entailing also twelfth- and thirteenth-century Anglo-French incomers."

By the fourteenth century, the first glimmer of a genuine and dis-tinct national character emerged as conflicts with the vastly more pow-erful English galvanized Scotland's various clans, aristocrats, and fiefdoms. Under King Edward I and his son Edward II, England strove to conquer Scotland and thus unify the island of Britain under English rule. After the fiery Scots rebel William Wallace, aka *Braveheart*, was defeated then later captured by the English, the Scots needed a leader who was both militarily skilled and politically composed. Enter Robert the Bruce, Scotland's most popular historical figure, who became King of Scotland in 1306. After absorbing several early military defeats at the hands of the English, Bruce decisively routed the heavily fortified and numerically superior English force in a momentous battle at Bannockburn on June 24, 1314. In the process, Bruce pierced the heart of English confidence and, thereby, its threat of dominance. Diplomatically under the reign of Robert the Bruce, Scotland entered the international stream by becoming Europe's first nation-state since the fall of Rome. Bruce died in 1329, but his legacy put Scotland ahead of any of its diverse parts. That legacy lives on.

Over the winding, treacherous course of five and a half millennia, the modern-day race of Scots has been sculpted from an exotic amalgamation of Celtic, Scandinavian, English, Irish, French, and Anglo-Saxon ancestry, ceremony, and custom. Doubtless, one of the greatest outcomes in the history of that gradual incorporation has been Scotch whisky, the Scots' distilled barley beer. If Scotch whisky, a magic of locality and a leading distilled spirit, has existed for roughly seven centuries, how long has distillation itself been lifting up the disposition of civilization?

Reaching the Boiling Point

THE LEGACIES OF great Scotch whiskies like Chivas Regal blended Scotch whisky, and The Glenlivet single malt whisky—and all of the world's whiskeys and distilled spirits for that matter—might not exist were it not for the early dabblers in distillation. As mentioned in Chapter 1, neither the medieval Scots nor their Irish neighbors invented distillation. A handful of nineteenth-century Scottish distillers, most prominently, George and John Gordon Smith, the father-and-son proprietors of The Glenlivet, significantly advanced the art to suit specific environmental conditions. But in the end, they were all talented and able perpetuators, not originators.

Before we can explore the founding families of The Glenlivet and Chivas Regal, a critical cornerstone in the foundation of the saga needs to be properly cemented into place. That matter is, Where, how, and when in history did distillation begin?

The word *distillation* comes from the Latin term *destillare*, which means to "drip down" or "trickle down." Archeological evidence currently points squarely at the Indian subcontinent as the probable cradle of distillation. Five hundred years before the life of Jesus demarcated

Western civilization's concept of ancient and modern eras of history, alchemists in what is now Pakistan regularly employed crude stills using botanicals—leaves, herbs, barks, seeds—in the search for medicines. So widespread was distillation in this region that archeologists speculate the biochemical process of distilling may be over 3,000 years old.

The aims of the earliest experiments with distilling ironically had little, if anything, to do with making potable alcoholic liquids for drinking pleasure. The ancients, who practiced primitive forms of distilling in China, the Indian subcontinent, Egypt, and Greece, were fascinated with making discoveries other than libations. Chinese aristocrats searched for potions that would prolong youthful vitality, enhance sexuality, or reverse aging. Indian physicians looked for improved methods of treating internal illnesses and topical ailments through distilled herbal medicines, ointments, and oils. Priests and courtiers in pharaonic Egypt longed to make perfumes and better cosmetics with which to combat the ferocity of the desert sun. Moreover, Greek alchemists desired among other pursuits to turn ordinary base metals into precious metals, especially gold. The simple stills of the ancient world didn't bubble to produce refined, complex elixirs like Chivas Regal or The Glenlivet. Instead, their purpose was to create enchanted concoctions that held therapeutic, magical, elemental altering, or even supernatural powers.

Distillation in the ancient world meant using stills made of earthen materials, most commonly, terra cotta, or ceramic. These primitive stills were poor and inefficient conductors of heat compared with modern stills, which are fashioned from natural or alloyed metals such as copper, steel, iron, and aluminum. Consequently, distilling prior to A.D. 800 was at best a haphazard and unpredictable exercise, with an unreliable outcome.

Arab alchemists and scientists residing in the Middle East ushered in the modern era of distillation. Abu Musa Jabir Ibn Haiyan, a renowned alchemist who lived in Kufa (present-day Iraq), invented the copper pot still, or *alembic,* in the last quarter of the eighth century A.D. Remarkably, the kettle-like, bulbous copper pot stills used today to distill Scotland's malt whiskies are based on Haiyan's 1200-year-old concept. The resourceful Jabir Ibn Haiyan, or "Geber" as the Europeans called him, wrote more than one hundred essays and treatises on

Traditional copper pot-stills are the heart of a distillery.

chemistry, metallurgy, and the importance of experimental investigation. Jabir Ibn Haiyan is the most important, if surprisingly ignored, figure of modern distillation.

Following closely in Jabir Ibn Haiyan's footsteps was the tenth-century physician, philosopher, and mathematician, Abu Ali al-Husain ibn Abdullah ibn Sina, known to Europeans as "Avicenna." Ibn Sina plied his trades of healing and teaching in Persia. An expert on the workings of the human anatomy, he authored over 450 books and essays, 240 of which are still in existence. His two most famous works are *The Book of Healing* and *The Canon of Medicine*. Ibn Sina utilized distillation in the preparation of medicines. His key role in furthering the science of distillation was to write authoritatively about the critical importance of corralling and condensing the steam in distillation. The vapors are the essence of distillation, the "spirit."

In view of the major contributions made by these two extraordinarily gifted men, little wonder that the word *alcohol* is derived from the Arabic term *al-koh'l*. Al-koh'l means "the antimony powder." Antimony is the friable, silvery powder that was used by Arabs of the Middle Ages as a base in eye cosmetics and perfumes. As it turned out, the Arabic influence on the spread of distillation was just beginning.

Moors, Monks, and Barbers

Distillation arrived on the European continent sometime after Tariq ibn-Ziyad's Berber Muslim army, the Moors, crossed the Strait of Gibraltar in A.D. 711 to invade the Iberian Peninsula. The Moors soundly defeated Roderick, Spain's last Visigoth king, and his legions soon after the assault. In a mere eight years, the Moors had conquered the breadth of Spain from Gibraltar to the Pyrenees. By A.D. 800, the sophisticated Moorish culture, which had accumulated and amalgamated the lost knowledge of ancient Egypt, Alexandria, Greece, and Rome, permeated the whole peninsula.

In the meantime, the rest of Europe languished in the late stages of the Dark Ages, the bleak, hopeless period that dawned with the collapse of the Roman Empire in the late fifth century and lasted until the turn of the first millennium. Relative to the rest of Europe, occupied Spain flourished under the Moors. During their domination, the Moors fostered an open and inclusive society that emphasized education, the arts, science, medicine, and technology. One of the foundational, indispensable technologies that took firm hold in Moorish Spain was distillation. Weary of their "friendly captives" status, however, the Spanish forcefully expelled the Moors in 1492 after almost eight centuries.

By A.D. 1000, the secrets of distillation had extended to other southern European regions. The earliest key non-Muslim advocate of distillation was the prestigious medical school operated by monks of the Benedictine Order in Salerno, Italy. The monks' pursuit of medicines to combat the horrific plagues that decimated the European population helped the school become a breeding ground for distillation experimentation. Its graduates dispersed throughout Europe and the British Isles, carrying with them the wonders of distilled liquids.

Other orders of Christian monks soon became adept in the distillation art, and they, too, fanned out across the known world, establishing monastic outposts that dispensed spirituous liquids to the ill, the sorrow-ful, and the depleted members of the local populace. The monks' near-mythical libations were thought to have restorative, healing powers that lifted and soothed the spirit. The Latin-speaking Christian monks not surprisingly identified their heady distilled concoctions as *aqua vitae,* which meant "water of life."

In addition to Christian monks, distinguished physicians of the pe-riod, most notably the thirteenth century French doctor and alchemist to kings and popes Arnaldus de Villa Nova, championed the production and application of distilled spirits in the treatment of a wide array of ail-ments. De Villa Nova was the foremost instructor of medicine and alchemy at medical schools in Avignon and Montpellier, France. His ir-reproachable reputation and influence within the courts of southern Eu-rope and the innermost layers of the Papacy advanced with credibility the awareness of aqua vitae in the highest circles of European society. Still other historical detectives posit that knights returning from the Crusades to northern Europe and the British Isles brought back the se-crets of distillation, suggesting that they had witnessed its making and application on their excursions through the Middle East. Whatever the truth from among the possibilities, a tidal wave of distillation interest and practice washed across the entirety of Europe and the British Isles from A.D. 1000 to 1300.

In the colder northern regions where grains, sugar beets, and pota-toes fared better than fruits, primitive vodkas and aquavits based in neu-tral grains and vegetable matter became cultural staples. During distillation in harshly frigid places like Russia, Scandinavia, and Poland, these raw, clear spirits were frequently flavored with grass, honey, fruits, or barks and seeds to render them more drinkable. To the south in the balmy Mediterranean Basin, where fruits and grapevines were bountiful, fruit- and grape-based spirits dominated and quickly spread. Italian wine-makers learned how to distill their spent pomace and unused juice from winemaking to make fiery grappa. In southern Spain, winemakers boiled a portion of their wines and created Spanish brandy. By the 1400s, farmer-winemakers in Gaul's (France) southwest district known as Ar-magnac were distilling grape brandy. Their grape-growing neighbors to the north in Cognac began their own brandy journey two centuries later. The Gauls-French described their immature, fresh grape spirits as *eaux-de-vie*, French for "water of life."

Around 1050 to 1100, Christian monks almost certainly exposed the Scots-Gaels of Ireland to the secrets of distillation. King Henry II of England invaded Ireland, circa 1170 to 1174. A vague, if tantalizing, report from his soldiers mentions the Scots-Gaels producing a potent libation made from "boiling," meaning distillation. Hearing the monks refer in Latin to their potent spirits as *aqua vitae*, the Scots-Gaels of Ireland understandably put a Gaelic spin on the term and called it *uisge beatha*. Author Charles MacLean in his book *Malt Whisky* (1997, p. 14) writes, "The Scots Gaelic for *aqua vitae* is *uisge beatha* (pronounced 'ooshkie bayha') which was abbreviated to *uiskie* in the seventeenth century, and to *whiskie* by 1715. The modern spelling—whisky—first appears as late as 1736."

Christian monks exported the system of distillation from Ireland to Scotland by the fourteenth century. The initial substantiation of its existence on the island of Britain, however, didn't occur until the waning years of the fifteenth century. A Scottish Exchequer Roll recorded in 1494 that a clerical member, Friar John Cor, of the Benedictine Lindores Abbey in Fife made a sizable purchase of barley malt in the amount of "viii bolls" for the purpose of making "aqua vitae." Since a boll amounted to 140 pounds, eight bolls of malted barley topped the scales at well over half a ton. As writer Michael Brander, author of *The Original Scotch* (1975, p. 5) states, ". . . it is clear at once that this was no small operation. Half a ton of malt producing probably in the region of seventy gallons of spirit was not required for private consumption. Obviously the monastic establishment . . . was distilling on no mean scale . . ."

As the 1400s rolled to a conclusion, another chronicling of Scottish aqua vitae appeared in the Lord High Treasurer's Accounts, dated 1498. Referring directly to an order placed by the Royal Court of King James IV, the High Treasurer's ledger accounts, "To the barbour that brocht aqua vitae to the King in Dundee be the Kingis command . . ."

The curious mention of "the barbour" in this official court entry is another indication of how deeply the making of aqua vitae had taken root in Scottish society by the end of the fifteenth century. The Guild of Barber-Surgeons was a powerful professional entity in Edinburgh at the turn of the sixteenth century. Their mission, as royally sanctioned by the King's "The Seal of Cause," was to maintain and promote the highest standards of surgical practice. Although nowadays the thought of getting an appendectomy from the man or woman who trims your beard and straightens your sideburns might be alarming, combining hair shaving and cutting with invasive and topical surgical procedures such as bloodletting and minor incisions was then considered normal in Edinburgh. The Guild of Barber-Surgeons was so highly regarded, in fact, that in 1505 King James IV bestowed on them the exclusive right to distill and peddle their aqua vitae for medicinal purposes within Edinburgh. The Royal Seal gave them a distilling monopoly within the capital of Scotland. One could say that in all aspects the Guild was the cutting-edge league of its day.

James IV had his own stash of peculiar interests that involved distillation. He owned a keen attraction for anything having to do with alchemy, medicine, and surgical procedures. The King needed copious amounts of aqua vitae for the experiments in which he attempted to locate and then produce through distillation the so-called fifth essence, aka the mysterious "ether." Alchemists, clerics, and mystics alike believed that the fifth essence was of celestial, or heavenly, origin. Accordingly, the elusive fifth essence was supposed to possess potent sway over all earthly matter and matters. The Lord High Treasurer's Accounts do not report on the success or failure of the King's findings. James IV also fancied himself a crack dental surgeon and was so proud of his dexterity that he actually paid his patients to have dental work performed. The mind boggles at how much aqua vitae must have surreptitiously been consumed by patients both before and after a tooth extraction, courtesy of His Majesty.

Nevertheless, since Scotland's *uisge beatha* became so officially recognized by the pillars of Edinburgh's community at the close of the fifteenth century, it requires no great leap of faith to speculate that distilling must have been occurring in urban Scotland for at least half a century. In rural western Scotland, the firing of crude stills may have been going on since the early 1300s.

By the middle of the sixteenth century, public perceptions of uisge beatha had begun to change. In addition to being widely employed as a medicinal liquid, uisge beatha started to be viewed as a social libation. Naturally, liberties turned to occasional excess. In *The Making of Scotch Whisky: A History of the Scotch Whisky Distilling Industry*, authors John R. Hume and Michael S. Moss write (2000, p. 23), "From the 1550s prosecutions for infringements of this privilege were common, suggesting that aqua vitae was becoming accepted as a drink as well as a tonic."

Legislation initiatives introduced in the Scottish Parliament in 1555 and 1579 suggest that the use of malted barley for the production of uisge beatha had greatly accelerated across Scotland in the second half of the sixteenth century. The two Acts addressed, in part, the mandatory shifting of malted barley for use in making bread and brown ale and away from the distilling of uisge beatha. Poor harvests and subsequent food shortages were the reasons parliamentarians gave for the restrictive legislation.

Doubtless, the staunchly independent Highland and island Scots scoffed at the dictates of a governing body with which they felt little, if any, connection. These sixteenth-century parliamentary edicts were the first of what would eventually become an onerous litany of measures to regulate and tax distilleries. As described in Chapters 3 and 4, these legislative actions and others would affect the lives and livelihoods— usually adversely—of Scots for hundreds of years. They would also contribute to an unprecedented era of illegal distilling and smuggling.

Royal and parliamentarian recognition, legislation, and acceptance, however, do not indicate in any way that Scotland's early whiskies were of good quality. The predecessors to the savory likes of Chivas Regal and The Glenlivet were very probably harsh and foul tasting. Whereas advancements in technique and technology as well as wood barrel maturation have made contemporary Scotch whiskies among the most refined of distillates, the uisge beathas of the King James IV era were rough-and-ready virgin spirits that were consumed straight off the still.

Today, Scotch whisky must, by law, age in oak barrels for a minimum of three years, but Scotland's first whiskies weren't allowed the luxury of time to mellow and evolve. Since hygiene wasn't an issue in the centuries that ushered in Scotland's religious Reformation (the split between competing factions within the Church that started in the early 1500s), stills and storage vats were likely to be fetid contraptions and containers that served as unsanitary playgrounds for harmful bacteria. Essentially, the majority of Scotland's early uisge beathas were, like those of Ireland, eye-popping moonshine whiskies notorious for their questionable safety records and ferocious personalities.

In defense of the Scottish distillers of the fourteenth, fifteenth, and sixteenth centuries, information about the intricacies of distillation was limited in both scope and availability; and it was passed on solely by word of mouth from father to son, uncle to nephew. There was no *Uisge Beatha for Dummies* instruction manual. The first book translated into English about distillation, *Das Buch zu Destilliern (The vertuose boke of Distyllacyon)* by Hieronymous Braunschweig, was printed in Europe in 1519 but didn't appear in Britain until 1527. Since most rural Scots of the period lived in far-flung, remote locations and spoke only Gaelic, this is a moot point. Anyway, as Michael Brander, author of *The Original Scotch*, observes (p. 7), "According to this book aqua vitae was regarded as purely medicinal and distillation was defined as: 'Distylling is none other thynge, but onely a puryfyeng of the grosse from the subtyll and the subtyll from the grosse'."

In 1559, Peter Morwyng published a tome titled *Treasure of Evonymous,* that described distillation in detail and lauded uisge beatha as bestowing a stunning inventory of benefits to imbibers. Gushed Morwyng, "It sharpeneth the wit, it restoreth memori. It maketh men merry and preserveth youth. . . . It expelleth poison. The smell thereof burnt, killeth flies and cold creeping beasts. . . . It is most wholesome for the stomake, the harte and the liver . . . it taketh away sadness . . ." (Michael Brander, *The Original Scotch*, p. 8).

Methinks Morwyng drinketh too much uisge beatha.

Make no mistake. The initial two to three centuries of Scotland's whisky distilling history were neither particularly notable nor filled with momentous breakthroughs. The Scots' early generations of uisge beathas were distant shadows of what was to come. After all, the farmer-distillers were unschooled and the conditions, materials, and equipment were unsophisticated and unkempt. Production was minute in comparison to modern times; the era's pot stills ranged in size from a scant four to five gallons only up to, if rarely, fifty gallons. At their finest, Scotland's early whiskies were pungent, throat-grating spirits that provided a quick buzz and a brief respite from the day-in, day-out hardships of Middle Ages Scotland. At their worst, they were bad tasting, fierce, skull-cracking brews. Alcohol poisoning was common and sometimes resulted in a painful death.

Scotch whisky's authentic trendsetters, superstar personalities, and innovators didn't begin appearing until the 1700s. Then, the hallmarks of the eighteenth and nineteenth centuries proved to be technological advances fed by a frenzy of ideas and a hunger for profitable gain.

While fully acknowledging Scotch whisky's humble, if dubious, beginnings, the crucial issue of historical significance at this juncture is that, by the reign of James IV and just beyond, the distillation of grain beers in Scotland was set on an irreversible course. That route would first establish distilling as the prevalent cottage trade of the common Scots in the islands, Highlands, and Lowlands. As momentum built on a local level, this populist skill and pastime would, over time, blossom into the powerful industry whose present influence reverberates around the globe because of brands like Chivas Regal and The Glenlivet.

The Thynge That Puryfyes the Grosse

Hieronymous Braunschweig's early sixteenth-century statement concerning distillation is as flawlessly precise as it is beautifully succinct. Distillation above all else *is* a purification process. At its most rudimentary level, distillation is the system of separating the biochemical properties of a liquid by boiling it, capturing the gaseous vapors, then cooling and condensing the collected vapors to create a distinctly new, high-potency liquid. This resultant distillate is the sanitized, decontaminated essence of the base materials that made up the original liquid.

Here is another way of understanding the primary purpose of distillation in terms that read less like a chemistry book. A natural disaster, such as an earthquake or flood, temporarily cuts off the water supply to a community. Once water service is restored, the first thing that municipal, county, or state authorities stress without fail is to boil all tap water prior to drinking or using it in cooking. Distilled water is purified water. Anyone who has ever boiled water in a kettle to make tea has practiced the initial step of the distillation formula.

Unlike a naturally occurring biochemical transition such as fermentation, distillation requires the hand, intellect and, most importantly, fire of humans. Numerous modern-day industries use distillation including oil refining, pharmaceutical production, cosmetics, and chemicals. To comprehend how distillation applies to the production of Scotch whiskies like Chivas Regal and The Glenlivet, it pays to begin with an accounting of whisky's base materials—the grosse, as Hieronymous Braunschweig would cite them—that ultimately undergo the rigors of the distillation process to extract their combined essence, or pure spirit.

Grain, water, and yeast are the three easily obtainable raw materials that constitute any whiskey made anywhere in the world, including the most prized and popular whiskey of all, Scotch whisky. At first blush, the value of this trio of commonplace substances seems modest. Though humble in worth, these ordinary elements become complex and extraordinary once they are carefully combined and processed.

Barley has customarily been the requisite grain for making malt whisky in Scotland. This is not because barley was the only grain that grew well in Scotland's finicky, sometimes atrocious, climate. Oats, rye, and wheat did as well. Farmer-distillers in the early period of distillation selected an ancient strain of barley that had four rows of spikelets, called *bere*, as their grain of choice. An alternative variety was two-row barley, which made smoother ales and whiskies according to some distillers, but bere proved to be first among equals. This was so for two reasons: Bere provided reliably large crop yields in poor soils and rainy climates, and its early ripening tendency accommodated farmers. Before being milled, the barley is allowed to partially germinate, thereby stimulating the grain's natural starches. This partial germination, which breaks down the cell walls, is called *malting*. Next, the malted barley is dried in kilns to halt the growth of the natural starches. The dried malted barley is then ground into powdery grist.

Water from a trusted source, such as a burn (stream) or a spring, is boiled and mixed with the malted barley grist in large metal vessels called *mash tuns*. Mashing converts the starches into maltose, a natural sugar. The soupy result is a walnut-colored, sweet-smelling liquid called *wort*. The wort is pumped into another metal tank, the *washback*, and yeast is injected. The introduction of yeast triggers fermentation. Over 48 hours, the innate sugar, or maltose, is transformed into carbon dioxide and alcohol. Fermentation changes the base materials into low-alcohol (7 to 8 percent), fragrant *wash* that is, for all intents and purposes, beer.

The wash-beer is then moved to a kettle-like copper pot-still, the *wash still*, and is set to boil. During the tumultuous first distillation, the vapors are forced to pass through a cold, coiled pipe, or condenser, also known as a *worm*. Since alcohol boils at 173.1 degrees Fahrenheit and water boils at 212 degrees Fahrenheit, the wash's alcohol vaporizes well before the water, causing a separation of properties. The alcohol vapors return to liquid form while traveling through the icy-cold worm. The moderate alcohol liquid (20 to 24 percent alcohol), or *low wines*, is pumped into the *spirits still* for its second distillation to further purify and elevate the alcohol level. Following the second distillation, the condensed vapors become a high-alcohol (70 to 72 percent), limpid distillate, the *spirit*.

After the second distillation, the biochemically altered base ingredients do not smell, feel, or taste anything like simple water, grain, and yeast. Through malting, mashing, fermentation, and double distillation on pot stills, the grain, water, and yeast unite to become a single liquid substance: pure grain alcohol, the crystalline liquid that once was called aqua vitae and uisge beatha.

All Scotch malt whiskies, including The Glenlivet and the ones that compose the Chivas Regal blend, have their origin in this sequence of events. Made in small batches in pot stills, malt whiskies are the oldest type of Scotch whisky and the sole variety made in Scotland prior to the 1830s when another kind of distillation—continuous distilling—introduced grain whiskies. Continuous distillation takes place in tall metal columns that never stop running, resulting in large volumes of spirit made from grains other than malted barley. Modern era Scotch whisky producers use both kinds of distillation.

The resultant transparent-as-rainwater liquid is deceptively compelling. When drawn fresh off the still, virgin spirit smells strikingly similar to a damp garden in June. Dewy scents of fresh flowers, green vegetation, and pine rush at you one moment; then yeasty odors of bread dough or dry breakfast cereal coyly tickle your attention the next. The potent (70 to 72 percent alcohol), immature fluid burns the tongue initially if tasted undiluted. But as the taste buds adjust to the virgin alcohol's racy nature, layers of ripe fruit and grain flavors emerge. Even at this nascent stage, it is possible to project how maturation, mellowing, and time can transform the razor-edged charms of the spirit into an alcoholic beverage of unusual virtuosity, nuance, and complexity.

Through heating, boiling, and cooling then, the grosse, as if by magic, is transformed into that which Hieronymous Braunschweig would call the subtyll. Then after a minimum of three years of maturation, out of the protective cocoon of the oak barrel flies the golden monarch butterfly of Scotch whisky.

George Smith, founder of The Glenlivet.

George Smith, Glenlivet, and Ancient Liberties

GEORGE SMITH, FOUNDER of The Glenlivet, Scotland's most illustrious single malt distillery, was born on March 8, 1792, on Upper Drumin farm in Glenlivet, Banffshire, Scotland. George was the sixth child and fourth son of Andrew and Margaret Gordon Smith. William (born 1777), Helen (1780), John (1782), Margaret (1785), and Charles (1789) Smith had all preceded George. Their father Andrew Smith was a respected tenant farmer, or "tacksman" in the vernacular of the time and place, who leased his land from the Duke of Gordon. The lease agreements were referred to as "tacks," hence the moniker conveyed on the leaseholder. As a major landowner in the pastoral district of Banffshire, the Duke's extensive land holdings in the eighteenth century included expansive tracts in the communities of Morinsh, Glenlivet, Strathavon, and Glenrinnes.

Glenlivet, the place, was then part of a "parish," or community, called Inveravon that also included parts of Morinsh and Strathavon. Approximately 2,240 people inhabited the secluded Inveravon parish in the 1790s, according to *The Statistical Account of Scotland*, a civic report

35

on population and local economics that was assembled parish by parish by administering clergy throughout the final decade of the eighteenth century. Virtually all the parish's residents including George Smith's family were farmers who cultivated grains like rye, oats, and the sturdy four-row barley called bere. Many kept livestock, such as the highly prized Black Angus cattle, as well as sheep and oxen. "It is said there may be about 2,500 sheep in the parish; some of them are of the Linton breed, with black faces and feet," describes the *Statistical Account*. "Every . . . farmer, if near hills, keeps sheep, but none have farms for that purpose alone . . ."

Recognized as one of Highland Scotland's most dazzling and bucolic river valleys, Glenlivet was a famous location long before The Glenlivet whisky was invented and became an enduring symbol of its place of origin. Glenlivet, or *Gleann-liobh-aite* in Gaelic, means "valley of the smooth flowing one" and was bisected into two areas by the Bochel, a camel-humped knob of land. To the north of the Bochel lay the Braes of Glenlivet, an isolated, bowl-like district in the 1790s; to the south was the Lower Glenlivet, where the majority of the region's farms and grazing lands rested.

The defining topographical features of this area of Banffshire both in the 1790s and today are its three networking rivers, the fast-flowing Spey, the Avon, and the Livet. The River Livet begins at the 1,100-foot high confluence of a couple of upland streams, the Suie and the Kymah Burns, then snakes for roughly nine miles through picturesque Glenlivet. Running to the northwest, the River Livet spills into the River Avon southwest of the town of Craggan. Finally, the River Avon connects with the River Spey, Scotland's most famous river, just west of the village of Ballindalloch.

Day-to-day existence in the parish held few guarantees except for frequent inclement weather and the need for hard work, peat for fuel, and plenty of strong, murky twopenny ale for drinking. The *Statistical Account* noted, "The fuel here used is peat, of which there is no scarcity in a dry year. . . . The climate in Glenlivet is colder than in Interavon; for in Glenlivet there will be a pretty deep snow. . . . The reason of this is because Glenlivet is higher and surrounded with hills more than Interavon is." In most winters, the snow would blanket the tundra-like, crusted ground, cutting off the glen's inhabitants for days at a time. Though the area was verdant and scenic, the timid, the slow, and the frail among the population did not survive for long in the long glen carved by the River Livet.

According to research conducted in the 1990s by historian Iain Russell of the Glasgow University Archives, members of the Smith family had leased land in Glenrinnes from the Duke as early as 1715. Typically, a Highlands tacksman leased scores of acres of arable tracts of land directly from the landlord and then sublet to subtenants the sections of the parcel that he and his own family didn't farm or use for grazing land. The tacksman paid the landlord an annual fee from income that was gathered both from his own farming profits and from the tacks of his subtenants. In this trickle-down, feudal system, tacksmen were also expected to pick up arms and organize small armies from the subtenants when the lord's property or prestige was at stake. Despite all these demands, established tacksmen like George Smith's father Andrew and grandfather, who was also named Andrew, often led comfortable lifestyles compared with the majority of Banffshire's small farmers, millers, craftsmen, or shopkeepers.

Prior to leasing the "Town and Lands of Upper Drumin with House, Gardens and Pertinents" in Glenlivet from the Duke of Gordon, Andrew and his wife Margaret leased a smaller property called Croftmartick, where they started their family. Realizing in 1783 as their dependents multiplied that they would require more living space, Andrew applied with a friend James Grant of Tamnvoulin for a larger property of the Duke's at Upper Drumin. The elevated parcel looked down on the River Livet from the hillside and boasted several homes, livestock shelters, pens, and work sheds. The Duke accepted their application. For an annual fee of £50 total, or £25 apiece plus one good wedder (a castrated ram) each, Andrew Smith and James Grant became the new tack holders of Upper Drumin in 1784. The Upper Drumin tack also stipulated that Smith and Grant were responsible for costs such as building maintenance and repair to the kirk (church), kirkyard (churchyard), schoolhouse, and "other necessary publick works." Soon after signing the tack, James Grant backed out, leaving Andrew Smith as the sole tacksman. The lease's term was for 19 years.

Going back in time a little further, genealogical evidence gleaned from archivist Iain Russell's investigations on the Smith family lineage suggests that a tacksman named "Thomas Smith or Gow (Smith was the anglicization of Gow, the Gaelic for 'blacksmith') . . ." appears in records, dated 1715, held by the Duke of Gordon's eldest son, Alexander, the fifth Marquess of Huntley. Russell posits in his unpublished papers that Thomas Smith, who had a son named Andrew, might well have been Andrew Smith's grandfather and, thereby, George Smith's great-grandfather. Though Russell's proposal is not irrefutable, no better recorded evidence has yet been unearthed. This information, then, indicates that by the time of George Smith's birth in 1792 the Smith family had become an integral part of the Duke of Gordon's estate and of the southern Banffshire community over the span of at least four generations.

In the late winter of 1792 what Andrew Smith's infant son George could not have known was that he was born in the epicenter of a monumental social earthquake. At its core, this deep-rooted upheaval concerned what the average Scotsman perceived to be his right to distill whisky unfettered by governmental interference, regulation, or taxation. Secluded, remote Glenlivet felt the seismic shudder more than most other places. What took place in Glenlivet over George Smith's lifetime sent political tremors across the whole of Britain, including deep within the walls of Parliament.

Moreover, 32 years after his birth, George Smith would initiate his own personal earthquake within Scotland's whisky trade. Andrew Smith could never have guessed that his fourth son would end up being instrumental in totally altering the landscape of whisky making in Scotland, changing it to the extent that even George's neighbors in the glen would turn into mortal enemies. Andrew Smith would die before his son became the most famous whisky distiller in all of Scotland.

Duties and Duty

A turbulent era of whisky smuggling and illicit distilling in Scotland began roughly 150 years before George Smith's birth at Upper Drumin and lasted nearly two centuries. The period from 1760 to 1840, in particular, proved to be the apex of illegal distilling activity. The seed of the problem was planted in the mid-seventeenth century when the Scottish Parliament passed the Internal Act of Excyse on January 31, 1644. That legislation put Scotland's farmer-distillers on official notice that the distilling of whisky was no longer a free, uncontrolled exercise. The Act of Excyse, ". . . imposed a duty of 2s. 8d. on 'everie pynt of aquavytie or strong watteris sold within the countrey,'" according to whisky author Gavin D. Smith in his book *The Scottish Smuggler* (2003, p. 3). The "2s. 8d." meant a duty of two shillings and eight pence to be paid on each pint of uisge beatha. In the 1600s, a "pynt" equaled roughly one-third of a gallon.

The overwhelming majority of seventeenth-century whisky distillers were ordinary farmers and subtenants who led hand-to-mouth existences within the trap of an archaic, yet effective feudal system. For the most part, the farmer-distillers were simply dealing with excess volumes of bere, Scotland's ubiquitous and vigorous four-row barley. Not only did distillation wisely utilize harvest surpluses of barley, it afforded the farmer-distillers a useful mode of currency or trade as well as a salable product that was growing in popularity. The imposition of a governmentally generated duty, then, came as a serious blow to their otherwise sturdy sensibilities. The Act of Excyse was an insult.

The Scots, a practical, modest, largely rural (well over 90 percent) and down-to-earth people, had since the first years of distillation considered whisky making to be an inalienable entitlement and not susceptible to taxation or official directive of any sort. Now, suddenly, their Parliament, a faceless body of aristocrats, lords, and landowners ensconced in faraway Edinburgh, had the temerity to tax whisky at the ambitious rate of over 6 shillings for each gallon produced. Village talk in rural Scotland, typically dry-humored and affable, turned sour and rebellious. Conversations between neighbors were colored by concern over the unexpected expense of whisky distilling. Was this Act passed to build up the treasury's coffers or, worse, to fund the king's army? The latter appears to be the primary motivation. The motivations of detached royals and their bidders, though, meant little to the struggling Scots.

Scotland's Population 1650 to 1850

Calculations on Scotland's population have suggested that between 1650 and 1750 the total number of Scots hovered around 1,200,000 to 1,300,000. This remarkably level sum remained flat primarily because of famines, ineffective health care, and epidemics. Then from 1750 to 1800, the total exploded to 1,600,000 as medicine advanced. By the 1840s, Scotland topped 2,600,000 inhabitants. Today's figure is just over 5,000,000.

But as history would depict, the Act of Excyse was just the launch, the initial volley, one might say, of what was destined to become a long, bitterly contested tradition of continual governmental meddling with whisky distillation. Over succeeding centuries, Scotch whisky would become the favorite duty target, a taxable pawn and cash cow of both the Scottish and English Parliaments to help finance potential wars, to pay the debts incurred by past conflicts on foreign soils, or to bail out Parliament when monies were mismanaged. As it turned out, from the late 1640s until the 1690s the Scottish Parliament did little to enforce the Act of Excyse. This relatively tranquil period witnessed the passing of a few Acts that tweaked the duties on distillation. They were minor and ultimately held toothless implications for whisky distillers. Consequently, Scotland's farmer-distillers were largely left alone to distill their country whisky as the seventeenth century came to a close.

Lulling calms can be deceiving. Dark, voluminous political clouds were gathering at Scotland's horizon as the need for tax revenues grew in Parliament. These towering thunderheads would spawn legislative downpours and gales whose winds would erode and buffet Scotland's fragile socioeconomic landscape. They would likewise shape the adult life of George Smith.

Meanwhile, whisky's popularity all across Scotland hurtled forward. This dramatic growth in consumption happened, in one part, because so much whisky was then being distilled in both cities and the countryside and, in another part, by the natural allure of whisky's mysterious nature. The native strong ale fermented from barley was turbid in appearance and spotty in quality. Its appeal to the masses was waning by the close of the seventeenth century. Scots, in general, were ready to glom onto a new potable.

Scotland's first large distillery, Ferintosh, founded in the 1660s and owned by Duncan Forbes of Culloden, produced the nation's first brand of whisky of the same name. Though the distillery, located in Ross-shire, was burned to the ground in the Jacobite insurrection of 1689, Forbes, a Whig party loyalist who was fiercely anti-Jacobite, rebuilt Ferintosh, which by the 1760s accounted for four major whisky distilleries coexisting on one property. Ferintosh was one of Scotland's first industrial complexes and proved to be a forerunner of modern whiskies.

Then, on May 1, 1707, one of political history's great marriages of convenience became reality. With Franco-Anglo relations on slippery footing and internal English Parliamentary wrangling between Tory and Whig at all-time high levels, the Treaty of Union of the Two Kingdoms of Scotland and England, also known as the Act of Union, joined the heretofore separate Parliaments of Scotland and England. To the dismay of most Scots, the Seat of Scottish government was relocated to London. In one calculated and artfully maneuvered stroke, the aristocracy of Scotland and the key political powerbrokers of England, the Whigs, created Great Britain. Unfortunately for Scotland's private distillers, they were expected to carry the extra baggage of increased excise duties that now extended to them through the Act of Union. Predictably, from May 1707, legislation on the taxation and regulation of whisky and whisky distilling accelerated at an alarming pace.

Six years after the Act of Union was implemented, the Malt Tax that had started in England before 1707 with the taxation of bushels of malt was introduced to Scotland. This policy adversely affected virtually all Scottish farmers, brewers, and distillers—in other words, just about every Scot. The timing of the levy could not have been worse. Feeble early eighteenth-century Scottish harvests and subsequent shortages of numerous food staples made the tax seem like an English-instigated punishment. Negative feelings and rhetoric in the streets of urban Scotland ran high against England and the Scottish MPs (Members of Parliament).

In 1725, the Malt Tax was increased. The upping of the Malt Tax incensed the starving Scots in Glasgow who quickly set upon the mansion of Parliamentarian Daniel Campbell, a Scot who had come down on the side of the increase. Cites Gavin D. Smith in *The Scottish Smuggler* (p. 5), ". . . the result was civil unrest, with eleven people being killed in June during Glasgow's Shawfield Riots. This was a tax on the everyday drink of 'twopenny ale,' and the Scottish people were not amused."

Despite the newly imposed duties, illicit distilling and whisky production in Scotland leapt forward at breakneck speed as twopenny ale, up to this juncture the nation's favorite tipple, was being replaced by *usky*, or whisky. During this chaotic period, Scotland's notorious dissidents, or *smuckellors* (archaic for *smugglers*), were not only the illegal distillers, but the transporters and merchants of illicit whisky as well. The English term *smuggler* is most likely derived from the seventeenth-century Dutch term *smokkelen* meaning "to sneak repeatedly." Smugglers are, in essence, individuals who cheat governments by covertly producing, transporting, and selling goods without paying customs or duties.

Sir Walter Scott's novels of the day reflected with searing accuracy the civil turmoil and the dark mood of the Scots in the early decades of the eighteenth century. Stories like Scott's *The Heart of Midlothian* also afforded readers vivid insights into the extent of smuggling. In Gavin D. Smith's book *The Scottish Smuggler* (p. 166), he prints some of Scott's most telling notes that formed the basis of *The Heart of Midlothian*. ". . . in those counties where it prevails, the cleverest, boldest, and most intelligent of the peasantry are uniformly engaged in illicit transactions, and very often with the sanction of the farmers and inferior gentry. Smuggling was almost universal in Scotland in the reigns of George I and II (1714 to 1727 and 1727 to 1760) for the people, unaccustomed to imposts, and regarding them as an unjust aggression upon their ancient liberties, made no scruple to elude them whenever it was possible to do so."

But Britain needed enormous infusions of cash to fund its conflicts in Europe and North America, such as the war with Spain (1739), the Seven Years' War (1756 to 1763), the American War for Independence (1775 to 1781), and war with France (1793), as well as the extension of Britain's colonial rule to India and Africa. The British Parliament, hungry for conquest and geopolitical influence, enacted customs legislation with a vengeance during the 1700s. The backlash was predictable, however, as whisky smuggling went to the next level with each new duty extension or increase. The potent combination of strings of poor Scottish harvests, a struggling economy, and rising taxes on distilling assured that smuggling activity in the eighteenth century would evolve from being a mere act of rebellion by a few indignant malcontents to become a widespread and socially accepted act of an entire desperate population.

The stage was set for the opening skirmishes of the historic guerrilla war between the smugglers, the landowners, and the government agents— the dreaded excisemen who were paid to ferret out the smugglers. The growing Andrew Smith family, contented on their farm at Upper Drumin with George, their new baby boy, were residing in Scotland's ground zero of whisky smuggling commotion—idyllic and remote Glenlivet.

The famous painting, Tussle for the Keg by John Pettie. *Credit*: Aberdeen Art Gallery & Museums Collections.

The Great
Era of Smuggling

FIRES OF DISCONTENT and indignation raged all over Scotland in the last quarter of the eighteenth century. The litany of woes for both common rural Scots and urban Scots mounted like piles of drying peat. To Scots like the Smiths of Glenlivet, it seemed as if every few years since the Act of Union in 1707, new Acts amending previous duty, grain, or distilling legislation passed through Parliament without any thought for the people being most affected. Each successive Act appeared to further tighten the legal noose around the neck of enterprising whisky distillers, limiting their freedoms and adding to their plight. Further sentiments were that Parliament was unjustifiably squeezing more tax money out of Scotland's private distillers to help finance Great Britain's war machine.

Both suppositions were founded in truth. From 1707 to 1781 no less than 19 separate pieces of Parliamentary legislation—dated 1710, 1713, 1718, 1725, 1727, 1729, 1736, 1743, 1746, 1751, 1757, 1759, 1761, 1762, 1772, 1774, 1779, 1780, and 1781—affected, among other issues, the selling or use of barley malt, the prime base material for whisky; the legal minimum size of pot stills; and excise duties on wash or spirits. As for Scotch whisky helping to subsidize British military actions: During this critical period of 74 years, Britain was neck-deep in three major foreign conflicts on two continents.

The bitter reality was that, to survive, the powerless Scots could do little in response to the deluge of legislation but protest and defy the law. Revenue Service excise agents, called "gaugers," were dispatched to Scotland's hinterlands to combat the obstinacy of the Scots by tracking down smugglers and collecting duties. Gaugers were paid bounties or percentages of their collections. Despite the gaugers and the battery of excise laws, distilling hit unprecedented heights in the 1740s and 1750s. Consumption of illicit whisky made totally from malted barley and a harsh concoction dubbed "malt spirit," a lesser whisky-like spirit composed of malted barley and unmalted grain, competed with twopenny ale as the common daily libation. Distilling hit the skids in the 1760s as disastrous crop failures curbed the making of whisky. But the worst was yet to come.

To the outcry and disgust of the farmer-distillers and city-distillers alike, private, unlicensed distilling was banned in 1781. Written within the legislation that prohibited unlicensed distilling were sanctions that gave gaugers the legal right to confiscate or demolish any illegal pot stills. Pot stills and their accompanying equipment were known then as *bothies*. Gaugers were also instructed within the bounds of their mandate to seize whisky stocks and other production-related equipment like storage vats and barrels. Even the horses and carts that transported the smugglers' whisky were fair game for the gaugers.

The next year, official records claim that gaugers seized 1,940 bothies, half of them in the Highlands. In addition to eight licensed stills, Edinburgh alone was estimated to have over four hundred bothies secretly pumping out thousands of gallons of illegal whisky each week. Statistical accounts also state that Scotland produced 264,000 gallons of legal whisky that same year in licensed distilleries like those operated by the Haig and Stein families. In 1783 and 1784—about the same time that Andrew Smith first leased Upper Drumin—massive, devastating crop failures and famine added fuel to Scotland's national crisis of morale. Riots broke out. In June 1784, an angry mob in Edinburgh descended on the Haigs' Canonmills distillery. Thinking that the stored barley, potatoes, and vegetables within the distillery compound were going to be used for distilling purposes instead of for food, the livid crowd, after once being rebuffed by armed guards, attacked a second time. A single rioter was killed by gunshot. The ringleaders of the riot were arrested, quickly tried and found guilty, publicly flogged as they walked through the streets, and sent to the colonies for 14 years. Scotland teetered on the brink of bedlam and anarchy.

Members of Parliament were loath to get dragged into a minor civil war over the duties imposed on distilling. In what could be described as an act of panic, Parliament did at that time the only thing it knew how to do well: Make matters worse by creating ensuing laws even more convoluted, punitive, and contradictory.

With the passing of the hastily patched together Wash Act of 1784, Parliament's ineptitude at dealing with the whisky distilling issue reached a zenith. Designed to douse the flames blazing in most Scottish hearts and minds, the Wash Act taxed only the fermented wash (at the rate of 5 pence per gallon) alone rather than the spirits and declared that 20-gallon pot stills, a typical size for the era, could be deemed legal on paying a yearly fee of £1 per gallon of cubic capacity. In an obvious, if transparent, attempt to appease the agitated Highland distillers, 17 Highland counties, including Banffshire, the home county of Glenlivet, were specified as being affected by the Wash Act. Parliament's intention was to convince the Highland smugglers that by legalizing their operations through licensing and paying duties they could enter the fold and, in time, prosper.

Another provision of this woefully ill-conceived Act, the "stick" part of the carrot-and-stick approach, provided for the stiffest penalties yet for illegal distilling. Additionally, if the offending person was a tacksman, or tenant, who was incapable of paying the fines, the holder of the tack (lease) was automatically held responsible. This enraged landowners, who were benefiting from illicit distilling because at least they were receiving lease payments from the profits generated by their tenants' smuggling practices. The skeptical Highlanders scoffed en masse at the Wash Act, ignored it and, more determined and united than ever in their cause, continued to pump out increasing volumes of illicit whisky in the secluded glens and hillsides.

To make matters worse for Members of Parliament that year, Lowland distillers, who harbored unfavorable opinions about Highlanders as it was, were outraged by the Wash Act's fine print, geared to entice the Highlanders. Feeling that their "hairy-kneed," tartan-wearing, rubelike Highland competitors were being given unfair advantages, the Lowlanders loudly cried "foul." On all fronts then—with Highlanders, Lowlanders, and landowners—Great Britain's MPs had badly miscalculated reaction to their actions . . . again.

The end of the 1780s witnessed both the dawn of the Industrial Revolution in Great Britain and the stunning rise of factory-like distilling in the Stein and Haig distilleries. The success of these ambitious, volume-oriented companies concerned the private distillers because of their might and ability to produce copious amounts of spirits. If this was to be the future of whisky making in Scotland, how could small distillers who made a few gallons of whisky a week hope to survive?

With the advantage of hindsight, it is reasonable to conclude that the eighteenth century was pivotal to the evolution of the whisky business in Scotland. This is so because the relentless governmental pressure and excessive legislation forced the cottage industry of home distilling to go underground. By becoming an outlaw industry, private distilling was doomed to failure after a few sputtering moments of glory. Only a fool would fail to recognize that Parliament's excise laws were designed to overwhelm and eventually break down the many small, private distillers while encouraging the fewer, larger companies to emerge and flourish. To what end? Because the few and the big were easier for lawmakers to contain, regulate, and drain of funds.

In 1793, one year after George Smith was born, more dire news spread throughout Scotland: Great Britain was going to war with France. And the hits just kept on coming.

Bladdermen, Bothies, Coffins, and Pony Trains

No matter how diligently one tries to romanticize whisky smuggling in Scotland's desolate Highlands, blustery islands, and along its craggy, dangerous coastlines, the cold reality of it all paints quite another picture. The artificial perception of ruddy-faced Highland lads attired in kilts sitting around a burbling pot still laughing as they hoist "anither cup o' kindness" is light years from the truth. Smuggling was a dirty and dangerous business. It took hold not because it was viewed as a frivolous leisure-time pursuit, but because Scotland and its inhabitants were in dire economic shambles. Scots were forced to make ends meet one way or another, often from subversive activities that operated outside the bounds of the law. That is not to say, however, that all smugglers were simple, wide-eyed, ordinary citizens turned illicit traders. There did exist a small, ruthless criminal element. The overwhelming majority of smugglers, though, were average citizens down on their luck.

Whisky smuggling hit stride by the early 1750s and kept accelerating throughout the length and breadth of Scotland until around 1830. About that time, the effects of the Excise Act of 1823 (legislation designed to at last undermine and destabilize private distilling once and for all) began to be broadly felt. By 1840, the Great Era of Whisky Smuggling in Scotland had, by and large, petered out. Parliament had been declared the victor by technical knockout. Though late nineteenth-century and early twentieth-century flashes of skulduggery flared up, these moments were softly rolling ripples on a placid pond compared with the massive, oceanic smuggling tsunamis of the Great Era.

For reasons already established—widespread poverty brought on by poor harvests, a lack of food, a roller-coaster ride of ever-changing regulations and duties, and a general distrust of London-based Parliament—normal Scots by the tens of thousands resorted to surreptitious illicit distilling for revenue generation. In its heyday—the latter half of the eighteenth century and the first quarter of the nineteenth century—smuggling became a self-perpetuating subculture, a wink-and-nod national cottage industry that touched nearly every Scottish life, young or old, city dweller or farmer. The more smugglers there were, the more whisky was consumed near and far, and the more money was to be made by smugglers and merchants. It was likewise during this flamboyant phase that Scotland's first noteworthy high-quality whiskies appeared. These were the harbingers of what was to come after 1824.

Most bothies, the compact, highly mobile, copper pot stills and accompanying equipment, ranged from 20 to 40 gallons in volume and were the property of cooperative proprietors. Typically, four to eight farmer-distillers owned and worked one bothy. As a practicality, the costs, workloads, and any fines incurred were equally divided. So, too, were profits. With multiple tenders available for supervision, the bothy could be percolating virtually nonstop. Everyone's hand was in the murky pool, even local officials, justices of the peace, landowners, and clergy. Farmers who weren't distillers furnished the barley to the smugglers, were maltsters, or were metalworkers who made stills or hauled illicit whisky to the Lowlands for sale.

To outwit gaugers, smugglers ingeniously concealed bothies beneath riverbanks, in shoreline caves, in the folds of undulating bogs, or deep within pine forests. Many were strategically situated adjacent to lime kilns or chimneys to conceal the telltale gray-silver trail of smoke, a dead giveaway for sharp-eyed gaugers. Journalist J. Gordon Phillips wrote five articles in April 1897, titled *The Origin of Glenlivet Whisky, With Some Account of the Smuggling,* for the *Distillers' Magazine and Spirit Trade News* monthly. Phillips interviewed scores of old smugglers, all residents of Glenlivet, who had been participants in the early 1800s. In the initial installment, Phillips described a typical streamside bothy: "The ingenuity exercised in the construction of these bothies was wonderful. Getting in beneath the banks where the bothy could be thatched down on the outer edge of the bank with heather so that it could not be distinguished, was a favorite plan, but sometimes they were constructed right under ground on a flat haugh." (A *haugh* is a low-lying, unusable flood plain next to a *burn*, aka stream or river.)

To no one's surprise, clashes between smugglers and gaugers increased as the smugglers strove to protect what for many of them had become a crucial source of income in otherwise hard times. In *The Secret Still: Scotland's Clandestine Whisky Makers* (2002, pp. 51, 52) author Gavin D. Smith reported, "Excise officers faced enormous handicaps when trying to execute their 'unpopular duties.' . . . The threat of violence was very real, and excise officers were sometimes kidnapped and held for weeks to prevent them from giving evidence in smuggling trials. . . . Physical assault went with the job . . ."

In 1815 near Glenlivet, smuggler Duncan McPherson attacked the gauger who had seized McPherson's bothy. Recounted the gauger, "He threatened me with immediate death if I offered to destroy any more, at the same time beating and bruising me to the effusion of blood, so far as medical aid was necessary." Other less-fortunate gaugers were murder victims, slain by knife, gun, rock, fist, boot, or club. Many were seriously maimed. Some simply disappeared in the bowels of the Highlands never to be seen again.

The gaugers were at a huge disadvantage for several reasons. They were, first and foremost, despised representatives of an unpopular government. They hurt the local economy by shutting down, confiscating, or destroying bothies. And, they were intruders who didn't know the lay of the land. To make matters even more difficult, they received little honest assistance from the tight-knit communities. In fact, the wily Highland Scots were known to routinely deceive gaugers by "informing" them of a supposedly working bothy. In actuality, gaugers would be sent to destroy an old, unusable pot still operation. After obtaining a reward—typically £5—for giving the excisemen the information, the informant would immediately purchase more copper to make brand-new equipment.

Smuggling was a dark avocation made up of several interdependent parts, the making of whisky being just one element of the process. For smugglers to realize a profit, they had to sell the whisky. Selling necessitated transporting it out of Glenlivet or other popular smuggling areas and discreetly marketing it. This stage of the process was called "disposal."

Groups of smugglers generally traveled south toward the major towns and commercial centers of Perth, Dundee, Stirling, and Edinburgh along well-established contraband routes that were previously marked and rutted to transport smuggled brandy and salt. Smugglers usually traveled in large caravans, called "pony trains," sometimes brazenly right in the open. In John R. Hume and Michael S. Moss's book *The Making of Scotch Whisky: A History of the Scotch Whisky Distilling Industry* (p. 53), they give an account of some findings from a report on smuggling dated 1790, ". . . traveling in bands of fifty, eighty or a hundred and a hundred and fifty horses remarkably stout and fleet [having] the audacity to go in this formidable manner in the open day upon the public high roads and through the streets of such towns and villages as they have occasion to pass."

The inventive smugglers devised all sorts of diversions and distractions to throw gaugers off the scent. Decoys carrying bundles, barrels, and boxes of nothing illegal were often sent ahead of pony trains to occupy the attention of gaugers while the smugglers took another parallel route. Both male and female smugglers concealed pig bladders filled with whisky beneath drapes of clothing as a means of transport. Others went to extraordinary lengths like staging fake funeral processions in which smugglers used empty coffins to transport gallons of whisky right in front of suspicious gaugers. Though tempted to halt the processions, the gaugers were frequently too wary to stop the "mourners" for fear of instant reprisals from the locals.

Not all smugglers were successful. Gaugers made hundreds of smuggling-related arrests, but convictions were harder to come by. Since Scotsmen from all quarters of society took part in smuggling, the general populace turned a blind eye to their activities. Impartial juries were hard to assemble. Sympathetic justices of the peace, like the infamous Auchorachan Justice William Grant, who was known as the "Cripple Captain" because of his wooden leg, frequently let off those who were arrested and brought before them by gaugers. For good reason. Local magistrates like the Cripple Captain were often themselves either smugglers or good customers. Besides, few Highland smugglers were caught in the act of distilling because word would rapidly spread throughout the glens when gaugers were first spotted by lookouts. Bothies were either moved or shut down in haste. Evidence against smugglers, therefore, was mostly circumstantial and slender.

Court cases involving smuggling sometimes took on an air of comedy. In Gavin D. Smith's book *The Secret Still: Scotland's Clandestine Whisky Makers* (p. 35), he recounts a story as told by nineteenth-century writer Alfred Barnard: "A capital story is told of an aged woman who resided near Hazelburn. She was of a rather doubtful character and was charged before the Sheriff with smuggling. The charge being held proven, it fell to his lordship to pronounce sentence. When about to do so he thus addressed the culprit, 'I daresay my poor woman it is not often you have been guilty of this fault.' 'Deed no Sheriff,' she readily replied. 'I haven't made a drop since I sent that wee keg to yourself.'" (For clarity's sake, the author has taken the liberty of paraphrasing the woman's heavily stylized retort.)

Then there's the oft-told story of the court case of the Speyside smuggler described only as Willie. When asked by the magistrate in Elgin if Willie had been caught in the act of distilling whisky, the arresting gauger admitted to the court that he had not. "But," asserted the gauger, "Willie had all the necessary equipment." After being found guilty, Willie was asked by the magistrate if there were any other crimes that he'd like to fess up to before sentencing. "Aye, your honor. Rape," replied Willie. "Rape?" bellowed the magistrate. "You're admitting to this court that you've committed rape?" Willie snapped back, "No. I haven't raped anyone, your honor . . . but I've all the necessary equipment."

For all the humorous anecdotes and larger-than-life escapades that revolved around Scotland's Great Era of Smuggling, the downside was that the pervasive widespread illegal, reckless behavior cast a patina of lawlessness over the Highlands. As recounted by Sir Robert Bruce Lockhart in his fine old book *Scotch: The Whisky of Scotland in Fact and Story* (1951, p. 21), writer John Wilson, who wrote under the nom de plume of Christopher North, traveled to the village of Tomintoul in 1815, just a few miles south of Glenlivet. Wilson depicted Tomintoul at the height of the smuggling era as "a wild mountain village where drinking, dancing, swearing and quarrelling went on all the time." This rowdy influence was not lost on all Glenliveters. It is worth pointing out that Wilson also thought that the whisky from Glenlivet was the finest he had ever tasted.

As it turned out, lovely Glenlivet, 14 miles long and 6 miles wide, was the most highly favored location in the Highlands for smugglers. According to Richard Grindal, author of *The Spirit of Whisky: An Affectionate Account of the Water of Life* (1992, pp. 29, 31), "In the small parish of Glenlivet alone it was believed that two hundred small stills were operated. . . . In the little glen . . . whisky of a special quality has been made for centuries. To ask why would be pointless, for no one could give a finite answer to such a question. Distillers have known it instinctively, which is why there were so many bothy stills in that tiny parish. One of these stills belonged to George Smith . . ."

Archivist Iain Russell's research about the inherent quality of illicit late eighteenth-century and early nineteenth-century whiskies from the place of Glenlivet compelled him to reckon, "The smugglers believed that the unusual climate of Glenlivet, the altitude of the glen, and the mossy water of the hill streams there, combined to give the whisky its unique character. As the excisemen rarely visited the glen, the locals could take a long time in distilling new spirits, running the whisky 'lazily' over a small fire. This was a luxury not allowed to other smugglers, constantly on the look-out for the gaugers. . . . Glenlivet whisky, fully matured and with its unique flavour, soon became a great favourite of the Lowland connoisseurs."

One nineteenth-century Glenlivet admirer by the name of James Hogg waxed, "The human mind never tires o' Glenlivet. . . . If a body could find oot the exac' proportion and quantity that ought to be drunk every day and keep to that, I verily trow that he might leeve for ever, without dying at a,' and that doctors and kirkyards [churchyard cemeteries] would go oot o' fashion."

Whatever the reasons, folly or fact, whisky from Glenlivet, the place, became the benchmark in the minds of seasoned whisky drinkers decades before George Smith obtained a license in 1824 for his family distillery at Upper Drumin. This prevailing wind, born of location, good base materials, and distilling artistry, propelled George Smith, the glen's finest distiller, and his The Glenlivet to unimagined heights.

The Glenlivet

ANDREW AND MARGARET GORDON SMITH insisted on providing good educations within their modest means for their children, especially their six sons. An industrious, robust, and quick-witted lad, George Smith attended school locally at Burnside of Deskie. The Upper Drumin tack was renewed in 1803—not by Andrew Smith, who was 61 that year—but by William Smith, the eldest Smith son, and the Smith boys' maternal uncle, John Gordon. Two years later for reasons that are unclear and immaterial, John Gordon extricated himself from the tack and was replaced by James Smith, who most likely was an uncle or older cousin of the half-dozen Smith brothers. One year later, James Smith assumed the responsibilities of the whole Upper Drumin tack when William relinquished his share. William, the speculation goes, wanted first to secure the Upper Drumin tack for the family but then moved on to establish his own life elsewhere in the glen.

Through all the leaseholder changes, young George remained either at or within close orbit of Upper Drumin. The years passed for the tall, strapping youth as he worked on the family farm. His ambitious nature and innate curiosity reached beyond tending livestock and grain cultivation, though. In 1814, the year George turned 22, he applied to become an apprentice of master square-wright John Davidson. "Square-wright" was the name bestowed on a highly skilled carpenter who worked predominantly crafting fine wood furniture. Davidson accepted the application, and George soon began learning a needed trade.

Though a report in the *London Scotsman* on September 19, 1868, described George as "a smuggler of the smugglers," no unambiguous evidence exists to support or deny George's involvement with illicit distilling during his youth. Deductive minds can, however, take the leap of faith that he at least learned the basics of whisky distilling from his father or from one or more of his older brothers, William, John, or Charles, or from a friend. As crucial events unfolded in the early and middle 1820s, it stands to reason that George was more than a mere dabbler, much more than a distilling neophyte by the time he reached the age of 30. It is wholly realistic, in fact, to conclude that George was a talented, if shrewd, smuggler whose clandestine pursuits remained cleverly concealed.

Parish records indicate that in 1816 George had a daughter, Helen, out of wedlock. The parish clerk did not record the name of the mother. The child's fate remains unknown. In 1817, George opened a new chapter in his life when he married Helen Stewart, a local girl who was the prized daughter of Lieutenant Stewart of Glenlivet. Lieutenant Stewart had served honorably with the 1st Royals and perished in Egypt at the Battle of Aboukir. George and Helen Stewart Smiths' firstborn, William, came on the scene in 1818, followed by Margaret in 1820 and, third and last, John Gordon in 1822. Presumably, George and Helen Stewart Smith occupied a farmhouse near to or in Upper Drumin, the leased family home since 1784. George's older brothers appear to have scattered to other parts of the glen by that time. George worked closely with James Smith to maintain and upgrade Upper Drumin.

For the next few years, circa 1816 to 1820, George toiled hard as a square-wright, a farmer and, very probably, a whisky smuggler. Even with smuggling in Glenlivet at record production levels and better whiskies fetching around six to seven shillings per gallon in the Scottish Lowlands and northern England, his opinion of smuggling's social and economic impact on the glen began to shift. As the risks of smuggling heightened, George was probably swayed by all the talk about the potential benefits to distillers of legalization.

Doubtless, the deeply held beliefs of Alexander Gordon, the 4th Duke of Gordon and the owner of Upper Drumin and many other properties scattered throughout Banffshire, Inverness-shire, and Aberdeenshire, influenced George's thinking. The Duke held that the unrealistically harsh strictures imposed on Scotsmen since the 1640s encouraged rather than discouraged smuggling. If the laws were liberalized, the Duke reasoned, then the production of illicit whisky would lose its primary purpose. In 1820, Alexander Gordon delivered a stirring speech in the House of Lords, recounted Gavin D. Smith (*The Secret Still: Scotland's Clandestine Whisky Makers,* p. 11), ". . . in which he reflected the views of many of his noble colleagues with estates in the north of Scotland. He promised that if the Government would expand upon the legislation of 1816 and 1818 and make it more favourable for illicit distillers to become legitimate, then he and his fellow landowners would undertake to uphold the law as diligently as they could, and evict anyone convicted of illicit distilling."

The gentry and a handful of tacksmen such as George Smith believed that smuggling had evolved from a just, if romantic, defense against an overreaching government to an anachronistic cancer that was jeopardizing many Scottish communities. For one thing, gaugers had grown more proficient; Parliament even dispatched mounted troops known as dragoons to assist the gaugers. Landowners were tired of having gaugers and dragoons scour their lands for smugglers. Tenants were being arrested and detained; sometimes they were convicted and incarcerated—and jailed tenants had trouble paying rent. In 1822, according to the *Scotch Whisky Industry Record* (p. 76), there were 4,867 smuggling-related prosecutions, a huge increase over the wild days of the 1780s and 1790s when a laissez-faire attitude ruled. Things had to change.

Mild as Milk, the True Contraband

Though the tide was now starting to turn against smuggling, illicit whisky received an unexpected and unintentional boost from none other than George IV, King of Great Britain. During a much-ballyhooed royal visit to Scotland in August 1822, word got out that the

King had become smitten with whisky, in particular, the highly re-spected illicit variety produced in or around Glenlivet.

Wrote Elizabeth Grant in her period tome *Memoirs of a Highland Lady 1797–1830*, "The whole country went mad. Everybody strained every point to get to Edinburgh to receive him. Sir Walter Scott and the Town Council were overwhelming themselves with the prepara-tions. . . . One incident connected with this time made me very cross. Lord Conyngham, the Chamberlain, was looking everywhere for pure Glenlivet whisky; the King drank nothing else. It was not to be had out of the Highlands. My father sent word to me—I was the cellerar—to empty my pet bin, where was whisky long in wood, long in uncorked bottles, mild as milk, and the true contraband gout in it. Much as I grudged this treasure it made our fortunes afterwards, showing on what trifles great events depend. The whisky . . . went up to Holyrood House, and [was] graciously received and made much of, and a remainder of this attention at a proper moment by the gen-tlemanly Chamberlain ensured to my father the Indian judgeship."

The King reportedly consumed whisky during his visit in a con-coction called the "Atholl-brose," a thick, sweetish mixture of whisky, honey and ground grain. His supposed appreciation of smug-gler's whisky instigated a national awareness of the superior quality of whisky from Glenlivet, which became something of a brand name for better smugglers' whisky. This wide recognition catapulted for-ward the mystique of Scotland's most famous glen, even though doubtless much of the illicit whisky touted as "Glenlivet" was pro-duced in other areas of the Highlands. His admiration of Glenlivet also led him to instruct his Home Secretary, Robert Peel, to request of the Board of Excise that they exercise clemency to smugglers. George IV clearly didn't want his whisky supply to be cut off.

The landowners had likewise become impatient with being held li-able for the unpaid fines of smugglers caught doing their handiwork on leased property. The Duke's eloquence, sensibility, and determination set the wheels in motion for a parliamentary committee, led by Lord Wallace, to further study the excise law issues from all sides. Two years after the Duke of Gordon's noteworthy and persuasive oratory, the Illicit

Distillation (Scotland) Act was ratified by Parliament. The ID(S) Act raised eyebrows immediately by elevating penalties to £200, an extraordinarily stiff sum for the era, for anyone apprehended while in possession of illicit whisky and £100 assessed to anyone owning an unlicensed pot still. Other provisions mostly dealing with permits went in the favor of small distillers. The 1822 Act, more than anything else, smoothed the path for what would eventually come to be known as the Act that thrust a lance through the heart of smuggling in Scotland, the Excise Act of 1823.

Lord Wallace's Commission handed Parliament all the ammunition they required to blow gaping holes in the foundation of whisky smuggling. The Excise Act, which astutely and broadly eased restrictions on virtually every major point of contention, became law in 1823. Ingeniously written to undercut the core arguments for smuggling, the Excise Act of 1823 called for significantly lower duties on whisky (2 shillings 3 pence per gallon), a fee of only £10 to acquire a license, a minimum pot still size of 40 gallons, duty-free warehousing for all whiskies and, with some reservations, the opening of markets in Ireland, England, and all other trading nations.

Allowing that the Acts of 1822 and 1823 castrated the smuggling subculture, they likewise did something else. In his book *A to Z of Whisky* (1993, pp. 60–61), Gavin D. Smith states, "The effects of the two new Acts were very soon obvious. The number of licensed distilleries in Scotland doubled in two years, and production of duty-paid whisky rose from two million gallons to six million gallons per annum. Illicit distillation fell dramatically during the next few years, with an astonishing 14,000 detections being made in 1823 . . . but only 692 in 1834, and six in 1874."

Addressing the bigger picture, Charles MacLean in *Malt Whisky* (p. 21) claimed with justification, "These changes laid the foundations of the modern whisky industry. No longer was it necessary to design and operate stills primarily to avoid paying tax; no longer need there be a difference in quality between legally produced whisky and illicit whisky and no longer was it so desirable to work outside the law. Distillers could now choose their own method of working; what strength of wash to use and what size and design of still would produce the best whisky."

Astonishingly, from 1644 to 1823 over 30 separate and amending pieces of distilling legislation had been drawn up and implemented, first by the Parliament of Scotland prior to 1707 and then after 1707 by the Parliament of Great Britain. The Duke of Gordon, who would in short order be landlord of Scotland's foremost licensed malt whisky distillery, The Glenlivet, operated by his esteemed tenant George Smith, and Lord Wallace together provided the impetus for the Parliament of Great Britain to finally get it right.

Meanwhile in Glenlivet, George Smith was about to make whisky history. But would it cost him his life?

Financial Woes, Bitter Foes

The Upper Drumin lease was set to expire in 1823. To complicate matters for George Smith, his landlord, the Duke of Gordon, was experiencing serious financial difficulties due in part to the dishonesty of his factor, or estate foreman, William Mitchell. The Reverend John Anderson caught the light-fingered, conniving Mitchell embezzling £3,200 from the duke, a staggering sum for the day. Anderson acted as the Duke's Commissioner, a kind of overseer/advisor of financial and legal matters regarding the duke's estates and holdings. Mitchell fell prey to an age-old modus operandi: He stole the duke's money to satisfy his own mounting debts. Because the losses were largely unrecoverable, Mitchell's nefarious actions threw the duke's estates into turmoil and jeopardized his financial status. George and Helen Stewart Smith were concerned about their uncertain living situation at Upper Drumin. Would the duke's financial troubles affect them renewing the Upper Drumin lease?

James Skinner, a sound and reputable young man with superb management skills, replaced Mitchell as the Duke's estate factor in 1823. Making his case to retain at least part of Upper Drumin under the new management, George proposed that he and a friend Peter Fraser share the tack. George's primary, if visionary, line of reasoning was that the Upper Drumin property could support a proper, licensed malt whisky distillery—a legal distillery that could produce larger volumes of superior whisky than the small bothies that dotted Glenlivet's countryside. The production of legal whisky would favorably affect the glen's barley farmers, George reasoned. Perhaps the opening of one legal distillery would even stimulate further interest within the Glenlivet community to swap smuggling for lawful distilling.

Because of their relationship with the Duke of Gordon, George Smith, Skinner, and Anderson were all acutely aware that the governmental wheels were in motion for Parliament to enact sweeping new excise legislation. They knew that in time it would be more profitable to operate a permanent, licensed distillery than to continue making illicit whisky on-the-run. Despite what some Glenlivet residents conjured up, there appeared to be little future in scurrying around the countryside with a pot still strapped to one's back trying to evade gaugers and troops. George contended to Skinner that the future of whisky making in Glenlivet and all of Scotland lay in legalization. To him, the future seemed inevitable and as crystal clear as fresh spirit off the still. George maintained with confidence that he could make a distillery at Upper Drumin a success.

Skinner, as it happened, was already a proponent of licensed distilling as a way to improve Glenlivet's sagging economy. In his report to Anderson, Skinner noted, "I have for some time back recommended in the strongest terms to all whom I believed possessed of the means to form joint companies and set on foot small legal stills, and I think I would have in several cases succeeded, but [for] the want of proper houses. . . . There is a tenant in Upper Drumin, who has a house he last year built for a different purpose, which will he thinks answer, and he proposes in a short time to commence. Indeed, he told me today that he had the intention of going to Elgin this week to obtain the requisite license."

On hearing of George's plans for Upper Drumin, the Reverend Anderson urged Skinner to grant the tack. Since George was of sound character as well as industrious and smart, Skinner quickly consented. George agreed to pay the Duke the annual sum of £9, while Peter Fraser agreed to pay £18. Green, hilly Upper Drumin was secured then for the next two decades. Feeling betrayed and embarrassed by the Mitchell misappropriation fiasco, Anderson yearned to right the Duke's financial ship. He and Skinner were fully cognizant that since the 1750s whisky making had blossomed into the glen's number one industry. At the minimum, one hundred illegal bothies were known to be bubbling away in the nooks and crannies of the glen in the early 1820s. Some unsubstantiated estimates doubled that total. If whisky making were legalized across the board, Anderson must have wondered, how profitable could a proper Glenlivet whisky distillery become, keeping in mind the glen's impeccable reputation? Additionally, under the leadership of a trusted and reliable tenant like George Smith, to what point could the Duke's long-range fortunes prosper?

There was another side to the story of legitimacy in Glenlivet, however. Consider for a moment the dilemma facing the smugglers who didn't have an influential patron/landlord in their corner. In the early 1820s, almost everyone residing in Glenlivet was somehow involved with smuggling at some step in the process. Some farmed the bere, the hearty barley that was turned into whisky. Others repaired the smugglers' copper pot stills, condenser coils, and storage vats. Many distilled whisky. Still others transported it. People embraced smuggling because everyone was consuming Highlands whisky and there was profit—meager, albeit, most of the time—to be reaped. Michael Brander, in *The Original Scotch* (p. 70), reports the words written by the Reverend Thomas Guthrie in 1818, "Everybody, with few exceptions drank what was in reality illicit whisky—far superior to that made under the eye of the Excise—lords and lairds, members of Parliament and ministers of the gospel and everybody else."

But trouble lay ahead. Most Glenliveters were not willing to cheerfully relinquish what had become a way of life for generations as well as a method of generating some income simply because the Acts of 1822 and 1823 had been passed. Acts of Parliament had come and gone before. Allowing for all the inconveniences, the overall success of smuggling, especially in Glenlivet, could not be denied. Illicit Glenlivet whisky had become the unrivaled gold standard. Whisky drinkers from Aberdeen to the Scottish Lowlands had learned to demand "the real Glenlivet" in roadside taverns and inns. More to the point, the Glenlivet smugglers, George's neighbors, were not prepared to naively trust a government that had arbitrarily changed the rules concerning distilling so many times.

Aside from harboring deep suspicions about the motives of their London-based government, the smugglers faced more immediate, potentially calamitous issues. For one thing, they were gravely concerned that suddenly growing numbers of legal distillers and whiskies could eventually drive the smugglers out of business. More legitimate whisky at low prices could destabilize their under-the-counter business. Another key reason for their resentment of those who were turning legal was that one provision in the 1823 Act authorized the stationing of excise officials at all legal distilleries, meaning an increased presence of gaugers in the glen. This provision infuriated the smugglers.

From those standpoints, the smugglers' reluctance to apply for licensing was understandable as was their disdain of those who did apply. But disdain is one thing and aggression is another. The smugglers had no assurance that going the legal path would pay as handsomely as staying a smuggler. Risks be damned and a pox on those who decided to turn legitimate, they fumed in the inns and taverns.

Despite local opposition and threatening whispers heard in the community, farmer and former smuggler George Smith traveled to Elgin in the late autumn of 1824 to apply for his license to distill legal whisky in Glenlivet. Some accounts cite George Smith as the first duly licensed distiller in the Highlands. That assertion is unsubstantiated and wrong. Licenses under the terms of the Excise Act of 1823 for other sites were applied for as early as the late fall of 1823, soon after the Act's passage. Cardow Distillery in Knockando (today known as Cardhu) possibly preceded George Smith's The Glenlivet as Speyside's first distillery to be licensed under the Act. Whatever the situation, in January 1825, the Supervisor of the Elgin Collection, John Anderson, notified his superiors at the Scottish Excise Board in Edinburgh that George's new distillery at Upper Drumin, "was about to commence."

George began producing fresh spirit sometime in the winter of 1825. Highland whisky in 1825 was sold unaged and raw, frequently in 10-gallon casks referred to as "ankers." In a revealing letter dated April 4, 1825, from James Skinner to the Reverend Anderson, who was anxious to sample George's whisky, Skinner noted, "I have ordered the four ankers of whisky which you mentioned from George Smith but his

A license from The Glenlivet.

demands are more than he can answer, and it will be ten days yet before he can send it. He says however you will not have cause to complain that the article is not equal to any smuggled whisky." If George had a backlog of orders, it seems certain that word of his excellent product had already spread throughout the glen.

George's two pot stills were at least large enough to meet the legal minimum of 40 gallons as specified by the Excise Act. Since they were 40-gallon stills or larger, George was producing at most 100 gallons of new Glenlivet whisky per week. Probably 50 to 60 gallons weekly was more accurate. Smugglers' pot stills, smaller and cruder, were no match in terms of volume for a pair of full-time pot stills. As George's fame grew, the ire of the smugglers against him escalated. An atmosphere of retribution hung over the glen like laden springtime clouds. The insect floating in the whisky was that George's optimism about the future of legal distilling in Scotland was shared by few of his Glenlivet neighbors.

When rumors circulated that some other reformed Glenlivet smugglers, for example, the infamous Peter McKerron, James McHardy, and James McPherson, were pondering going legitimate, blatant threats were made to their faces. Legal distillers were derisively labeled as "blacklegs" by the angry smugglers, who looked on them as turncoats, opportunists, and colluders with the government. Peter McKerron, who broke ranks with the smugglers in 1823, spoke openly about the intimidation tactics by neighborhood smugglers. The smugglers made it clear to McKerron that if he applied for a license they would destroy his distillery operation. McKerron's distillery at Whitehouse in Aberlour was a brief affair. James McPherson obtained a license shortly after George Smith. While McPherson was transporting a cache of his legal whisky south in 1826, a band of smugglers assaulted him in Glen Gairn. Concerned that emboldened smugglers would inflict worse damage than a moderate beating next time, McPherson shut down his distillery.

Suspicious fires destroyed several upstart legal distilleries throughout the Highlands. The Banks o' Dee Distillery in Aberdeenshire went up in flames in 1825, the victim of arson. Its proprietor was nearly incinerated in the blaze. Smugglers razed James McHardy's distillery at Corgarff Castle in 1826. News of other distillery closures at Croftbain, Braeval, and

Stobbie in Glenlivet and Coul and Achfad in Morange echoed through-out Banffshire.

Years later in a newspaper interview, George Smith described the hazardous years of 1824, 1825, and 1826 in Glenlivet, "When the new Act was heard of in Glenlivet and in the Highlands of Aberdeenshire, they [the smugglers] ridiculed the idea that anyone should be found daring enough to start distilling in their midst . . . the desperate character of the smugglers and the violence of their threats deterred anyone for some time. At length in 1824, I, George Smith, who was then a robust young fellow, and not given to be easily 'fleggit,' determined to chance it. I was already a tenant of the Duke and received every encouragement from his grace and his factor Mister Skinner. The outlook was an ugly one, though. I was warned by my civil neighbors that they [smugglers] meant to burn the new distillery to the ground and me in the heart of it."

His mortal enemies were soon to discover that George Smith of Upper Drumin was not a man who easily caved in to bullying and coercion. Come what may, George Smith was in Glenlivet to stay as a fully licensed distiller of fine malt whisky. Why else would he start packing pistols?

Timely Passages

THE SAME YEAR, 1824, that George Smith acquired the license from the Board of Excise in Elgin for his distillery at Upper Drumin, James Chivas was 14 years old. James Chivas was born on December 20, 1810, to Robert (1767–1847) and Christian Chivas (1775–1842) at his parents' Strathythan farm at Overtown of Dudwick in Ellon Parish. The sixth of thirteen children by Robert and Christian Chivas, James, like his siblings Alexander (1801), Robert (1802), Adam (1804), William (1805 or 1806), Ann (1807), Nathaniel (1809), Elizabeth (1812), John (1814), Christian (1815), Jean (1817), George (1819) and Christian (1827) worked on the family farm and attended local Strathythan schools. The second Christian Chivas of 1827 was so named in honor of the first Christian Chivas (1815) who died at the age of two.

Generations of the Chivas family had been residing in the Strathythan area of Aberdeenshire for centuries. Genealogical research delving into the pedigree of the lyrical family name Chivas (pronounced SHI-viss) that began in the 1950s and spanned the rest of the twentieth century confirmed the family's long-standing presence in the parishes north of Aberdeen. There have been numerous variations on the name Chivas, including Shivas, Schivas, Sheves, Chewis, Sevas, Civis, Sivis,

Chivish, Scheeves, and Scives. In the early years of ancestral research, historians in Aberdeenshire thought the name was rooted in Norman origins. But in 2000, Glasgow University archivist Iain Russell deflated that theory when he unearthed more detailed information. Russell sent a memo to Colin Scott, the master blender of Chivas Brothers charged with tracing the Chivas lineage, claiming, "There is no evidence that [the name Chivas] has anything to do with any Normans or their pals who came to Scotland—rather it appears to be from an old Gaelic place-name . . ."

A place-name authority, Simon Taylor, at the University of St. Andrews informed Russell in 1996 that he believed Chivas was far more likely to have been derived from the Gaelic phrase for "a narrow place," *Seimhas*, pronounced shave-ASZ. In Russell's mind, this made sense because two famous structures, the older a medieval castle built in the thirteenth or fourteenth century and the younger a fortified edifice called the House of Schivas constructed in middle of the sixteenth century, were strategically situated at narrow points on the banks of the River Ythan. The River Ythan descends from its source high in the Grampian Highlands winding through a pastoral district that used to be the Barony of Schivas on its way to the North Sea. The Barony of Schivas, located directly north of the city of Aberdeen, was the stronghold of the Schivas/Chivas clan from the thirteenth to the eighteenth century.

Russell discovered that the House of Schivas, which still stands, was erected close to where the old castle/fortress stood. Further on in his memo to Colin Scott, Russell explained, "So Schivas is probably from 'Seimh as' . . . which describes its important location, at a narrow, fordable stretch of the River Ythan . . . 'Our' Chivas family [meaning the creators of Chivas Regal] were almost certainly descended from people who lived in or near Schivas." In the same memo from 2000, Russell posits another intriguing possibility about the source of Chivas, "Of course these things are partly conjecture. . . . So it's worth bearing in mind (and you may find that this is useful in some situations) that 'seamhas' (pronounced shevus) is a Gaelic word for 'prosperity' or 'good luck'—I checked that in my Gaelic dictionary!"

A viewing of the accumulated data for this book as well as further independent investigation concurs with Russell's conclusions. Nonetheless, whatever the name's derivation, the Chivas clan was well established in northeastern Scotland in the medieval era of kings, dukes, barons, feudal armies, and castles. While it was a widely known surname in Aberdeenshire by 1400, Chivas would become a household name on a global basis five and a half centuries later.

Sparked by the Industrial Revolution, Scotland in the 1820s and 1830s was an expectant nation bursting with commercial, financial, and technological potential. In *The New Penguin History of Scotland: From the Earliest Times to the Present Day* (2002, pp. 349, 350), historian Bruce P. Lenman points out, "Scotland in the early nineteenth century was not yet an industrial society. It was an agrarian one which had experienced a dramatic expansion in industry and commerce. . . . Obviously, Scotland shared after 1707 in the progressive globalization of European commerce, far more so than it had before the Union."

Like anywhere in Scotland in the first half of the 1800s, life on the Chivas family farm in rural Aberdeenshire was tedious, grueling, and confined. Livestock, mostly sheep, needed endless daily tending and herding plus seasonal birthing. The fields required long hours of plowing, planting, and harvesting. The average day began at least an hour before dawn and lasted well into the early evening. By 1824, the Robert Chivas farmhouse burgeoned with children. Its rafters rang with a cacophony of domestic racket and familial interaction. Robert Chivas's main concern was whether the farm could support his expanding family.

William Chivas was the first sibling to escape Strathythan, deciding to go to sea in the late 1820s. Remembering later in life about his departure as a young man from the only home he knew, William said, "A big country loon, I left my parental roof with only a few shillings in my pocket, two shirts in my bundle, and my good mother's blessings and a Bible." Eventually, William advanced through the ranks to captain a merchant vessel, traveling to the Indian subcontinent and the Orient.

When his older brother William left the farm to seek his fortune by roaming the oceans' trade routes, James took note and started to ponder his own future. Farming, while it was all that he knew, held little attraction for him. News of the astounding growth and opportunity in the seaport city of Aberdeen, located just a 20-mile hike to the south, kept ringing in James's ears. His older cousin Alexander Chivas resided in

Aberdeen, after all, working for a bank, so James at least had a family contact of some influence in place. In late 1835, he confided to his younger brother John that he was considering pursuing his destiny elsewhere. John, who had also been fantasizing about adventures away from Strathythan, liked the idea of striking out from Ellon Parish and decided to join his older brother. Their departure would lighten the load somewhat for Robert and Christian in that there would be two less mouths for which to provide food. Plenty of siblings would remain to help operate the farm.

The following year at the respective ages of 26 and 22, James and John Chivas, two more "country loons," waved goodbye to their parents and brothers and sisters as they began their long trek to the place of their dreams, Aberdeen. No Aberdeenshire train line existed in 1836. No stagecoaches ran north-south routes from Aberdeen to Fraserburgh. Robert had no horses. James and John had no choice but to walk the 20 miles. Aberdeenshire's rural lanes were rutted, muddy, and in atrocious condition. The road designated nowadays as "A92" was their probable route. Their march was slowed doubtless by overflowing bundles of clothes and books and perhaps by inclement weather. It likely took them two to three days at the minimum to reach the northern reaches of Aberdeen. Finally, James and John approached the north bank of the River Don and the spectacle of the massive, single-arch Union Bridge, the first stone bridge they had ever seen. One can imagine them silently standing at the lip of the bridge and peering in awe across the span at broad and cavernous Union Street, the bustling, noisy commercial heart of Aberdeen.

For the naive, young, but clever and ambitious Chivas brothers, there was no going back then to Ellon Parish. Scotland's sparkling and dynamic Granite City awaited them on the south side of the River Don and across the Union Bridge.

An Extraordinary Symphony in Grey

The Earth's greatest cities have customarily been built on or within spitting distance of navigable bodies of water, either flowing rivers, estuaries, deep harbors, or large lakes. Aberdeen is a coastal city facing east toward the grey-green, humbling North Sea and the sunrise. The city is advantageously situated between two roughly parallel rivers, the River Dee to the south and the River Don to the north. Both rivers flow east in their final stretches and belch fresh water into the North Sea. Unlike other major Scottish municipalities that exist in relatively close proximity to rival cities, like Edinburgh and Glasgow or Dundee and Perth, Aberdeen dwells within the cultural or economic aura of no competing metropolis. It is an old municipal entity that was famously favored by Robert the Bruce in the fourteenth century following his upset victory over the English at Bannockburn.

The travel book *Lonely Planet: Scotland* (p. 309) describes Aberdeen as ". . . an extraordinary symphony in grey. Almost everything is built of grey granite, including the roads, which are paved with crushed granite. . . . The name Aberdeen is a combination of two Pictish-Gaelic words, 'aber' and 'devana,' meaning the meeting of two waters. The area was known to the Romans, and was raided by the Vikings when it was an increasingly important port, with trade conducted in wool, fish, hides and fur."

Aberdeen is defined as much by its remoteness in northeastern Scotland and the encircling caress of pastoral Deeside as it is by its two rivers, fine deep harbor, and estuary. By the time that James and John Chivas set out to walk the score of miles from Ellon Parish to the city in 1836, Aberdeen, embracing the concept of the Industrial Revolution, was exploding with ideas, with new granite building construction, with wide new streets and bridges, with new manufacturing industries, and, just as important, with thousands of eager new faces.

The fresh faces were largely supplied by the surrounding countryside from hamlets and towns like Dyce, Kintore, Old Meldrum, Newburgh, Inverurie, Peterculte, and Ellon, where living conditions were necessarily colored by frugality and challenge. Over a significant 100-year span, Aberdeen's population zoomed from around 15,000 in 1750 to 72,000 in 1850. According to the book *Aberdeen 1800–2000: A New History* (2000, p. 47), edited by W. Hamish Fraser and Clive H. Lee, ". . . the growth of the textile industry the first three decades of the new century (the 1800s) brought spectacular rates of growth of close to 30 percent per decade . . . in the first half of the nineteenth century, population increased by two and a half times to reach 71,973 by 1851."

Transportation was a nagging problem for Aberdonians in the early 1800s. Only 10 stagecoaches serviced the Aberdeen area in 1820 with three of those regularly rumbling south to Dundee. Prior to the 1850s when the Great North of Scotland Railway finally connected Aberdeen to Scotland's cities in the south, the seaport was Aberdeen's primary lifeline to the rest of Scotland, England, and the world. Fishing was a major industry in the 1830s. The city's natural deep harbor fostered an industry related to fishing and shipbuilding. By the turn of the nineteenth century, Aberdeen boasted seven shipyards that mostly produced small, quick vessels, typically less than 100 tons, that were employed both for fishing and for short-haul sailing south to London and east to Europe.

By 1800, Aberdeen was gradually becoming a financial center as well, boasting several banks. In 1815, the Aberdeen Savings Bank opened its doors, thereby promoting the concept of preserving assets in a safe, nearby, and accessible place. The North of Scotland Bank, which dedicated its resources and services to the local community in the northeast, was founded in 1836. Manufacturing likewise took firm hold in Aberdeen in the first half of the nineteenth century. In 1825, John Moir & Son began canning edibles like trout, crab, lobster, and salmon. Small textile factories producing linens opened. Aberdonians also quarried enormous amounts of granite in the 1800s, a trade that employed hundreds of men. London was the primary market for granite. The Rubislaw Quarry opened in 1740 and was still going strong a century later.

Aberdeen was also a vibrant, progressive city of printed information from 1800 to 1850. In the historical account titled *The City and Its Worlds: Aspects of Aberdeen's History since 1794* (1996, p. 101), edited by Terry Brotherstone and Donald J. Withrington, local historian Iain Beavan observed, "The 1830s and early 1840s kept local printers busy. The output of the local press in the 1830s was almost double that of the previous decade, and this increased activity was sustained into the 1840s. It was also very much a period of the local periodical and newspaper, with about 45 titles launched between 1830 and 1845."

The most popular dailies included the *Aberdeen Herald* (1832–1876), *Aberdeen Banner* (1840–1851), *Aberdeen Journal* (1828–1852), and the *Aberdeen Observer* (1829–1837). During the 1830s, the *Journal's* circulation totaled approximately 2,400 copies while the *Herald's* was about 1,300. Aberdeen's newspapers were filled with the advertisements of purveyors of clothing, exotic imported foods, satin hats ("Your head! Your head! Take care of your head!!!" bellowed one advertisement in the *Herald*), fine linens and cloth, as well as handmade furniture.

Along with the economic boom came the development of a vigorous middle class that had disposable income to spend on amenities and luxuries. Shops along Union Street, King Street, and Castle Street, the three main commercial avenues, catered to this growing economic force. As they grew accustomed to the layout of the city, James and John Chivas passed by the numerous storefronts of specialty vendors like Samuel Martin, Hatter to the People, at 34 Union Street, and William Edward, fine grocer and wine seller, at 47 Castle Street. With each passing week, it was evident that James and John had made a wise decision. Aberdeen was home.

In 1801, John Forrest unlocked the door on his grocery shop for the first time. Located at 47 Castle Street, Forrest's storefront was within sight of Castlegate, the traditional center of Aberdeen and the site of the old demolished castle. "In the course of the nineteenth century, Aberdeen grew outwards from its historic centre around the Castlegate and the harbour and expanded along the channels marked out by the new streets and their hinterland," wrote historian John S. Smith in the opening chapter of *Aberdeen 1800–2000: A New History* (p. 25).

Mirroring the bright economic fortunes of Aberdeen in the early nineteenth century, Forrest's retail business rapidly grew. In the 1820s, he hired a bright, energetic young man by the name of William Edward to manage his shop. In 1828, six years prior to the arrival in Aberdeen of James and John Chivas, Forrest died. William Edward wasted no time and purchased the shop from the deceased proprietor's family. He promptly bought the next-door cellar at 46 Castle Street, thereby almost doubling his shop's space. That same year, Edward identified himself for the Aberdeen Post Office Directory as a grocer, wine, and spirits purveyor and provision merchant.

Inside the Chivas Brothers shop on King Street.

Seeing an opportunity to become a "total service merchant" to Aberdeen's thriving wealthy citizens, Edward advertised in local newspapers that he was now additionally acting as an employment agency for domestic help. Edward astutely concluded that since the prosperous middle and upper classes of Aberdeen and Deeside formed the core of his retail customer base, providing reliable servants would only further solidify his client relationships. For a fee, Edward and his staff began staffing affluent households with qualified cooks, housemaids, butlers, grooms, laundry maids, nannies, and nursemaids. Edward moved his shop to 49 Castle Street in 1834. Three years later, Edward, seeking even larger quarters to house his retail and service placement businesses, relocated to 13 King Street.

In 1838, Edward's banker friend Alexander Chivas introduced him to his young and inexperienced cousin James Chivas. Edward hired James as his assistant and thereby started a business relationship that would alter the course of Scotch whisky history forever.

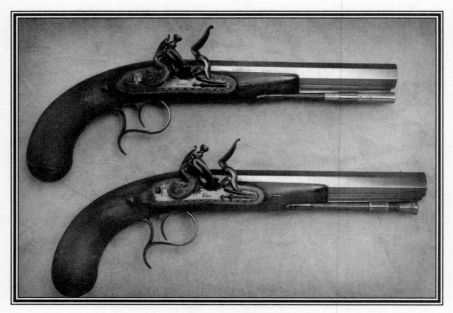

George Smith's famous pistols.

Smoking Guns and Castles Three

DESPITE THE VERY real possibility of violence befalling his newly opened Upper Drumin Glenlivet Distillery or, for that matter, his person, George Smith distilled whisky in 1825 within the limits and the nominal protection of the law. In weekly volumes of around 40 to 80 gallons, George supplied his legal Drumin Glenlivet whisky to the Duke of Gordon and other Banffshire gentry as well as to the few local merchants who would sell his crystalline, heady, and superbly satisfying spirit. George carted the remaining spirit in 10-gallon ankers to the south of Scotland where the Drumin Glenlivet was gaining a solid reputation alongside other popular top-quality malt whiskies like Underwood and Kippen. All along, George kept thinking that with time the smugglers, his rankled neighbors, might come round to his reasoning and that of the small number of other legitimate Glenlivet distillers.

Less than a year after opening the Drumin Glenlivet Distillery, disturbing news of a different nature struck. In early June 1825, arrest warrants were issued by the Acting Supervisor of the Grantown District for George's older brothers, John and Charles. While conducting a raid on the brothers' bothy near Upper Drumin, gauger William Thomson was physically attacked by the Smiths. Consequently, John and Charles were charged, as the Board of Excise records depicted, ". . . for an assault committed upon William Thomson, Officer, when making a private Distillery detection." Peculiarly, no further account has been uncovered in the Board's records with regard to a trial. Whatever the brothers' fate, it can be safely assumed that the incident did not enhance George's standing with the Glenlivet gaugers. With smugglers circling like sharks around Upper Drumin, George desperately needed the local excise officers on his side. He cannot have been pleased with the stupid and ill-timed exploits of John and Charles.

Trudging on in the face of his brothers' legal troubles and mounting threats from smugglers, George focused on making good-tasting whisky. Vouchers filed with the Board of Excise by gauger David Thomson (a relation to William Thomson, the gauger set upon by George's brothers?) report that during the 13-week period of January 7 to April 1, 1826, George produced a total of 904 gallons of whisky. That is slightly more than 69.5 gallons on average per week. The *Scotch Whisky Industry Record* (p. 82) claimed, "Production at Upper Drumin [was] up to 100 gallons per week" later that year. With production rising, sales must have been climbing. That same year, Aberlour Distillery, operated by James Gordon and Peter Weir, became fully licensed and George's neighbor William Grant opened Aucherachan Distillery in Glenlivet.

Spirits Soaring

The *Scotch Whisky Industry Record* (Table A.2, p. 559) reported on the total amount of recorded spirits as measured in liters of alcohol made in Scotland during the 1820s. These randomly selected years chronicle the dramatic growth of distillation in Scotland following the implementation of the Excise Act of 1823:

- 1820: 8,506,745 litres
- 1823: 8,001,721 litres
- 1824: 15,332,228 litres

- 1825: 21,343,374 litres
- 1828: 26,253,737 litres

Distilling totals remained below 30 million litres until 1850 when they reached 30,201,723 for the first time. Figures, of course, do not reflect all the illicit whisky that was still being produced in the 1820s and early 1830s by stalwart smugglers.

But choppy waters lay dead ahead as an unexpected whisky glut in late 1826 and 1827 undercut the meager gains made by George in his first full year of operation. A poorly timed lowering of duty on all varieties of foreign spirits spurred the overabundance of whisky, both legal and illegal. Suddenly, Scotsmen were flocking to rum and away from their native distillate. The recession in the whisky market proved more devastating to fledgling legal distillers like George Smith than to the smugglers. As sales dropped as if pushed off a table, George's debts mounted.

James Skinner, the Duke of Gordon's factor, became aware of George's plight as evidenced by a letter to the Reverend Anderson. In it, Skinner explained, ". . . Dram drinkers are getting Rum at the same price as whisky in Tomintoul. And having been denied this beverage for a long time from its high price, many are now preferring it to their native mountain dew. George Smith the distiller has lately been in the South Country with a cargo of Whisky, and complains so much on the decline of his market there that I am told he has refused delivery of some bere he sometime ago bought from the tenant of Bogarrow."

As Skinner's note illustrated, George's financial situation had become so dire by March 1827, that he was forced to turn down a barley delivery that was already paid for. His actions point to a severe drop in distilling activity caused directly by the plummeting demand for whisky. The alarmed Skinner, a fervent advocate of both legal distilling and of George's distillery at Upper Drumin, revealed in his March 8 letter to Reverend Anderson the inherent complications of legal distilling. "[George] commenced the Business the First in the Country under every disadvantage. He was not the master of his business, legal distillation requiring much greater care than the System of Smuggling to extract the quantity of Spirits required by Law from the grain. He commenced, as he now admits, when he was upwards of £100 behind and had about £300 to lay out in utensils and houses upon credit. And from want of money to go to Market for his grain was obliged to buy at Disadvantage."

To make matters worse, Skinner informed Anderson, two other legitimate Glenlivet distillers had recently shut down their operations due to mounting debt and soft demand for whisky. Indicated Skinner, "I am sorry to mention that George Smith the Distiller at Upper Drumin has become so embarrassed in his circumstances that he has intimated to me he will be unable to go on." Before closing his letter Skinner recommended that the Duke consider providing assistance to George, one of the estate's most reliable tacksmen, to help him weather this fleeting storm and to bolster his confidence.

In actions that depict the seriousness of the situation, Anderson responded to Skinner via letter on March 9. After discussing not only George's predicament but likewise the welfare of local barley farmers and greater Glenlivet in general, Anderson and the Duke decided to financially bail out George. They suggested to Skinner that George approach his creditors with the full but secret backing of the Duke and propose that he pay off his debts in two graduated parts within the timeframe of nine months from the agreement. The Duke would silently guarantee £500. As a show of good faith to the Duke and the Reverend Anderson, Skinner urged George also to auction off his cattle and related equipment as well as to relinquish another leased piece of property at Minmore Farm to raise some much-needed cash. In return, Skinner would free up an additional £100 of the Duke's money as compensation. George's creditors wouldn't receive the full sum of the debt, but would get enough in shillings on the pound to close the matter.

Said Anderson in his missive to Skinner, ". . . my view in this is to try to support the man who is represented to be active, industrious and of honest character under his present difficulties and to enable him to carry on the distilling himself which, for various causes, he can do more advantage than any other person."

After meeting with his creditors to present the debt satisfaction proposal, George informed Skinner that he had met with success. His debt would be satisfied by early 1828. The distillery at Upper Drumin would remain open and operating. With a bit of operating capital at last, George would be able to purchase barley and pay in cash rather than credit, thereby skirting the quagmire of debt. Skinner was elated. His plan had worked. By mid-May, an obviously pleased Reverend Anderson wrote to Skinner applauding his deft handling of the affair. "That poor man's business you have conducted with great judgment, and have brought so far to a very satisfactory conclusion. The Duke must advance another hundred pounds to support him, and enable him to carry on his operations to advantage."

Without the intervention, aid, and encouragement of James Skinner, the Reverend John Anderson, and the 4th Duke of Gordon in the spring of 1827, George would have been left no choice but to close Drumin Glenlivet. If that had happened, whisky drinkers in later decades would never have known the seductive whisky made by the greatest of all the Speyside distillers.

Old Minmore, Pistol-Packing Distiller

All the while that George Smith was dealing with his grave financial travails, threats from smugglers continued to haunt him. Knowing that George was experiencing money trouble, the smugglers smelled blood in the water. They became bolder in their menacing behavior toward legal distillers. In March 1827, George pleaded with the Board of Excise for more protection in the glen. The Board responded, saying, ". . . every protection will be afforded him at the expense of the Revenue upon sufficient proof being adduced to convict the parties from whom he [the accusing distiller] has sustained loss on account of being a legal Distiller."

As more licenses were being applied for at the Board of excise, lawlessness increased in Glenlivet in the late 1820s. Greater availability of fine legal whisky was slowly loosening the smugglers' hold on the whisky trade. Smuggling in the Scottish Lowlands had been virtually stamped out by 1827, but in the Highlands it continued. Trapped in a vicious circle of hostility and destruction, many Highland smugglers were unable to accept the inevitable collapse of illicit distilling and thereby were mired in a dying cause. Before 150 to 200 additional British troops, the Dragoons, were sent to Banffshire in 1828 to assist the gaugers in flushing out the remaining smugglers, George and his legitimate cohorts were left largely to defend their properties and themselves with whatever means they could afford.

In 1868, George Smith, in an interview in the *London Scotsman,* recalled: "The laird of Aberlour [fellow legitimate distiller James Gordon] had presented me with a pair of hair-trigger pistols for ten guineas, and they were never out of my belt for years. I got together two or three stout fellows for servants, armed them with pistols and let it be known everywhere that I would fight for my place to the last shot. I had a good character as a man of my word and, through watching by turns every night for years, we contrived to save the distillery from the fate so freely predicted for it. But I often, both at kirk [church] and market had rough times of it among the glen people; and if it had not been for the laird of Aberlour's pistols, I don't think I should be telling you this story now. . . . The country was in a desperately lawless state at this time."

The greatest threat of violence to legal distillers from smugglers existed when shipments of legal whisky wended their way south to Perth and Dundee through the desolate glens and hillsides. By all accounts, George appears to have fired his pistols in self-defense no more than twice. He relied as much on his wits as his pistols. Writer J. Gordon Phillips, who contributed articles in the 1880s and 1890s to the *Distillers' Magazine and Spirit Trade News,* was an acquaintance of George Smith. Phillips wrote of "Old Minmore," as George Smith came to be known later on in life, and his adventures on the whisky transport trail. He depicted George as, ". . . a man of tact and resource . . . who did not believe in extreme measures if others could be employed, and he often got out of a tight place where another would have failed and blood been shed."

One dark autumn evening in the unfortunately named village of Spittal of Glenshee, George strolled into a roadside inn that was full of ill-tempered smugglers, drinking and eating. The sight of George Smith entering stilled the smugglers. Recognizing many of them as Glenliveters, George pleasantly greeted them. Their snarls and rude whispers compelled him to quickly request a room for the night. The innkeeper, sensing trouble, refused. The smugglers howled in delight. Acknowledging his precarious position, George looked straight into the faces of the smugglers and said, "Would you boys join me in a dram on this cold night?"

Surprised at George's offer, the smugglers murmured amongst themselves. Finally one shouted, "I'll be hanged if I would drink with such as you!" Others chimed in, "Nor I!"

"I'm sorry about that, boys," answered George as the shouting continued. Thinking fast, George turned back to the anxious innkeeper, whose eyes were doubtless out on stalks, and said, "Fine sir, bring out a half-dozen bottles of your best."

J. Gordon Phillips picked up the story from there, "The landlord stared and so did the smugglers. Half-a-dozen bottles! Why, there were not more than a dozen smugglers present altogether and supposing they all took a share of the whisky, it meant a half bottle each. . . . He went for the whisky and returned in a few minutes. Mr. Smith drank the first glass. He drank to their health and his words, as near as I can remember as repeated to me were—'Here's to ye, boys. You need not be afraid of me. I thought you knew me better. There's surely room enough in this country for the licensed and the unlicensed . . . we are a' neighbors, and I wish you a' success and a safe return home.'"

Phillips reported that the smugglers reluctantly downed the first glass of high-grade whisky, then warmed on the pouring of the second and were civil to their Glenlivet neighbor by the third. Grateful to George for so cleverly defusing the tense situation, the innkeeper prepared a room. The smugglers temporarily pacified, George went to bed for the night, his pistols cocked, a wood bench propped against the door.

On two other known confrontations between George and smugglers, the blast of gunfire and the acrid scent of smoke filled the air. One incident, again near Glenshee on the "smugglers' road" between Braemar and Blairgowrie, was recounted in the *London Scotsman* newspaper on September 26, 1868. Said the account, "Minmore [George Smith] was driving his carts one day down the Spittal of Glenshee, when he was set upon by about a score of fellows returning to the north from . . . Perth market. He gave the rascals a dram all round, but when they wanted another cask wherewith to make merry at their leisure, he naturally resisted. They seized a cask, and he had to fire one of the Laird of Aberlour's pistols at the foremost, and confront the remainder with the other on cock, before he succeeded in convincing them that he knew how to take care of his property."

The other occasion involved a particularly nasty and vindictive smuggler by the name of Shaw. Once more spending the night in the heavily frequented inn in Spittal of Glenshee, George caught sight of Shaw and his band of thugs as he passed through the dining area on his way to his room. Shaw certainly noticed George, for he began objecting to George's presence and decrying his "treachery." In the wee hours as the candlelight dimmed, Shaw and his bunch stealthily crept into George's room, surrounding the bed and locking the door behind them. George lay still but awake. His pistols were cocked and at the ready concealed in the pitch darkness beneath the bedclothes. Shaw, according to George's account, pulled a large, ominous-looking butcher knife, stained with blood, out of his clothes. He leaned over George and softly uttered, "This gully [knife] is for your bowels."

Deciding that this was an appropriate time to make use of his pistols, George uncovered the pistol in his right hand and aimed it directly at Shaw's forehead. Swearing aloud with cold conviction that unless Shaw and his gang vacated his room without delay, he would create for Shaw a brand new hole between his eyebrows. George then discharged the pistol in his left hand into the fireplace across the room. Stunned and alarmed by the flare of the gun barrel and the explosion echoing in the chimney, Shaw and his chums bolted from George's room. Smoke from the gun hung like a fog in George's room as the innkeeper came running in. He likely encountered George sitting on the side of the bed, staring fondly at the Laird of Aberlour's two gifts, one still warm from firing.

With the roads from Glenlivet to Perth so active with legal and illegal whisky trafficking, it is reasonable to assume that George had other dangerous encounters in which his pistols served him. With more British troops arriving in 1828 and 1829, the violence lessened as more smugglers applied for licenses. Even with the Dragoons' higher profile in the glen, though, George continued to carry his pistols well into the 1830s. This was especially true when his itinerary had the place-name "Spittal of Glenshee" entered on it.

The meteoric dalliance with inexpensive imported rum soon abated. To the relief of whisky distillers large and small, homegrown malt whisky once again came front and center in the eyes of Scotsmen. By the late 1820s and early 1830s, more legal malt whisky was entering the market-places of Scotland's metropolitan areas. Sold for prices that rivaled or beat frequently inferior illicit whisky, legitimate, handcrafted malt whisky was gaining a steadily expanding following. One, in particular, was proving to be the benchmark for all Highland malt whisky. One was coming to be known as "the real Glenlivet." And, only one became the subject of a popular verse:

Glenlivet it has castles three
Drumin, Blairfeldy, and Deskie,
And also one distillery
More famous than the castles three.

But, it was still early days in George Smith's escapades with his Drumin Glenlivet Distillery.

ORDER OF GREEN CLOTH

These are to Certify that I have Appointed

Mess.rs James Chivas
and Alexander John Clipperton Chivas

trading as Chivas Brothers

into the Place and Quality of Purveyors of Grocery to
Her Majesty at Aberdeen.

To hold the said Place so long
as shall seem fit to The Lord Steward for
the time being. This Warrant is strictly
personal and will become void on the Death,
Retirement, or Bankruptcy of the person
named therein.

Given under my Hand this
twelfth day of June 1884 in the
Forty seventh Year of Her Majesty's Reign.

Sydney

Lord Steward.

A Chivas Brothers Royal Warrant.

From On-the-Job Terror to Purveyor to Her Majesty

WILLIAM EDWARD'S GRAND provisions emporium at 13 King Street in Aberdeen was a showplace for all the best in meats, fish, and fowl; vegetables and juices; dried and fresh fruits; cheeses from Great Britain and continental Europe; breads, cakes, and pastries; pickles, relishes, jams, and preserves; cigars and pipe tobacco; and wines, ales, and spirits. The storefront boasted tall, street- and sidewalk-facing windows where alluringly displayed delicacies and unusual treats enticed strolling Aberdonians. The grey-silver building of Number 13 sparkled on sunny days because of the silvered granite. It was bookended, fortuitously according to Edward, by the pillars and porticos of a monolithic pair of public works edifices. Their grave and officious countenances accentuated the friendly, reassuring warmth of the neat shop owned and operated by Aberdeen's politest and most attentive merchant.

Young James Chivas must have been more than slightly overwhelmed on his inaugural day in Edward's well-stocked grocery shop located near the quick-beating heart of Aberdeen. Still not having cleared all the hay strands and barley buds from the linty pockets of his heavy, dark, woolen clothes, James's initial weeks with William Edward had to be frustrating one day and exhilarating the next, a delightfully agonizing period of tough enlightenment. Call it on-the-job terror for the earnest man who had been reared in dozy Ellon Parish in Strathythan. Robert and Christian Chivas's bucolic farm had been James's safe haven for 26 years. During those first weeks in William Edward's employ, the Overtown of Dudwick family farm must have seemed 10,000 miles away. The vibrant pace of Aberdeen, a purposeful, urban commotion pitched to the tune of the Industrial Revolution, must have appeared to be at least five notches and 10 miles per hour faster to James than the deliberate, lulling tempo that had gently pulsed through Ellon Parish. There must have been moments when James and John felt as though they could have just as easily landed from the Planet Mongo as from the northern wilds of Strathythan.

Still, under the tutelage of William Edward, James's trainee phase must have likewise been an exciting and edifying period of discovery. There was so much for James to learn. The dark wood shelves were filled ceiling to floor with wonderful sounding, if mysterious, edible and drinkable goods. Unworldly but poised, James must have had a million questions spewing through his head like a Highland burn bursting its banks in spring. *Are Sauternes from France much different from Champagne? Is Madeira the same as Marsala? Where does Montilla come from? Are all wines from Bordeaux necessarily red? Is Cognac a French or Spanish wine or spirit? Are the whiskies that we carry legal?* That was just the imposing libations department, the area of the store that held a special fascination for James. What about the shop's completely perplexing tea and spice sections? *What exotic part of the Earth does Assam tea hail from? And Dimbula and Shui Hsien come from where? How should I reply if a customer asks for my recommendation with cocoa, mocha, and chocolate? I should know the country of origin of cinnamon, nutmeg, allspice, and saffron.* And, on and on.

But, while the demands of his retail education were weighty, the physical rigors of farming and the innate subtle rhythms of country life had instilled in James mental durability, unblinking persistence, and calm steadfastness. James would not allow himself to become a victim of attrition, defeatism, or self-doubt. These common afflictions, the bane of some people, simply were not options for him.

Aberdeen was alive with commerce in the 1830s. The *New Statistical Account of Scotland*, taken in 1831, lists 208 grocers and wine and spirits merchants, 193 vintners and innkeepers, 7 wholesale and 12 retail tea purveyors, 3 opticians, 1 civil engineer, and 6 pawnbrokers, which the Account described as "a lucrative but not commendable occupation."

Meanwhile, his brother John had landed, with the help of their cousin Alexander, an apprentice's post at the wholesale warehouse owned by the Shirres family. DL Shirres & Company dealt primarily with footwear and clothing. Both gainfully employed by 1838, the Chivas brothers were making an admirable go of it in Aberdeen. At the minimum, they owed their cousin and their employers their best efforts—not to mention their parents, Robert and Christian. James and John were firmly planted in Aberdeen. They knew after their first year that they were in Scotland's Granite City for the long haul. No matter what, they would survive there. The key question then was: Would the brothers each discover a niche from which to flourish in northeast Scotland's burgeoning metropolis and seaport?

A New/Old Purveyor on the Block

Following the demise of her uncle King William IV in 1837, Alexandrina Victoria ascended the throne of Great Britain at the age of 18 becoming Queen Victoria. She thereby launched the longest reign (1837–1901) in the history of the British monarchy. Four years later in March 1841, the respected Aberdeen grocer, employment agent, and wine and spirit merchant William Edward died while on a trip to the island of Madeira. Over the tenure of their brief professional relationship from 1838 to 1841, William Edward and James Chivas had developed a strong and close personal bond as well as a professional one. Edward, with his keen entrepreneurial spirit and business sense, had come to appreciate his trusted assistant as an honest and straightforward employee.

James's sunny optimism, diligence, and capacity to effortlessly beguile even the most demanding clients impressed Edward, whose main objective had always been the total satisfaction of his clientele. Edward drummed into James that contented customers became regular clients, the lifeblood of any retail operation; and further, through personal endorsements happy regular clients begat new patrons. Edward built his business on that circular philosophy. James embraced it and, in fact, took it to the next level. Resourceful and gracious, James added his personal dimension of "Please leave the matter with me and I'll have it done." James's knack of focusing his undivided attention on each customer's welfare helped the shop's revenues rise steadily during 1839 and 1840. Such personal attention meant long hours in the shop, but the sharp rise in business made the time worth it. Little wonder why William Edward came to view James as indispensable.

By the time of William Edward's unexpected passing, James had built a loyal customer following of his own at the busy purveyor's shop. Details of Edward's will and the dispersal of his estate have yet to be discovered. Hence, there were no data about an heir apparent for the King Street shop. With the fate of Edward's retail operation now uncertain, James at the age of 31 made a major decision. He quickly entered into a partnership with another food and wine merchant Charles Stewart, forming the firm of Stewart & Chivas. Stewart had previously owned a food and wine shop at 39 Woolmanhill Street. Together, they had the resources, the experience, the energy, and the physical ability to take over and operate the already successful shop at 13 King Street in the manner in which its patrons were accustomed. Within a short time, James and Charles did what was necessary to legally acquire the shop.

Stewart & Chivas advanced and promoted the concept of "one-stop shopping" by bringing the world to Aberdeen. Their notepaper publicized that they could provide "every article that families in the country may require . . ." Their inventory included ". . . curious brandies, French liqueurs, green and dried fruits, teas as imported, hams, tongues, cheese, pickles and fish sauces, wax and sperm candles . . ." While customers were waiting for their food and wine order to be packed for delivery directly to their residence, they could have Charles or James hire them a new cook, carriage driver; or housemaid, or sell them a new badminton set for the lawn.

The late William Edward's sacred business credo of properly and politely servicing the customer continued to be practiced at full tilt at 13 King Street. Indeed, James believed not just in satisfying all patrons to their delight but, moreover, satisfying them to their *astonished* delight. James and Charles brought a modern perspective and fresh passion to the 40-year-old business. At the sophisticated food and wine shop of Stewart & Chivas, all consumer wishes and even some of their whims were made possible.

In the distribution of duties between Charles and James, the young Chivas took responsibility of the wine and spirits department, expanding it significantly from the time of William Edward's proprietorship. James took an especially strong interest in whisky, Scotland's native libation. Customer interest in intensely flavorful Highland malt whisky, made in minute batches in pot stills, had been vigorous throughout James's three-year tenure with William Edward. James was well aware of the already legendary malt whisky made at George Smith's Drumin Glenlivet Distillery, the one people called "the real Glenlivet," as well as many others produced just to the west of Aberdeen. James, therefore, made the stocking of top-notch malt whisky a priority and a personal mission.

Regrettably, the small volume of the majority of pot stills meant that the supply of fine malt whisky was finite and painfully irregular at the best of times in the early 1840s, and patrons' demand often outdistanced the inventory. In view of the uneven availability of malt whisky, James astutely began purchasing ankers, the small 10-gallon wood casks, of malt whisky from Highland distillers or their brokers, storing them in the shop's cool, dry cellar. Shortly after Stewart & Chivas came into being, James very likely started, perhaps initially as a diversion, to experiment with mixing some of the Highland whiskies together in proportions that enhanced the virtues and downplayed the rough edges of each whisky. These early blending dalliances in the King Street cellar honed James's acute senses of smell and taste, abilities that would serve him famously in the near future.

But another pivotal whisky-related mid-nineteenth century occurrence would affect the partnership of Stewart & Chivas in ways Charles and James never thought possible: the coming of continuous distillation and grain whisky, courtesy of the column still, and in their wake, the momentous emergence of blended Scotch whisky.

Stein and Coffey: The Innovators

With the introduction and gradual acceptance in the 1830s and 1840s of the groundbreaking column still distillation system, the face of Scotland's whisky industry changed for all time. Scotsman and distiller Robert Stein of Kilbagie Distillery in Clackmannanshire nudged the ball down the hillside when he invented the initial column still system (aka patent still, Stein still) in the middle 1820s. He patented his revolutionary design in December 1827 (patents #5583 and #5721). Stein's cousin John Haig, proprietor of Cameron Bridge Distillery in Fife, saw the future in the design and installed a Stein still in 1830–1831. The Haig family, among the first to blend malt whisky and grain whisky, is one of the oldest and most venerable clans involved with the Scotch whisky trade.

Stein's rudimentary single-column design was refined and, in virtually all distilling experts' minds, perfected by Irish distiller Aeneas Coffey. Owner of the Dock Distillery in Dublin, Coffey patented (#5974) his single-column still device (aka Coffey still, continuous still) in 1830 after ending his long career as an excise officer. After being exposed to scores of squat, potbellied, and often troublesome copper pot stills during his tenure as a gauger, Coffey pondered new ways to make distilling more efficient and simpler for the contemporary distiller.

Aeneas Coffey's motivations are still debated in some quarters. Was he solely looking to improve on the painstakingly slow and cumbersome workings of the customary pot still? Was he trying to revolutionize the whisky industry? Did he want to trump Robert Stein? Or, was he simply attempting to supply lots of high-strength alcohol (90 to 95 percent) to the highest bidders? Writer Gavin D. Smith posited in his book A to Z of Whisky (p. 35), "Coffey's original intention was probably to sell the comparatively pure grain spirit produced by his apparatus for industrial purposes rather than for domestic consumption. He proceeded to manufacture stills of his own design, selling them to several Scottish whisky and London gin distillers, the latter finding the strong neutral spirit of the *Coffey* still ideal for their product. The basic design of the still remains unchanged."

In Coffey's radical new system, the still was originally constructed of one metal column, cylindrical in shape. The base of the column was named the *analyzer* and the second tier was called the *rectifier*. Each section enclosed a series of chambers separated by perforated metal plates. The Coffey still was later redesigned into two columns—one the analyzer, the other the rectifier. In laypersons' terms, here's how Coffey's ingenious, double-column system worked:

First, the fermented, cold wash was pumped into the top of the first column (the analyzer). As it tumbled down the column chambers, the wash was met by intense heat that warmed the dripping, descending wash. By the time the hot wash reached the bottom of the analyzer, it was near the boiling point.

Second, the heated wash was transferred via pipes to the top of the second column (the rectifier). As the wash cascaded down through the perforated plates, it was met by fast-ascending steam. The steam separated the components of the hot wash, specifically, the alcohol from the water and chemical compounds. That action sent the clouds of vaporous alcohol climbing through the chambers as even more oils and other impurities, such as congeners, fell away. As the alcohol vapors bounced off the successive levels of plates, more impurities were fractionally stripped away.

Third, by the time the vapors were condensed back into liquid form, what exited the spout was crystalline, high-alcohol, neutral grain distillate, or spirit. The raw final product, neutral grain spirit, bore little resemblance to the spirituous product of pot stills, which was always lower in alcohol and more intensely aromatic and flavorful. As to the practical advantages of column still distilling on a broader scale, writer David Daiches captured the essence of the impact of continuous distilling in his book *Scotch Whisky: Its Past and Present* (p. 66): "Aeneas Coffey's invention had obvious commercial advantages over the pot still: it can produce more whisky quickly, more cheaply, in much greater quantities and in a continuous process."

This basic, industrial, continuously operating distillation format was the exact opposite of the traditional, labor-intensive, stop-and-start technique of bulbous pot stills, which had to be shut down after every distillation, cleaned, and refilled before the next. Another underpinning rationale from a business standpoint behind column stills was that they allowed distillers to use cheaper unmalted grains, such as maize, wheat, oats, and rye, to produce a potable spirit. The malting of barley for malt whisky added another step and hence more expense to the old-fashioned pot still process. The sheer ease with which distillers could make huge volumes of good quality grain spirit increased, in time, the overall availability of Scotch whisky.

The most significant outcome of first Stein's and later Coffey's system started to take shape in the late 1840s and 1850s when pioneering whisky blenders, such as Andrew Usher, John Haig, John Walker, Matthew Gloag, George Ballantine, William Teacher, John Dewar, and Francis and Walter Berry, began combining the ethereal whiskies from column stills with meatier, more charismatic Highland malt whiskies from pot stills. Through their individual and combined efforts, they launched the high-flying, dynamic era of blended Scotch whisky. In the tranquil eye of the blended whisky hurricane stood James Chivas, the provisions merchant known as an unrelenting pursuer of the finest quality.

A Timely Royal Push

Born in Kensington Palace in May 1819, Victoria became the successor to the British throne in 1837 because her three deceased uncles, all royal heirs themselves, sired no legitimate children. Queen Victoria married Prince Albert, her first cousin, in 1840. The young, energetic, and engaging queen visited Scotland for the first time in 1842 at the age of 23, starting a lifelong enchantment with the Deeside Highlands to the west of Aberdeen. Prior to the arrival of the royal party, the queen's servants quizzed the local gentry about which food and wine merchants they employed to provide the best provisions. On receiving several word-of-mouth recommendations, the royal household retained the services of Stewart & Chivas in Aberdeen. Supplying the royal party with all their food and libation needs for the duration of the queen's Deeside holiday, James and Charles, sticklers to detail, must have made a good impression on the queen's staff.

The next year in the late summer of 1843, the queen and her large entourage again visited Deeside at an old, available estate called Balmoral. The 11,000-acre estate, located roughly half way between Braemar and Ballater in the valley of the River Dee, boasted breathtaking Highlands vistas, acres of rolling fields, woods and meadows, superb fishing and hunting as well as a dilapidated and drafty fifteenth-century castle. The stunning scenery of Deeside, so contrary to that of congested and polluted London, inspired the young monarch, whose natural talent of creating images with pen and paper improved on her trips north.

Based on the success of the previous year, Stewart & Chivas were again hired to provide everything needed for a second royal visit. James and Charles cheerfully and efficiently satisfied all the royal household's requests, no matter how trivial. *Shoe polish, brooms, and a new cook? No problem. Leave it with us. A new wheel for the carriage? We'll contact our local smithy and he'll be out by the end of the day. The doors need repair? Not to worry, we know Aberdeen's finest carpenter. He's one of our best clients. The queen craves scallops? We'll have the freshest ones delivered to the kitchen first thing tomorrow morning.*

Either by the conclusion of the second royal visit or shortly thereafter, James, sitting at his desk in the King Street shop office, received a heavy envelope stamped with the seal of the Office of the Board of Green Cloth. Puzzled but excited, he called for Charles. When Charles arrived, James showed him the unopened envelope and smiled. "Open it," urged Charles. The document stated:

> By Virtue of the Power to me given I hereby appoint James Chivas of Aberdeen to the Place of Purveyor of Grocery to Her Majesty in Ordinary.

He is to have and enjoy all the Right, Profits, Privileges and Advantages to the said Place belonging during my Will and Pleasure.

Given under my hand this second day of August 1843 in the Seventh Year of her Majesty's Reign.

Liverpool.

Entered in the Office of the Board of Green Cloth the second day of August 1843.

Chas. Hill.

Seven years later in 1850, Stewart & Chivas was appointed Royal Grocer to the queen's mother, the Duchess of Kent, whenever the Duchess resided at her home in the Highlands, Abergeldie Castle.

There's a Warrant Out . . .

Royal Warrants had expirations, which may explain why some of the Warrants first granted Stewart & Chivas and then Chivas Brothers appear to be renewed. Changes in shop ownership likewise brought the issuance of updated appointments.

1843: "Purveyor of Grocery to Her Majesty in Ordinary." Stewart & Chivas are registered in the Aberdeen Post Office Directory as "Grocers to Her Majesty."

1850: Stewart & Chivas are appointed Grocers to Her Royal Highness the Duchess of Kent, the queen's mother.

1863: "Purveyor of Grocery to His Royal Highness, the Prince of Wales." Stewart & Chivas has now become Chivas Brothers, with James Chivas as the principal.

1884: "Purveyor of Grocery to Her Majesty at Aberdeen." James and his son Alexander, principals of Chivas Brothers, add this Royal Warrant to their list.

1896: "Purveyor of Oilery Provisions to Her Majesty at Aberdeen." Principals Charles Howard and Alexander Smith, trading as Chivas Brothers, obtain this appointment.

1901: "Purveyor of Provisions to Her Majesty at Aberdeen." Warrant is bestowed upon Charles Howard and Alexander Smith, trading as Chivas Brothers. Queen Victoria dies.

1902: Charles Howard and Alexander Smith, trading as Chivas Brothers, are awarded the Royal Warrant as "Italian Warehousemen to His Royal Highness, the Prince of Wales."

1910: "Purveyor of Provisions to His Majesty, Edward VII." Charles Howard and Alexander Smith still own and operate Chivas Brothers.

1911: Chivas Brothers, owned by Charles Howard and Alexander Smith, awarded Royal Warrant, "Italian Warehousemen to Her Majesty, Queen Alexandra."

1923: William Mitchell now operates Chivas Brothers and is appointed "Purveyor of Scotch Whisky to His Majesty, George V."

1936: Amendment to 1910 Royal Warrant removes the names "Charles Howard and Alexander Smith" and replaces them with "William Mitchell."

1940: "Purveyor of Provisions and Scotch Whisky to His Majesty, George VI." Chivas Brothers now owned by James Meikle.

1955: "Purveyor of Whisky and Provisions to Her Majesty, Queen Elizabeth II" and "Provision Merchants to Her Majesty, Queen Elizabeth, the Queen Mother" awarded to Chivas Brothers.

1975: Chivas Brothers instructed to remove the Royal Warrant from Chivas Regal by year's end.

As to why Chivas Brothers was forced to relinquish their official appointment in 1975, two theories exist, according to archivist Iain Russell. One theory postulates that the Royal Family decided to reduce their associations with firms that pedaled alcoholic beverages as a subtle example of their concern over ardent consumption of alcohol. The second hypothesis focuses on the Royal Family's disdain of a series of print advertisements that carelessly, at least in the eyes of the royals, made light of the association of Chivas Regal and the British monarchy.

In 1848, Prince Albert leased Balmoral for the queen and their growing family. In 1853, Victoria and Albert purchased the rambling estate outright for £31,000. Following the purchase, the old castle was thought too cramped and rundown for the royal family and their staff. Architect William Smith of Aberdeen designed a new castle with the help of the prince. The old edifice was dismantled. The mammoth new castle, which today acts as the late summer residence of the present royal family headed by Queen Elizabeth II, was constructed from local granite and completed by 1858. Every summer, every royal holiday from 1848 to 1894, Stewart & Chivas provided all the provisions, consumable and nonconsumable, to the royal party as they joyfully lounged away their late summers at Balmoral. Even after Prince Albert's death in 1861 at the age of 42, Victoria headed up to Balmoral with at least some of her nine children. Balmoral played an important role for the long-grieving queen until her own passing in 1901. There was even talk of a romantic dalliance with a local Scotsman by the name of John Brown, who had been Albert's ghillie, or fishing guide.

Beyond the direct positive effect of the Royal Appointments, the queen's influence and powerful persona encouraged the evolution of a whole new stratum of customers for Stewart & Chivas. Victoria and Albert's widely publicized and chronicled family trips to Deeside instigated a rush by the English aristocracy to own estates in the northeastern Scottish Highlands. Naturally since the queen employed Stewart & Chivas as her food and beverage purveyors, the newly landed gentry felt the pressure to stay in step with their queen and dutifully followed suit. Stewart & Chivas and their famous victuals had become such a phenomenon that by the 1860s their business reached far south into England as the nobles returned home in the autumn.

The affluent English likewise brought with them a fervent, unquenchable thirst for the whisky of Scotland. Accustomed in large measure to gin, port, brandy, and wine, they made it clear to James that they fancied a tamer, smoother whisky than that offered by most of the Highland malt distillers. As orders for Scotch whisky climbed, James spent more time in his office mixing various sample whiskies in an attempt to find a proprietary blend worthy of the Stewart &

Chivas name as well as a blend that would fulfill the desires of the moneyed English.

Business was booming in the first half of the 1850s when the inaugural whisky brand from Stewart & Chivas, Royal Glen Dee, debuted. Royal Glen Dee, James's first publicly sold whisky and the forerunner of Chivas Regal, garnered early popularity. A few years later in the 1860s James followed up with his second blended Scotch, Royal Strathythan, so named to honor his home district. With sales of Royal Glen Dee and Royal Strathythan soaring, James knew instinctively that the future of the shop at 13 King Street had just turned liquid.

Assembled distillery crew at The Glenlivet in 1903.

Panicked Grouse and the
End of a Defining Era

SHOPTALK AMONG HIGHLAND malt whisky distillers in the early 1830s was seasoned with the unnerving news of the new-fangled contraption confusingly dubbed the "Coffey still" or "patent still" or "column still" or "Stein still" or, as the skeptical Highland distillers most likely reacted, ". . . whatever the accursed bloody thing is called." Word trickled into Glenlivet with increasing frequency that the mysterious machine, depicted through innuendo and gossip as a kind of über-still, was said to never stop running and, as a result, continuously produced light-bodied, very high-alcohol wheat, oats, or maize spirits in unbelievably copious volumes. Was this apparatus evil incarnate? Accustomed to making minute quantities of robust, flavorful spirit in arduously tended pot stills, some Highlanders had heard that Coffey stills stood towering and narrow, 10 stories or more high. Others derisively scoffed at the new concept, saying, "Whoever invented them mus' be daft. Wha' fools wa' drink such a foul, flimsy dram made fro' oats or maize? Much less distill it? S' madness, s' wha' it is."

But the rumors that flew like panicked grouse at the crackle of gun-fire didn't decline. Another common claim held that a handful of Low-land distillers were even talking about blending the weak but plentiful column still spirits with Highland malt whiskies to develop a milder, less feral type of Scotch whisky that might appeal to the masses. "Mixing [Highland malt] whisky with that [column still spirits] would be like marrying a prince to an idiot's daughter. It'll never happen in my life-time," one Highlander colorfully predicted in an article in the *Aberdeen Observer* in August 1835. In their idyllic remoteness, most Highland malt distillers knew precious little and cared even less about the changing eco-nomics and coming revolution in the whisky distilling industry.

Yet, the bravado of the Highland malt distillers was understandable. Legal whisky making was a booming cottage industry in 1832, the year that the Coffey still was officially sanctioned by the Customs & Excise Board. On the heels of the implementation of the landmark Illicit Distil-lation (Scotland) Act of 1822 and the Excise Act of 1823, an atomic ex-plosion of licit malt distilleries mushroomed all over Scotland. Wrote John R. Hume and Michael S. Moss in *The Making of Scotch Whisky: A History of the Scotch Whisky Distilling Industry* (p. 75), "Between 10 Oc-tober 1823 and 9 August 1824, no fewer than 79 new stills were commis-sioned. The number of licensed distilleries in operation grew swiftly from 111 in 1823 to 263 by 1825. Most of those who registered were encour-aged to do so by their landlords. No doubt drawing on the skill of the 'Glenliveters,' Captain George Smith with financial assistance of his landlord, the Duke of Gordon, opened a licensed distillery on his farm at Upper Drumin in Glenlivet to supply high-quality malt whisky to the growing Lowland industrial centres."

Following the path of George Smith's Drumin Glenlivet Distillery, other fabled malt whisky distilleries like Macallan, Fettercairn, Longrow, Balmenach, and Mortlach, also began in 1824. In 1825, the Board of Ex-cise offices in the Highlands were besieged with applications for legal distilleries. Remarkably, 121 opened for business in that benchmark year alone, including famous ones like Ben Nevis, Port Ellen, Strathisla, Kip-pen, Glencadam, and Glenury. In 1826, 29 more started up, including

Aberlour and Pulteney. The surge continued until 1835, a year when just a single malt distillery, Lochruan, was licensed.

For the Highland smugglers, the sharp increase in legal malt distilleries in the Highlands in the 1820s and early 1830s plus the steep penalties imposed by the two Acts (1822 and 1823) collapsed the tent of Scotland's once-thriving whisky smuggling industry. With the abundance, indeed the glut by 1835, of cheap legal whisky, the majority of illicit distillers admitted defeat, shut down their bothies, and either applied for distillery licenses or took up another trade. The socioeconomic effect on the Highlands of this shifting tide was telling as entire hamlets once devoted exclusively to whisky smuggling vanished from 1825 to 1840. Former smugglers packed up their families and belongings and relocated to cities in the south, especially Glasgow, Edinburgh, Stirling, Perth, and Dundee, to find work and start over. Still other disenfranchised Highlanders immigrated to Canada and the United States, where skilled workers, tradesmen, and farmers were needed in the frontier territories.

By 1839, the year that George Smith's Drumin Glenlivet Distillery was producing 200 gallons of spirit per week (*Scotch Whisky Industry Record*, p. 98), smuggling was being conducted only on a minor scale by a widely scattered handful of diehards hunkered down in the remotest glens. According to Glasgow University archivist Iain Russell, existing public accounts describe how small amounts of illicit whisky from Cabrach Strathavon were still being sold as "Glenlivet whisky" in the south of Scotland in the late 1830s, but the Highlands' notoriously combustible Era of Smuggling was largely doused by 1840. To the relief and gratification of both Parliament and the Highland land barons, the near two-century-long epidemic of illicit whisky making had been eradicated through the slow-dripping antidote of legislation.

The termination of large-scale smuggling and the introduction of continuous distillation fed the trend toward industrial-type licensed distilleries that were sizable enough to meet the bursting public demand for Scotch whisky. Around 1840 to 1850, the modern era of Scotland's whisky industry commenced. The "rascally liquid," as Scotland's foremost rebel-poet Robert Burns once referred to whisky, was poised to evolve from an accidental rustic brew into a sophisticated, calculated libation. Moreover, Scotch whisky was about to emerge not only as an international commercial powerhouse, but likewise as the most beloved and enduring native symbol of Scotland.

Robert Burns's impassioned cries of "Freedom and Whisky gang thegither, Tak aff your dram!" were suddenly ringing echoes of the rambunctious and admittedly romantic eighteenth and early nineteenth centuries, when Scots viewed the unfettered distilling of whisky as an inalienable right and a free exercise of their heritage. As the second half of the 1800s dawned and as the sons of George Smith and James Chivas were groomed to carry the reins of the family businesses, Scotch whisky, Scotland's *uisge beatha,* turned into a crucial and multifaceted industry.

PART TWO

The Sons

John Gordon Smith, son of George Smith.

A Father's Dreams

PROSPERITY HEAPED NEW opportunities on the family of George Smith in the 1830s and 1840s. Business contacts established by George in the early 1830s with wine and spirits merchants blossomed into mutually beneficial relationships as sales of Drumin Glenlivet whisky soared. Retail shops like Aberdeen's Durno & Michael and Harvey Lumsden; Leith's R & J Cockburn; Andrew Usher & Company in Edinburgh; and Cowie of Keith sold substantial amounts of "the real Glenlivet" to their well-to-do clientele. Locally, with the help of James Skinner, the Duke of Gordon's factor, regular customers, including the Duke himself as well as other Aberdeenshire, Banffshire, and Morayshire gentry, came to openly prefer George's whisky to those of other district distillers and were willing to wait for their orders to be fulfilled. Drumin Glenlivet whisky became renowned as far away as Glasgow and Edinburgh by 1835 due, in part, to George's many personal trips ferrying scores of ankers of whisky by cart to middlemen in Perth and, in part, because of enthusiastic word-of-mouth advocacy by customers. Ultimately, however, it was the extraordinary quality of George's fresh and savory malt whisky that propelled it forward.

George offered customers two varieties of Drumin Glenlivet at different "proof" levels in the 1830s and 1840s. The concept of "proof" remains a common point of confusion to this day. Proof is defined as *the measure of alcohol content in a beverage*. In the nineteenth century, all malt whiskies, including George's prized Drumin Glenlivet, were dispensed straight from the barrel to the goblet without any reduction in strength. The English invented the idea of proof in the seventeenth century for the purpose of assigning accurate duties according to alcoholic potency. The rule guiding the taxing of alcoholic beverages was simple: the higher the alcoholic content, the stiffer the duties.

From the mid-1600s to 1818, excise officials routinely determined the alcoholic strength of beverages by mixing a portion with gunpowder, lighting it and gauging the intensity, the color, and the duration of the flame. An elongated, long-lasting, bright white-yellow flare meant that the beverage was "over-proof"; a steady, short, blue-yellow flame designated proper proof; and a smoldering, smoky ember with little or no flame declared the beverage to be under-proof. Then in 1816, Bartholomew Sikes, an excise official, perfected the hydrometer, a device that measured the specific gravity of liquids. From 1818 on, excise officials calculated alcoholic strength with a hydrometer.

To the British, a "proof spirit" contains 57.1 percent alcohol and 42.9 percent water. Yet in the United States, proof signifies 50 percent alcohol, 50 percent water. To Americans, when a spirit is called "86-proof," it signifies that the alcohol by volume content is 43 percent, or half of the American version of proof. No wonder the notion of proof has tangled consumers' minds worse than a bowl of cooked spaghetti.

Anyway, George's popular frontline Drumin Glenlivet whisky, sold at a per gallon price of 10 shillings, registered at what was described as "11 percent higher than proof," which in the imperfect environment of the period probably meant that it hovered at from 60 to 65 percent alcohol. This robust whisky, hardly a timid wallflower, was George's best seller and was almost certainly cut with water by the majority of malt whisky drinkers. For people with even stronger constitutions and perhaps cast-iron intestines, he also sold a flamethrower, high-octane version of Drumin Glenlivet at what was depicted as "25 percent over proof" for 12 shillings and sixpence per gallon.

The rational betting today is that the description "25 percent over proof" was misleading because two distillations in copper pot stills create a spirit between 68 and 72 percent alcohol. It is doubtful that George ran a third distillation since that ran firmly against Highland tradition and distillery scheduling. So, the more powerful version was very likely a full barrel-strength edition that bubbled along at around 70 to 72 percent alcohol. To give an idea of how toe-curling and teeth-bending these nineteenth-century malt whiskies were, bear in mind that most Scottish whiskies nowadays are reduced from barrel strength to 40 to 43 percent alcohol.

Typically, transactions in this era were concluded in the neat and clean handover of hard cash. To both individuals and shopkeepers, George gave a discount of sixpence per gallon on orders of 50 gallons or more. As demand increased, so did production and activity at Upper Drumin. In the face of fast-rising sales, George's coffers doubtless were swollen with currency by the late 1830s. What to do with the profits? Expand the family holdings.

George's ardor for Glenlivet, his beloved Valley of the Livet in Banff-shire, and the success of his Drumin Glenlivet Distillery compelled and en-abled him to lease more nearby farmland for his family business. In 1838, George assumed responsibility for the tack on the Castletown of Blairfindy farm whose leaseholders had fallen on hard times. Described the Duke of Gordon's factor, James Skinner, in a letter to the Reverend John Anderson, the Duke's estate overseer, "The widow of the present tenant's father and a son by a second marriage (an idiot) are both in the place and objects of charity, and I have got George Smith to agree to provide them with a house and four Bolls of Meal yearly during the remained of the lease."

The following year, 1839, George took on the available 19-year tack of Nevie farm, an expansive tract of rolling hills and pastureland that George envisioned as prime grazing land for sheep and cattle, cattle breeding being his other keen commercial interest. He installed his in-dustrious elder son William as the new laird of Nevie. The next year, the tack on Minmore, a prime parcel that lay down the hillside from Upper Drumin came up for lease. George and William acted quickly and signed on as joint-tacksmen of Minmore farm. By the end of 1840, the Smith family was cultivating approximately 800 acres of arable land and con-trolled over 10,000 acres of pasture in Glenlivet.

To personally concentrate on developing Minmore and Castletown of Blairfindy for their purposes, George asked William to manage the Drumin Glenlivet Distillery, in addition to his Nevie farm responsibilities. William agreed, though while shaking hands on it with his father, he might have felt vaguely and inexplicably uneasy about the arrangement. George reportedly took a particular liking to their enthralling new acquisition, Minmore. From a description in an article printed in the *Elgin Courant*, dated July 18, 1862, one could understand something of George's enchantment. "Minmore lies on the west side of the Livet, and seems to occupy nearly the whole countryside. Like the other large farms near it, it is divided into extensive parks chiefly by stone dykes [walls]. One can see in this district at a glance the advanced, thorough system of management which characterizes the estates of the Duke of Richmond [Duke of Gordon]—every nook improved, which is necessary to make the parks square and regular, every wet rig drained, steadings slated, and all in the best of order, a great portion of the parks enclosed with substantial stone fences—everything, in short, thoroughly done at first, and tidily kept . . ."

Another newspaper account from the 1870s called Minmore, ". . . a large and fine-lying farm . . . not, as might be supposed, in a narrow Highland glen, but in a rolling country, braes [hills or slopes] rising behind and beyond braes to the shaggy mountains in the distance."

George's bright and energetic younger son John Gordon selected a markedly different path from his pensive, homebody older brother, William. After completing his required terms at Blairs College in Aberdeen, John Gordon worked first for the Caledonian Bank in Elgin. By the time that Minmore came under the control of George and William, John Gordon was preparing to move to Edinburgh to work for John Shand, a highly respected city lawyer and a cousin of the Reverend John Anderson. The plan was to take courses in law while in the employ of Shand. In 1841, John Gordon relocated to Edinburgh.

George, like any father and man of means, had a dream of leaving the family affairs in the capable hands of his two heirs. In his reveries, George pictured William as the on-the-ground manager of the family's distilling and farming businesses and John Gordon, skilled in banking and law, as the family planner, counselor, and investor. But a father's dreams, sent aloft in what may appear to be ideal conditions, nevertheless own fragile wings.

Family Letters and Raps at the Door

William, born in 1818 and thus still a young man in the early 1840s, shouldered his distillery and Nevie farm duties quietly in his father's presence so as not to shake his faith in him. Though coached by his father to operate the family businesses, the strains of running the distillery and simultaneously bringing Nevie farm up-to-speed mounted on William. The whisky side of the family business was booming and William's daily obligations to Drumin Glenlivet cut severely into his time for dealing with the upgrading of Nevie. Gathering and purchasing the materials, distilling the whisky, storing the whisky, transporting the whisky, dealing daily with curious and lingering distillery visitors, dealing with staff, maintaining the voluminous accounting and inventory books, expanding to meet demand, and keeping vendors happy required days that started prior to sunrise and concluded long after sundown. William's travails and dissatisfactions are captured, poignantly at times, in riveting letters between him and John Gordon when John Gordon was residing and working in Edinburgh.

What was worse and, in fairness, perhaps unknown to George was that the seeds of illness were beginning to sprout in William's lungs by the time that George made him manager of the distillery. William's feelings of being overwhelmed and of being alone at the helm were evident in one telling letter to John Gordon in February 1842. Wrote William of his escalating anxiety, "I find, with looking after the distillery, going from home, and one thing or another, in place of being able to balance off these old accounts, I have great ado to keep up the books and were it not that I observe some method . . . in my way of going to work, I could not do it all, as every month I find adds a little more weight to my shoulders."

By this time, his father's schedule had become crowded with other interests, especially the breeding of Highland cattle. Perhaps George blindly left William to sink or swim on his own at Drumin Glenlivet.

Continued William in his letter, "Father used to help me greatly, but as I now never look near the farms, he finds enough to do to keep them in working order. There are so many people going and coming to the Distillery with whom I have to do business that it is very seldom indeed I can put pen to paper, except with candle light, and consequently I get up . . . by 5 or 6 o'clock and bring my books and answer letters, over breakfasttime and before I am troubled with dubskelpers [time wasters].

"I would think nothing of doing business with business people, every half hour of the day, but as you are no doubt aware of the Glenlivet way of doing business is none of the quickest. A good honest farmer from Braes comes in, sits down by the cheeck o' the chimney, lights his pipe, and begins to ask you what is to be done now . . . when he is cut short by a rap-rap at the door. And in comes his neighbor, who immediately takes possession of the opposite chimney nook, and between them they manage to crack by the time, till their number is perhaps augmented three-fold . . . when the shades of evening begin to appear, some one will say 'Speak a word, Mr William.' . . . The above is only what has to be gone through I may say daily, and it is part of my work which I *hate*, but cannot escape."

In his correspondence to his younger brother, William was clear about what kind of help he needed: "What I am most in want of just now is a clever person to assist me in squaring up old accounts . . ." It appears from the correspondence still available between William and his brother, written during the years 1841 to 1846, that the "clever person" never materialized. Did George veto the hiring of a distillery assistant, or was he blithely unaware of William's deep frustration? The letters fail to shed ample light on this point.

With the distillery's rapid and prodigious success came accompanying problems on several key fronts. One of the most annoying glitches for William was having to placate irate merchants who were receiving less than the full amount of whisky that they had paid for. Mysteriously, a portion of the shipped whisky was disappearing somewhere between Upper Drumin and the final destination in the south of Scotland. Highland malt whisky was frequently shipped in barrels on small commercial vessels from the seaport of Aberdeen to the docks of Leith in Edinburgh.

Not surprisingly, it was the Drumin Glenlivet whisky that always seemed to have the biggest share filched from it.

William's annoyance at this regular but unpreventable pilferage was revealed in another letter to his brother. A resigned William, who knew where the problem lay, wrote about the nuisance in a letter to John Gordon, dated May 17, 1843, "My Dear Brother, I should have written you before now, as I do not remember having done so since I re'd [received] your letter of 29th April (I keep no copies of the letters I send you) and I write now, not that I have any news worth sending you, but in order that I may be out of your debt, as I am anxious to hear from you . . . it is impossible to prevent the sailors from drinking out of the casks while on board ship. Another thing, they are always worse on us than others, as the 'Gallant Tars' know the quality of our shipment! Their manner of extracting the whisky is by slacking a hoop of the cask and introducing a small tube by means of a hole bored with a gimlet [small tool for boring holes] and when they have taken their turn they drive a pin of wood into the hole then bring the hoop to its old place. I cannot find nay way of preventing this . . . it has been going on regularly since ever we shipped whisky . . ."

The incidents involving the sailors, or Gallant Tars as William called them, surfaced because of John Gordon's complaints in letters to William that Edinburgh customers that he personally had cultivated were giving him grief over the missing whisky. During his five-year tenure in Edinburgh, John Gordon acted as something of an agent for Drumin Glenlivet. In fact, John Gordon frequently ended up acting as the emissary between William and the clients, sometimes venting the ire of clients if they felt that they were being gypped on a shipment or if they thought that the quality of the whisky was inconsistent or if shipments were tardy.

In a letter dated June 27, 1843, the severe backlogging of whisky orders at the distillery came to the forefront. In the missive, William pleaded with John Gordon to employ his attorney's gift with words to pacify particularly disappointed Edinburgh customers, contritely and patronizingly writing, "I wish you would call on the parties and try to make some apology for me, in order to endure them to take the whisky. I will not however forward it till I know how they feel on the subject. I would not care too much for losing the present orders, but I would like if possible to make friends with the parties, so that we could call upon them for future orders. I will endeavour to write them plausible letters, and then your calling on them with a fine face, and a story such as lawyers are capable of delivering, may solder matters . . ."

William's seemingly cavalier attitude, or perhaps his mismanagement of the situation, rankled John Gordon, who fired back a scathing letter that did nothing less than dress down William. Answered John Gordon, not bothering to cloak his irritation with his brother, "I am not willing [to confront the client] for the simple reason that it is unbusinesslike. . . . First, I say you *could* have supplied these orders, *if not,* you could have written to the parties at the time they should have been supplied, stating that it was impossible to do so at that time owing to the weather, etc., but that you valued their esteemed custom too much to let any such cause be the means of losing it, and that you would just do yourself the favour of keeping their order till a more convenient season—specifying an exact time at which it would be executed, to convince them it was not an *indefinite* put off.

"Secondly, if I say I am anxious to further your interest, it is not the way to do so, to be the palliator [easer of tension] of culpable neglect. If you wish to do business the transactions must be carried through in a businesslike way, and to encourage them to be done otherwise is not my province. To do that is not the means in which I desire to be of use to you, because to do that would be doing you no essential service."

William could not have been pleased to receive that blunt and unsupportive response from his confidante and closest ally. With each passing year, William's despair grew deeper.

Yet another burr buried deeply beneath William's saddle was an agreement hammered out by his father with the Edinburgh merchant Andrew Usher, who had bought malt whisky from George since he turned legitimate in 1824. Opposed to the transaction, William bristled when his father returned from Edinburgh in early January 1843, signed agreement in hand. The arrangement spelled out that Andrew Usher & Company was to receive 600 gallons of whisky per month, a large chunk of the distillery's monthly volume, and that Usher was to get an extra commission on successful sales to other clients. William thought that Usher already was making a healthy profit by selling Drumin Glenlivet at retail for 21 shillings per gallon when paying less than 10 shillings. Adding a commission as a sweetener seemed absurd to William. He argued bitterly to his father that Usher's overall compensation was excessive.

What is also moderately enlightening but not conclusive about this turbulent episode is that George engineered the deal in Edinburgh with Andrew Usher, apparently without William or even John Gordon present. This begs the questions, Had George so little confidence in William's ability to concoct and close a deal like this that he decided to push ahead with it alone? Did George merely consider William as the onsite manager of Drumin Glenlivet and nothing more? Or was the sole driving force behind the deal the friendship of more than 20 years between George and Usher and, therefore, no reflection on William at all? Whatever George's motivation, it was William who was left to deal with the prickly and, by some accounts, arrogant merchant over the ensuing few years as the particulars of the vaguely written agreement were debated, often heatedly, point by painstaking point.

Usher then began running print advertisements without William's approval or prior knowledge, to which William sternly objected. In the copy of the advertisement, Usher & Company describes Drumin Glenlivet as "The Real Glenlivat Whisky." Vexed by the incorrect spelling of Glenlivet as well as the extra commission, William first expressed dismay to John Gordon in a letter, then relented, saying, ". . . they have no right to any commission as they run no risk, nor does it come within the pale of their agreement . . . as to the advertisement which appeared . . . I think they went wrong . . . to advertise . . . there is no doubt they are overstepping the agreement, in the way they are going on with the advertisement, but you are aware, that with such good customers, it would be ridiculous for us to *quarrel* in trifling a matter as such as the writing of an advertisement, that is when the error is not very glaring."

For the remainder of 1843 and well into 1844, William continually locked horns with Andrew Usher over the existence of and size of the commission as hazily stipulated in the contract. Though they wrangled over the terms of the agreement, they remained steadfast business partners, one the supplier of Scotland's finest malt whisky, the other the aggressive merchant of whisky. But in one September 1843 letter to John Gordon, William lamented, "I do not know how matters [with Usher] are to end, it gives me a great deal of trouble. . . . If Mr Usher comes up today, I will do everything I can to heal matters, but I am determined I will not give my calm consent to an agreement so ruinous as the one proposed."

History confirms that the tumultuous business relationship forged between George Smith and Andrew Usher in the 1820s, further cemented in 1843, and then vigorously fought over by William and Andrew Usher, nonetheless championed the cause of The Glenlivet at a critical stage.

Who Was Andrew Usher?

Born in 1782, Andrew Usher, George Smith's friend and business associate and William Smith's nemesis, was an influential Edinburgh wine and spirits merchant who opened his shop in 1813. Many whisky historians cite Usher, along with W. P. Lowrie and Charles MacKinley, as being one of the innovators who started mixing together malt whiskies from different distilleries for the express commercial purpose of discovering a style that was more accessible than the robust, cask-strength, single distillery Highland malts. In doing this, Usher ushered in (sorry, but I had to do it) a new era for Scotland's whisky trade. Described spirits writer Stefan Gabányi in his book *Whisk(e)y* (1997, pp. 338–339), ". . . the creation of a *cuvée*, already central to the cognac business, was considered a waste of time in Scotland. Usher was one of [the] first to experiment systematically with this technique." In 1853, Usher introduced the initial brand associated with The Glenlivet, Old Vatted Glenlivet, an amalgamation of different Drumin Glenlivet malt whiskies mixed with the malt and grain whiskies of other distilleries that was designed to appeal to a broad audience. Andrew Usher died in 1856.

In one advertisement in the June 14, 1844, edition of the *Morning Post,* an Edinburgh publication, the copy speaks glowingly of The Glenlivet and its debut in the vast London marketplace, saying, ". . . This whisky produced in the district of Glenlivet [note the correct spelling], upon the estate of His Grace the Duke of Richmond ['Gordon' had become 'Richmond'], in the Northern Highlands, and pronounced by all connoisseurs to be by far the purist [spelling] and finest spirit made in any part of these dominions, is now, for the first time, publicly introduced into London, under the patronage of his Grace. Andrew Usher & Co., of Edinburgh, sole consignees, beg respectfully to announce that they have established a depot for the sale of this unequalled whisky, in its native strength and purity, at No. 1 Northumberland Street, Strand, where supplies of this, and every other whisky of deserved reputation, will in future be received direct from Andrew Usher & Co.'s, bonded warehouse in Scotland. By his Grace's permission, the Ducal arms, on the seal and label, will distinguish the Real Glenlivet from all others. Price 21s. per gallon for cash."

Despite the rancor displayed in the early 1840s, the relationship between the Smiths and Andrew Usher & Co. continued for decades and thousands of gallons of whisky to come.

An Old Enemy and Peculiar Ways

John Gordon, born in 1822, four years after William, was experiencing his own personal troubles, mostly financial in nature, while dwelling in Edinburgh between 1841 and 1846. City life was far more expensive than everyday life in Glenlivet. John Gordon's meager salary at John Shand's law office was barely covering his expenses. Letters from John Gordon home to William, his married sister Margaret Smith Grant and his mother Helen frequently implored them to send some funds to help bridge the periods between paychecks.

In one letter to Margaret, dated July 21, 1842, John Gordon divulged indirect insights into the difficulties facing his brother at Drumin Glenlivet, who either was too busy to write back or in a fit of pique unwilling to do so. Wrote John Gordon perplexedly, "I have written William twice of late and both letters required to be answered but up to this time he has not favored me with one. I have been very anxious to know if Father intends to come up soon as if not I would ask him to send me some money to *keep my pockets* [full] on my journey home. I requested of William to send me some about six weeks ago which he wrote me he would do but as yet has not found it convenient to do so. You need not of course mind this as I will settle with him myself in my own peculiar way. [Do] not let him know you are aware of it at all but I wish you to let me know if Father is coming to Edin [Edinburgh] before the middle of August . . ."

With regular financial boosts from his family John Gordon made the most of his time in Edinburgh, working hard for John Shand and increasing his knowledge of law. By all accounts of the existing letters, William and John Gordon did not appear to be especially close, but rather had a formal and reserved connection. Though he concluded his letters routinely by saying, *Yours most affectionately,* William always signed his letters to John Gordon, *Wm. Smith.*

John Gordon noticed in late 1842 that William began referring in his letters to his "old enemy," his tuberculosis, which with alarming frequency was preventing him from working at Drumin Glenlivet in 1844 and 1845. In the summer of 1846, George urgently summoned John Gordon home. Perhaps attempting to finally bridge the gap that had developed between them, John Gordon nursed William in his final days. When William finally succumbed to his old enemy, John Gordon witnessed the fathomless grief of his parents and the concern of his father over the future of the family businesses. He decided to finalize his business in Edinburgh and return home to Banffshire. To complete his legal training, John Gordon moved to Elgin and began working for the firm of Grant & Gordon. At weekends, he traveled home to Minmore where his parents and sister resided. The important thing to George and Helen Smith was that their lone remaining son, John Gordon, was close to home again.

New Directions and O.V.G.

By his own admission years later, George was devastated by the death of his elder son. To salve the wound and maybe some vestiges of guilt, George, a strong, tall, and strapping man at age 54, busied himself with cattle breeding and once again with the inner workings of Drumin

Glenlivet Distillery. Business was so brisk, in fact, for Drumin Glenlivet malt whisky that George expanded the operation at Upper Drumin twice by 1849. Soon thereafter, John Gordon came home from Elgin for good. George gave him Nevie as a residence and a job at Drumin Glenlivet. But orders continued to swamp the limited capabilities of Drumin Glenlivet Distillery.

In 1850, George and John Gordon leased another property, Delnabo, located a mile southwest of the nearby village of Tomintoul. The object of taking on yet another tack, the family's fifth such commitment, was purely to enlarge the Smith family's distilling operations. A gentleman named, oddly enough, John Gordon founded Delnabo. The attraction to the Smiths was that the property had a working distillery. Gordon had gone bankrupt in 1849 and the tack, with four years remaining, became available. George and John Gordon immediately renamed the distillery Cairngorm-Delnabo and began working it to supplement the volume of Drumin Glenlivet. John Gordon was named Cairngorm-Delnabo's manager.

Records from a census taken in 1851 portray George as a "distiller and farmer" who resided at Minmore farm with his wife Helen as well as his daughter Margaret and her three children, George, Isabella, and Helen. George was named as an employer of 28 people, including domestic help, distillery help, and farm workers. John Gordon was listed as a farmer, presumably at Nevie, and described as an employer of eight laborers. Charles Smith, whose relation to George (if any) remains unknown, was cited as the manager of Drumin Glenlivet Distillery.

By mid-century, Drumin Glenlivet's fame was spreading far and wide. Charles Dickens, Great Britain's most illustrious novelist of the nineteenth century, was not known as a serious drinker, but evidently he understood good malt whisky. In a letter to a friend written in 1852, the great author and social observer wrote, "A man in Edinburgh supposed to be unparalleled in his whisky education has just sent me what they call in the City of London 'a small parcel' of what he recommends as rare old Glenlivet. Try the accompanying specimen . . ."

Then, a major and momentous breakthrough for the distillery operations—and Scotch whisky in general—occurred in 1853 with the introduction by Andrew Usher & Co. of Usher's Old Vatted Glenlivet, or O.V.G. Usher's regular whisky clients in southern Scotland and England had kept telling him how much they had wished that malt whisky from the Highlands would stop melting their fillings and be less aggressive in the mouth. The enterprising Usher had heard from the mid-1840s on of other merchants in Aberdeen (James Chivas, no doubt), Edinburgh, and Glasgow trying out different combinations of malt whiskies and grain whiskies in attempts to find a smoother, less harsh whisky, a sort of middle-ground whisky whose personality was friendlier than those of the individual malt whiskies.

Mixtures of different malt whiskies were referred to as "vatted malts" while combinations of malt and grain whiskies were simply called "blended whiskies." Usher's final product ended up being Old Vatted Glenlivet, whose core element was Drumin Glenlivet malt whisky. While the exact ingredient whiskies of O.V.G. are not known, some whisky historians postulate that the whisky comprised six to eight whiskies, the majority malt whiskies. Usher's O.V.G. immediately became a hit and "the first commercially marketed blend," according to author Phillip Morrice in his book *The Schweppes Guide to Scotch* (1983, p. 37).

With production at both Smith-owned distilleries at full throttle but cumbersome because of the dual locations, George and John Gordon, in either 1855 or 1856, decided to ask the Duke of Gordon and Richmond for permission to erect a new, modern facility just down the hill from Upper Drumin on the Minmore property. The Smiths wanted a single plant that would be large enough to handle the increase in business. Realizing the financial advantages in the face of escalating whisky consumption, the Duke gave his blessing for them to draw up plans and survey the site.

In 1857, the Provost Grant of Elgin honored George and presented him with a silver plate valued at £200. Lauded the Provost in his introduction, "You were the first to engage in such an undertaking [legal distilling] in this district. The difficulty and opposition which you had to encounter were such as few would meet, and still fewer could overcome. You had the prejudices also of the district to meet and combat; but you had the courage and fortitude to do both, and soon manifested to all that you were the best friend of your countrymen, by affording them a ready market for their produce [the barley grown by the shire's farmers], and saving the expense and trouble which they would otherwise have to incur in disposing of the produce of their farms."

Coincidentally in 1858, the Drumin Glenlivet Distillery sustained significant damage from a fire. This event spurred the builders at Minmore to speed up construction. In early 1859, operations at Cairngorm-Delnabo were shut down. Workers moved the salvageable equipment from Drumin Glenlivet and Cairngorm-Delnabo to the spacious new building, and The Glenlivet Distillery at Minmore, the finest of its kind in Banffshire, opened.

About the same time that the distillery became an operational reality, the new company of George & J.G. Smith was formed and legally sanctioned. George Smith had, at last, given full recognition to one of his sons, indeed, his lone remaining son. Now, in William's memory, it was time to take The Glenlivet to the world.

James Chivas, left, in front of the King Street shop in 1862.

The Chivas
Brothers Company

THE FLOOR OF THE celebrated Stewart & Chivas fine provisions shop at 13 King Street in Aberdeen throbbed with continual foot traffic during the early 1850s. The shop's air, seductively perfumed by exotic wares like cinnamon, coffee beans, tobacco, and pastries, billowed with the amiable chatter of sales staff and patrons pleasantly engaged in commercial transactions. Stewart & Chivas had become much more than just the most trusted place to buy the best produce, cigars, whisky, spices, tea, and bread in the whole of northeast Scotland; it had become a destination for people visiting the Granite City from England, France, Spain, Germany, Portugal, Ireland, and Italy. A mere handful of provisions purveyors in London, Paris, Lisbon, Rome, and Madrid could match the eclectic inventory of Aberdeen's Stewart & Chivas. Certainly, none could top their whisky offerings.

Prior to 1850, Aberdeen had been accessible solely by stagecoach or by ocean-worthy vessel. The opening of the Aberdeen Railway in 1850 linked the city to the south. Then in 1854, the Great North of Scotland Railway connected Aberdeen with the northwestern villages and towns of Aberdeenshire all the way to Huntly. The introduction of regular rail-way transport allowed visionary Aberdonian retail purveyors, like Stewart & Chivas, to actively pursue mail-order accounts, particularly in northern England and Scotland's affluent south.

Ensconced in the eye of the whirling commercial hurricane, James Chivas calmly spent greater amounts of time embellishing the wine and spirits department in response to the growing interest in the whisky made in Scotland. The outright triumph of Royal Glen Dee and Royal Strathythan gratified James and confirmed his belief that the home-grown whiskies of Scotland would be a hot-ticket item for many years to come. On the heels of obtaining their first Royal Warrant in 1843, whisky orders came flooding into the shop from society's elite. Earls, generals, dukes, admirals, and princes, not just from Britain but also from continental Europe, became regular whisky customers.

To meet the exploding on-premise and mail-order sectors of the business, Charles and James needed more space for order fulfillment, inventory storage, and whisky blending. Consequently, they expanded the store first to include the adjacent spaces at numbers 9 and 11 King Street and then, later, up to number 23 King Street on the other flank. In 1851, James, a courteous but demanding overseer, moved his residence to the second floor of 21 King Street, thereby solidifying his lordly presence quite literally over Stewart & Chivas.

Three years later at the mature age of 44, James married a vivacious and attractive young woman by the name of Joyce Clapperton. They resided in the spacious 21 King Street second-floor flat and in 1855 welcomed their first child, Julia Abercrombie Chivas. One year later, their first son, Alexander James Clapperton Chivas, was born. Although James was happy and settled with Joyce and their two children, signs of strain between him and Charles began to show by mid-1856. More than a decade and a half after the firm was created—and for reasons that remain unclear—Charles decided to leave Stewart & Chivas. He started up his own wine and spirits and food provisions shop in a commercial area known as the Adelphi.

Had the strong-willed and fastidious James become the dominant partner, perhaps assuming a bit too much command and control for

Charles's liking? Or, had James's relocation to King Street made Charles suspicious of his motives? Maybe James's outright success with his whisky blends or perhaps his popularity with the store's clientele didn't sit well with Charles. It is entirely possible that all these things wrapped up in personalities and goals contributed to the split. Regrettably, most of the company papers, personal letters, and other business-related materials that might have divulged clues to the breakup were consumed in a catastrophic office fire in 1929. Whatever the underlying causes, the 16-year-old partnership of Stewart & Chivas was formally dissolved in 1857.

That same year, two other important familial and business-related events occurred that would affect the Chivas family and the family business: First, Joyce Chivas gave birth to Williamina Joyce Shirres Chivas, James and Joyce's third child; and second, on the corner of Erb and Caroline Streets in Waterloo, Ontario, Canada, entrepreneurs William Hespeler and George Randall established the Granite Mills & Waterloo Distillery, the company that Canadian whisky man Joseph Emm Seagram would purchase in 1883, marking the official beginning of the Seagram legacy in the annals of beverage alcohol. As described in later chapters, the Seagram Company would show a consuming interest in Chivas Brothers by the halfway point of the twentieth century.

Keen to find a suitable partner to help him deal on a managerial level with the growing provisions business, James looked first to the logical selection, his younger brother John who had done exceedingly well over the two decades spent at D.L. Shirres & Company and was now a partner. John agreed to leave Shirres providing that he became a full partner in the provisions business. Without hesitating, James agreed and suggested that the name of the new entity be Chivas Brothers. John was delighted and excited about entering a family firm, not to mention one with such built-in cachet. The company known as Chivas Brothers officially appeared for the first time in the 1858–1859 Aberdeen Directory. It would appear there for over a century.

The sole drawback—and not an inconsiderable one, at that—to bringing John into the family business was his total lack of retail experience. Having worked as a manager in a wholesale warehouse company and therefore behind the scenes, John, in his mid-40s, was unaccustomed to dealing face-to-face with highly expectant and demanding customers. Neither was he familiar with the physical demands of the mercurial daily pace nor the long hours that such a thriving enterprise routinely devoured. John's first weeks must have reminded James of his own start with William Edward 20 years earlier.

Though John was a savvy businessman, his apprenticeship proved difficult. Nevertheless, his natural good humor, inherited Chivas-family grace, and willingness to learn eventually made him a valuable asset to the store. John's skill as a behind-the-scenes manager likewise served the company well as he assumed the role of overseer in the crucial backroom order fulfillment, ordering, and inventory areas. James, the obliging person most regular patrons wanted to see, remained the public face of Chivas Brothers. Also in 1859, the family of James and Joyce Chivas grew by one with the birth of James Joyce Chivas, the fourth and final child for the James Chivases.

From existing advertisements printed in Aberdeen newspapers of the era, one gets a sense of what Aberdonians were purchasing around 1860 as well as how much they were spending for foodstuffs and libations. Loaf sugar sold for 10 pence per pound; common black tea was garnering 3 shillings to 3 shillings, 6 pence per pound; finer loose pekoe tea went for 4 to 6 shillings per pound; coffee beans from Jamaica fetched 1 shilling, 8 pence per pound. Guinness's Extra Double Stout sold for 4 shillings, 6 pence per bottle; rum ranged from 9 to 14 shillings per gallon, while brandy garnered a steep 32 shillings per gallon because of stiff duties. Ordinary Highland malt whisky sold for 6 shillings, 6 pence per gallon; finer malt whisky at 11 percent over proof brought in 8 shillings per gallon; and the malt whisky from George Smith's new Glenlivet distillery at Minmore, considered Scotland's crème de la crème, sold for 20 to 22 shillings per gallon.

With business booming at Chivas Brothers in the early 1860s, tragedy struck in June 1862 when John Chivas unexpectedly died at the age of 48, less than five years after joining James in the provisions business on King Street. Condolences poured in from all over Scotland and

England. James was shattered. Only the unwavering support of Joyce and his children and the Chivas Brothers staff helped him overcome his deep despair.

The Bishop's Empty Jars

After his period of mourning, James plunged back into work. Placing more day-to-day responsibilities on his handpicked staff and department managers in the mid-1860s, James set about opening up new overseas mail-order markets and developing new blends of proprietary whiskies. Through the 1870s, business continued growing as more Royal Warrants were bestowed and even more noble families purchased estates in Aberdeenshire, Morayshire, and Banffshire, most of whom automatically retained Chivas Brothers as their exclusive providers of victuals and beverages during the stalking and shooting seasons.

Throughout the late 1860s and early 1870s, Alexander Joyce Clapperton Chivas, James and Joyce's elder son, and James Joyce Chivas, their youngest child, typically spent school holidays with their father in the shop, stocking shelves and helping out in whatever capacity they could. Alexander's easy manner with clientele and staff and his fascination with the mechanics of retail were not lost on his observant father. The younger son, James, although congenial and bright, appeared less interested and more easily distracted than his older brother. Though still a little boy, in his father's view James showed scant early promise in retail. Alexander, therefore, became the ordained son and the focal point of James's grooming. Indeed, James arranged for Alexander to spend time in Portugal, Spain, and Bordeaux, France, during his teenage years. There he absorbed the fineries of the Continent while also learning about the wines, spirits, and foods he would later be selling at Chivas Brothers. This exposure helped Alexander develop acute senses of smell and taste.

The 15-year span from the death of John Chivas in 1862 to 1877 proved to be a stunning period of achievement and expansion for James and the Chivas Brothers shop. Existing scraps of correspondence from devoted customers of the era depict the relationships that James had

assiduously cultivated. In addition, the letters described the types of services, running from the mundane to the wildly unorthodox, that Chivas
Brothers routinely provided. For example, when the fussy Marchioness of
Aberdeen was told by her Haddo House staff that her piano was being
sent to Aberdeen by sea from London, there was only one thing to do:
She contacted James Chivas to have him arrange for a trustworthy man
with a solid wagon and good team of calm horses to transport it from the
docks of Aberdeen to Haddo House.

An existing letter from the Earl of Fife, lord of Duff House in Banffshire, illustrates another odd request made of James by one of his customers:

> Mr. Chivas
>
> I want you to send a small band here on Friday week the 14th to
> play at a ball. I am anxious that you should get a really good one
> if you can. The band which used to come here in former years
> under the direction of Mrs. Wiseman left a *very great deal* to be
> desired, although she herself played well. It will only be required
> for that one night.
>
> Yours faithfully,
>
> Fife.

Simultaneously, orders for James's blended whiskies went off the
charts. The Earl of Enniskillen placed an order for "four gallons of
Strathythan" to be sent to a friend in Ireland. The Earl of Sydney's brief
note asked for ". . . as usual an old and ripe whisky." A courteous missive
from Lord Ashley informed James that the London-based noble,
". . . would be much obliged if Messrs. Chivas would send him one of
their 'smoked and pickled tongues' to try." Before signing off, a scribbled
note from Ashley at the bottom read, "Also a sample Bottle of their
'Lochnevis Whisky 20 years old!'" James had added two other personally
blended whiskies, Royal Loch Nevis 20 Year Old Whisky and Chivas
Brothers Old Highland Whisky, to his whisky roster in the late 1870s.

The new whiskies that he developed in the King Street cellars and offered to Chivas Brothers patrons sold well.

But as in all retail operations, not all transactions went smoothly and without hitches. There was the sticky problem with the Anglican Bishop of Aberdeen that the staff talked about for many years. The good bishop, the story goes, took a rather, shall we say, robust liking to James's first blended whisky, Royal Glen Dee. At the time whiskies were sold to patrons in stoneware jars. The jars were meant to be returned to the purveyor by the patron for refills. Unfortunately, the bishop kept failing to return the stoneware jars along with his new orders for more Royal Glen Dee. Not liking to have orders dent his profits, James had one of his staff deliver a note to the bishop, politely requesting that he return the accumulated jars with the courier. The courier returned with only a hastily scratched note from the embarrassed bishop. The bishop responded by sheepishly admitting that he hadn't realized the terms of the arrangement and, thinking that the jars were worthless once they were empty, smashed them to pieces. Said the mortified cleric, ". . . whereas some people had fairies at the bottom of their gardens, visitors to the Palace garden [church garden] would find only the broken sherds [shards] of Messrs. Chivas Brothers' whisky jars."

Fragments of other remaining documents from the late 1870s indicate that James was exporting large volumes of whisky abroad and across into England. One such note cryptically cites "Glen-Dee" as having ". . . given so much satisfaction in England . . ." while another shred of burned-edge paper mentions a ". . . large stock of WHISKY, in Casks" which Chivas Brothers was ". . . prepared to execute orders for exportation free of Duty."

By late 1879, James decided to take a chance by opening a satellite provisions shop near the bulging and tony new western neighborhoods of Aberdeen. By midyear, the new Chivas Brothers branch was christened at 20 Union Place, an extension of Union Street. In James's mind he knew that there was only one person who could adequately manage and guide the shop to prosperity, his able, charming, industrious, and eager 23-year-old elder son Alexander.

A Wastrel in Their Midst

Having worked as both a cashier and a floor sales assistant for his father in the King Street shop, Alexander Chivas was ready to take on the managerial duties in 1879 of what his father termed "the west branch" of the Chivas Brothers retail empire. Though he had a vigorous, educated, and intelligent younger brother, Alexander had to accept, in large part, the sole responsibility for guiding the new enterprise. James, the second son, was then 20 years of age, but displayed scant interest in the family retail business, preferring instead late nights and thus even later mornings. Young James's wanderlust and unreliable nature did not allow him to spend enough time in the King Street shop learning the fundamentals of retail.

To the deep disappointment and disgust of his father, who had always hoped to have both of his sons involved in the family business, young James evolved into a notorious wastrel, ladies' man, and high liver. He declined numerous invitations from his father and older brother to enter the family trade, however much of a pillar of the Aberdeen community the firm of Chivas Brothers had become. The younger James's spend-thrift habits bred serious money woes that resulted in 1880 in a bitter row between Alexander and the boys' father. To allay some of his irresponsible younger brother's debts around Aberdeen, Alexander dug deeply into his own finances—monies that were linked to the business. Alexander, too, had lived an active social life before accepting the managerial spot at 20 Union Place and was sympathetic to his brother's propensities. Alexander believed that with his encouragement and support perhaps James would mend his ways.

James the father somehow caught wind of the sibling bailout through the Aberdeen social grapevine. He immediately checked the status of Alexander's personal company account with the Chivas Brothers bankers and found it overdrawn. James reportedly did the nineteenth-century equivalent of "going ballistic" and, in the process, reprimanded his elder son more severely than his younger son. James argued that only young James should be held accountable to his own debts, not his brother, not his family, not the company, and that Alexander showed poor judgment by intervening. Neither was the senior James pleased about having this negative babble floating around the gossip mills of the staid and tightly buttoned-up Anglican Aberdeen community. The critical importance of the impeccable reputation he and their uncle John had built, brick-by-brick, from the late 1820s triggered James's anger as much as the financial losses from his sons' reckless behavior.

Even in the frosty aftermath of this unseemly internal and embarrassing episode, young James defiantly refused to knuckle under to either his brother's entreaties to work with him or his father's demands to settle down. The familial friction ebbed and flowed over the next few months as the family's emotional equilibrium teetered on the brink. Alexander and his father spent long, most likely tense days together dealing with the daily operations of two shop locations.

Finally, feeling castigated, misunderstood, and disregarded, young James departed Aberdeen and emigrated from England to the shores of the United States of America in the summer of 1881. Making his way from the eastern seaboard to the conservative heartland city of Milwaukee, Wisconsin, James made the acquaintance of another Scotsman and former Aberdonian, Alexander Mitchell, who was a leading Milwaukee banker and railroad executive. Mitchell, liking James's buoyant personality and joie de vivre, helped him get settled in southeast Wisconsin's Scottish community. James soon found employment as a secretary/clerk at one of Milwaukee's top medical insurance concerns.

In December 1882, James Joyce Chivas, doubtless to the speechless shock of his family and scores of young women in and around Aberdeen, married Emma Grosskopf in his adopted city. In what must have seemed like a textbook case of cruel irony to his older brother and his father, James was listed in the Wisconsin Marriage Index for 1882 as a "clerk" for the Northwestern National Insurance Company. Suddenly a respected member of a faraway community, James was elected in 1883 as an honorary member of the Robert Chivas Post No. 2 in Milwaukee. Robert John Chivas, an Aberdonian born in May 1842 and likely a distant blood relation, served as a decorated lieutenant in the Union Army in the American Civil War. Robert Chivas was killed in action while his unit was advancing on confederate troops in Mission Ridge, Georgia, in the autumn of 1863. For young James Chivas, the payoff for relocating to the United States was being allowed the opportunity to reinvent himself.

Meanwhile back in Aberdeen, the west branch of Chivas Brothers, managed by Alexander, purred along like a finely tuned and carefully primed machine after three years in business. In 1883, Alexander reported to his father that the growing outlet required more space to accommodate the upswing in business and received the okay to move across the road to 35A Union Place. With Aberdeen expanding westward, Union Place eventually connected with Union Street a few years later and the store's address changed again, this time to 501 Union Street.

Alexander, an adept administrator, hired a competent and trustworthy staff. Like his father, he believed that if an employer treats his employees honorably, the workers will respond by exhibiting loyalty and good performance. This was especially true with Alexander's right-hand man, Alexander J. Smith. The "two Alecs," as they were called, worked well together, and by 1884 Alexander J. Smith had become the de facto manager of the west branch. After the relocation of the west branch, Alexander Chivas shuttled back and forth between King Street and Union Place.

With local, national, and international sales of Royal Glen Dee, Royal Strathythan, Chivas Brothers Old Highland Whisky, and Royal Loch Nevis reaching new heights on an almost annual basis, James began tutoring Alexander in the subtle skills of whisky blending back at the King Street cellars. Alexander would sit next to his father as James meticulously "built" a blend from scratch, demonstrating how through sniffing dozens of cask samples he identified, first, the right whiskies to include in the blend and then, second, the correct ratios. James imparted to Alexander the understanding that the final blend needed to accentuate each whisky's virtues, thereby generating a whisky that was better than the sum of its parts.

The key to blends as opposed to unblended malt whiskies, James instructed his son, lay in consistency. Once a customer became comfortable with a particular taste style, say like that of Royal Strathythan, they typically remained devoted to that brand for many years. So, it was critical that the creation of each batch of Royal Strathythan, or whatever brand it was, replicated the flavor profile of the previous batch to the point where the batches were nearly identical. Blended whiskies were popular with the majority of patrons now, James told Alexander, because they were reliable, time after time.

Alexander realized only then how challenging it was to repeat a specific taste profile. Only then did he comprehend why his father logged so much time in the cellar every time the stock began running low on one of the Chivas Brothers whisky brands. Alexander came to see that a good whisky blender needed the combined abilities of an alchemist, a scientist, a whisky drinker, a wizard, and a chef. A whisky blender, in essence, had the difficult task of painting the same picture each time, frequently using different colors of paints. These were among the lessons on whisky blending that James passed onto his son during the first half of the 1880s.

By the dizzyingly busy winter holiday season of 1885, Alexander grew concerned about his father's health. In the furious bustle of the King Street shop, James appeared to tire easily, some days by midday. To help his father, Alexander spent part of virtually every day at the main shop. In the cold and damp of early 1886, James was ill and in bed at home most of the time. By late spring, the Chivas family doctor suggested to James and Joyce that they take some time away from the shops and Aberdeen. Alexander arranged to have them spend some recuperative weeks at a lovely country house in Bridge of Allen.

James Chivas died July 9, 1886, at the age of 75. Hailed from every quarter as Scotland's quintessential retail merchant, James's legendary willingness to please any and every Chivas Brothers customer, no matter what the request, was characterized sharpest in the obituary printed in the *Aberdeen Journal*. "A kindly, warm-hearted man, perhaps no tradesman in the town took so much trouble to oblige his customers, quite apart from self-interested consideration. People, in fact, applied to Mr Chivas for everything, and it went hard with his own feelings if he disappointed them. . . . As a simple, upright, and sincere man, Mr James Chivas will long be affectionately remembered by a large group of friends."

James's burial site is in St. Peter's Cemetery on his beloved King Street. Beneath a St. Andrew's Cross, the tombstone inscription reads:

"Sacred to the Memory of James Chivas, J.P., Merchant in Aberdeen and for upwards of forty years Churchwarden of St. Andrews Church who died at Bridge of Allen July 9, 1886, aged 75 years and is buried here. *The memory of the just is blessed.*"

With both the original Chivas brothers now deceased, the burden lay on the shoulders of Alexander Chivas to keep the family business operating briskly and efficiently. Regrettably, Alexander's younger brother James would not make things easy for him, even from a distance of 4,000 miles. In every family there hides a black sheep.

Such a Character as the Late Mr. Smith

IN THE WAKE of the death of William Smith, George and John Gordon Smith remained committed to dealing with the present by expanding and improving the family land and business holdings. In the Glenlivet community, the building of the new distillery and the acquisition of the additional farms had markedly elevated the Smith family's status and wealth during the 1850s. Nationally, the Smiths continued to enjoy the respect and acclaim bestowed on Scotland's most revered malt whisky distillers.

The Glenlivet Distillery at Minmore farm was, by an account published in the *Elgin Courant* in July 1862, a fully self-contained operation. The article gave readers a candid and precise glimpse into how Minmore functioned on a daily basis just prior to the era of electricity, telephones, and hydraulics. The report described Glenlivet's most illustrious farmers and distillers: "The barley produced upon the farm is all manufactured [malted] at the distillery, and a great proportion of the oats grown upon it is required for feeding horses and for supplying the meal used on the

135

farm and at the distillery. . . . The number of cattle kept at Minmore varies from 130 to 150 . . . there are twelve pure West Highland cows, with long wide horns, and shaggy hair of enormous length, and of all shades of colour. . . . Some of the cows have been prize winners. . . . The Messrs Smith have generally twenty work horses [including massive Clydesdales] at work. . . . There is a blacksmith's shop in the steading, and all the year round a blacksmith is kept, who does the work of the farm and distillery, and in harvest or on any busy occasion, makes himself generally useful."

The lengthy account even depicted what life was like for the male workers at Minmore. Indicative of the times, female employees were mentioned only in passing and then as being subservient to the men. The Smiths, who valued aptitude and initiative as much as physical strength in their employees, hired capable and bright individuals to help make The Glenlivet malt whisky and to tend the farm's award-winning cattle. According to the *Elgin Courant,* "There are in all no fewer than fifteen man-servants on the farm. . . . The men get all their meals in the kitchen, breakfast before six, dinner at eleven, and supper at six. . . . Their sleeping room is in a loft above [the sitting apartment]. . . . The men are all of an intelligent well-to-do class, who in their own spheres enjoy not a little of the innocent pleasures of life during their spare time in the evenings. When their work is over, they come in to supper cleanly washed and trimly dressed, and after enjoying the evening repast, retire to their sitting apartment and have their newspapers and books for those disposed to read, and various harmless amusements for those who wish to avail themselves of them."

The water for the main house and for the distillery came from a pristine subterranean source, called Josie's Well, the same water source used in the distillery today. The new state-of-the-art, two-story Glenlivet distillery was shaped in three sides of a square that measured 135 feet in length and 28 feet in width per wing. One upper section was the grain loft, where the barley was stored. Immediately below was the malting barn, where the barley was partially germinated before being steeped in water. The Glenlivet crew used from 740 to 850 bushels of malted barley for each new batch of whisky.

On the second floor of the middle section sat the kiln, where the damp, partially germinated barley was dried over fires fed with coal (a transported fuel) and local peat from a nearby field. Below the kiln in the center section stood, ". . . the mash tun, the boiler, the stills, the furnaces, the spirit and low wine vats, and the brewer's room." These core machines and large storage containers formed the heart of any distillery of the period and, therefore, required a central location. The bright, shiny, squat-bottomed copper pot still used for the first distillation, the Wash Still, held 2,000 gallons—a humongous capacity for the era. The capacity of the pot still for the second distillation, the Spirits Still, totaled 1,200 gallons. As explained in Chapter 2, smaller pot stills are required for the second distillation because reduction and the separation of compounds in the Wash Still decrease the total liquid volume.

The ground floor of the third section of The Glenlivet Distillery at Minmore contained seven cavernous storage vats, with capacities that ranged between 2,500 and 3,000 gallons. The remainder of the ground floor of the third wing acted as the bonded warehouse. The second floor space was taken up by the offices of George & J.G. Smith as well as those of the excise officer who, by law, had to reside on the premises during production periods to ensure that the Smiths were abiding by the legal tenets of distilling established by the Board of Excise.

The Smiths operated the distillery five to six days a week to keep up with the demand from merchants such as Andrew Usher & Co. and others in Scotland's main municipalities. In the spring and summer of 1863, the Smiths built four additional storage warehouses on the property because warehouse space in the third wing had been overflowing with aging whisky since the end of the previous year.

Also in 1863, the Strathspey Railway opened a station in the village of Ballindalloch, a mere eight miles from Minmore. A train traveled daily from Ballindalloch south to the town of Tomintoul. George wasted no time in applying for the permits necessary to build a supply store at the station. Casks of The Glenlivet were soon being transported to the railway station at Ballindalloch on wagons drawn by stately teams of Clydesdales owned by the Smiths. Running southeast to northwest, the Strathspey Railway also connected the hamlets of Boat of Garten and

Craigellachie. The underlying purpose for the Strathspey Railway was the east-to-west linking of the crossroads towns of Grantown-on-Spey and Keith. From Keith, rail links to Aberdeen became a reality. In George's mind, reliable railway transport not only would aid the distribution of The Glenlivet to Aberdeen and from there the cities in the south of Scotland, but likewise would cut down or eliminate whisky conveyance to southern marketplaces by slow horse-drawn carts.

Public Houses, False Prophets, and Pretty Views

By 1867, when George Smith turned 75, The Glenlivet malt whisky had become so closely identified with its creator that mentioning one almost automatically meant inclusion of the other. An advertisement in the *Aberdeen Journal* run and paid for by an Aberdonian merchant named Mister Sheed illustrated the point: "Glenlivat Whisky. Mr Sheed begs to call attention to his large stock of matured old and very old Glenlivat Whisky from the celebrated distillery of Mr George Smith, which is acknowledged to be the finest spirit made, and unrivalled in the trade. Forwarded, in cask or in bottle, to all parts of the United Kingdom and abroad free of duty."

As the fame of The Glenlivet spread like wildfire over tinder-dry underbrush, remarkably the Smith's distillery remained the only whisky operation within the valley of the Livet. According to *The Scotch Whisky Industry Record* (p. 120), the Duke of Richmond, who had come by the 4th Duke of Gordon's properties through inheritance, said in a letter dated November 6, 1865, "The District of Glenlivet, a part of the Gordon property in Scotland, belongs to me. My tenants George and John Gordon Smith, whose distillery of malt whisky is called 'The Glenlivet Distillery,' are the only distillers in the Glenlivet district—Richmond."

The reputation of The Glenlivet had become so impeccable and prevalent that it even floated in the royal consciousness of the British Crown. After a coach excursion through Banffshire, Queen Victoria wrote in her personal daily journal on September 24, 1867, of the atmospheric communities she had experienced, "... we changed horses and

November 6. 1865.

The District of Glenlivet, a part of the Gordon property in Scotland belongs to me

My tenants George and John Gordon Smith, whose distillery of malt Whiskey is Called "The Glenlivet" "Distillery" - are the only distillers in the Glenlivet district —

Richmond.

Duke of Richmond letter, November 1865.

drove on, entering *Glenlivet* through the small village of *Knockandhu*—*Blairfindy Castle* on the left, just behind the celebrated *Glenlivet Distillery*. We drove on for six miles; pretty country all along, distant high hills and richly cultivated land, with houses and cottages dotted about. . . . Sir Thomas said he would ride across [the bridge] with the ponies and meet the Duke [of Richmond], while his head keeper was to come on the box with Brown [the widowed queen's suspected lover-companion John Brown] and show us the way. . . . We drove on for an hour and more, having entered *Glen Rinnes* shortly after *Tomnavoulin*, with the hills of *Ben Rinnes* on the left. . . . The day became duller, and the mist hung over the hills; and just as we sat down by the roadside on a heathery bank, where there is a pretty view of *Glenlivet*, to take our tea, it began to rain, and continued doing so for the remainder of the evening."

In the September 19, 1868, edition of the *London Scotsman* an obviously enchanted reporter breathlessly observed, "There is hardly a public house in Scotland or England which does not announce for retail the 'finest Glenlivat whisky pure from the still.' . . . There is but one Allah, and Mahomet is his prophet. There is but one Glenlivet, and George Smith, better known as 'Minmore,' is its distiller. . . . In his youth he was a smuggler of the smugglers."

Later on in the flattering article, George Smith, a polite and robust elderly gentleman, is physically described by the impressed correspondent as, ". . . a man of some seventy-five years of age, but still a powerful, close-knit man. His breadth of shoulder and depth of chest are immense. . . . His face is broad, fresh and healthy. From under the shaggy snow-white eyebrow glimmers out the shrewd, acute yet kindly eye. In the knotted brow, surmounted with the wiry white hair, there is something indicative of an indomitable resolution, while the lower face is broad, open and good-humoured. Such is the personal appearance of the father of Highland licensed distillation."

To no one's surprise, the overwhelming renown garnered by a single distiller's malt whisky inspired imitation from Highlands competitors. Some newer malt whisky distilleries in neighboring districts like Morayshire, however, were unrepentant about copying the flavor traits of The Glenlivet. An article in the publication *British and Foreign Spirits* in

1864, observed, "The new Speyside distilleries were often merely imitators; at Craigellachie, for instance, 'The Glenlivet' characteristics, which were much admired, were reproduced—namely, the 'pineapple' flavour which was the original old Glenlivet style from the sma' still days."

In outlandishly brazen attempts to hitch their whisky wagons to that of the most famous distillery in the Highlands, other distillers started to identify their whisky in part as "Glenlivet" by tacking on the place name to their own proprietary distillery name. Malt whiskies from distilleries with names such as Miltonduff-Glenlivet and Glenfarclas-Glenlivet began appearing in retail merchants in the 1860s.

Concerned about the rash of shameless mimics, the Smiths began to voice concern over the growing confusion in the marketplace about what was and what wasn't the "real Glenlivet." The random and, in their eyes, fraudulent use of the word "Glenlivet" by malt whisky distillers who were not located in or even near Glenlivet was muddying the waters. The Smiths decided to make public their awareness of any Highland distillers who were misrepresenting their whiskies at the expense of The Glenlivet. George and John Gordon paid for the following advertisement that appeared in the liquor trade publication, *Wine Trade Review,* in 1868: "Glenlivet Whisky. Messers. George & John Gordon Smith of The Glenlivet Distillery beg to intimate that Glenlivet is a district which belongs exclusively to his Grace the Duke of Richmond, and their Distillery was the First, and is *now* the Only Licensed Distillery in Glenlivet; and they respectfully caution the Trade and the public against other manufacturers of spirits offering the productions of their distilleries under the name of 'Glenlivet Whisky'. Finely matured and new whisky in casks of any size; and by Messers. Andrew Usher & Co., West Nicholson Street, Edinburgh. Sole Agents South of the Tay [river]."

George and John Gordon, the foremost malt whisky distillers in Scotland, were suddenly and rudely made mindful of the dangers that success can inadvertently generate. Despite the irritations from distilling colleagues, the distillery at Minmore operated at full capacity all through 1868. The leased farms at Nevie, Delnabo, Minmore, and Castleton of Blairfindy likewise worked at full-tilt. The Smith family businesses as devised, built piece-by-piece and fostered by George were flourishing. As 1869 dawned, John Gordon, the younger son of George and Helen Smith, was not aware that his tidy, safe world was about to be tipped upside-down.

A Man of That Kind

In 1869, Helen Stewart Smith, the daughter of the war hero Lieutenant Stewart of the 1st Royals, beloved wife of George Smith and mother of John Gordon Smith, Margaret Smith Grant, and the late William Smith, died in Glenlivet. In the face of losing his lifelong mate, George, still strong-willed, spry, and resilient, remained fully engaged in the family businesses, assisting and advising his son John Gordon on a daily basis. He encouraged John Gordon to hire George Smith Grant, the 24-year-old son of John Gordon's sister Margaret and William Grant of Ruthven. With his wife's death and his own age creeping up on the number 77, George acknowledged that it was time to begin grooming the next generation of future ownership. George Smith Grant launched his career as an office clerk at the distillery, sharing space with his kindly grandfather and more demanding uncle.

The next year, 1870, John Gordon and his father traveled to London together to officially register the name "Glenlivet" as their proprietary trademark. They did this on February 5 in the Stationers Hall under the existing laws that loosely governed the ownership and protective rights of names and trademarks. Their action, though, did little to stem the tide of competing distilleries employing the name "Glenlivet" in their title. If anything, the number of malt whiskies from the Highlands incorporating the name Glenlivet increased.

On returning from London and seeing that his grandson was fast learning the routine machinations of the whisky and cattle trades, George decided to fully retire from the family businesses in the late summer of 1870. Enjoying generally good health into his late 70s, George was nevertheless unaccustomed to leisure time. He told John Gordon that he intended to spend his time reading, riding in his carriage across the thousands of acres he controlled in Glenlivet, and visiting with distillery guests and old friends in neighboring villages. During the nearly five decades he spent guiding the family distilling and farming interests, this industrious man viewed leisure pursuits as rare, almost trivial, luxuries.

The regional census of 1871 confirmed George's formal withdrawal from the firm of George & J.G. Smith since he was listed in the records as a "retired farmer." John Gordon Smith was cited as a "distiller and farmer." Young George Smith Grant was registered as a "general clerk." At The Glenlivet Distillery at Minmore, John McConnachie was identified as the distillery manager, Alexander Gray as the stillman, and James Stuart as the maltman. The distillery's annual production was logged at 93,000 gallons, or slightly less than 1,800 gallons per week. Export markets for The Glenlivet Distillery were listed as Europe, North America, South America, Egypt, and India. The Glenlivet, by then an authentic worldwide brand of Scotch malt whisky, fulfilled George's vision, born in 1824 when he applied for his license. Moreover, the results were significantly richer in scope than he had imagined.

In early December 1871, two years after his wife's demise, George Smith, died peacefully in his Minmore home; he was 79 years old. The cause of death remains uncertain. Of the many obituaries dedicated to the founder of The Glenlivet, one of the best, oddly from an unidentified publication, read, "We have this week to announce, and that with deep regret, the death of Mr. George Smith, farmer and distiller, Minmore, which event took place in his dwelling-house on the afternoon of Monday last. Deceased was only a few days confined to his room, and the cause of his death was no lingering disease. Nature was exhausted at his patriarchal age, and he passed out of the world with tranquility and Christian resignation, surrounded by his sorrowing family."

While the international recognition of stature as a legendary master distiller was secure, George Smith had proved to be a man of enormous talents in farming, cattle breeding, and land husbandry as well. These skills were depicted in the same lengthy account of his life. "His whisky was a certificate of his skill as a distiller over the world, but out of the district few perhaps know to what extent Mr. Smith carried on farming, and how he added field to field in the way of improvement. On his farms, from first to last, he has reclaimed more than 300 acres of waste land, and now leaves his son with more than 800 acres of arable land and some

10,000 or 12,000 acres of hill pasture, on which 2,000 or 3,000 sheep can be kept. . . . One thing Minmore specially excelled in which we have mentioned only incidentally—the breeding and rearing of cattle. He had a great fancy for Highlanders, and, when cattle shows came into fashion, short-legged mountaineers with long hair and horns came to them from Minmore that no cattle of their breed in this part of the country could equal."

Like all people of historical, social, and industrial impact, George Smith owned a multifaceted personality—at one moment, complex, distant, and unfathomable, at the other instance, straightforward, amicable, and simple. Although the existing cache of family letters provides circumstantial evidence that George inexplicably acted blindly toward his emotionally distraught and physically ailing older son William, it seems clear that he recognized his failing and behaved differently with John Gordon. The character traits most frequently cited in George Smith's obituaries were his foresightedness, his innate ability to see potential and seize opportunity, and his charitable nature to employees and total strangers.

"Education cannot make a man of that kind," continued the same account. "The secret of his success must be born with him. . . . Some men will rise to eminence in whatever condition they are placed. . . . To strong inborn common-sense Mr. Smith added quickness of perception. He saw through men and things intuitively, and with a sound judgment he formed his plans and perseveringly carried them out. His intellect was clear and penetrating in a remarkable degree, foreseeing results that would have escaped the attention of ordinary men. . . . Minmore never passed a beggar, even when hurriedly driving on the highway. . . . If he had not the silver, he borrowed from his driver or post-boy, and handing it to the poor, used to remark, 'It is never lost that is given to the poor; we get a blessing with what remains.'"

Neither did George Smith forget those people who had once worked for him but had retired. The *Banffshire Journal*, dated December 5, 1871, recounted the sermon given in George's honor at the parish church in Glenlivet. Said the officiating minister of George Smith's caring ways, "He had an open, honest, manliness of character, which was very refreshing to meet with, and his word in any transaction, even when he might be the loser, was as good as his bond. His hand was always open to the poor and needy; and from what I have learned, not a few in Glenlivet were assisted by him. He knew life; and to the last, he did not fail to sympathise with those who were suffering under the difficulties of life. And what more worthy of imitation can be pointed out in his life than the cases of those who, after having spent their strength in his service, were kept and cared for by him when they were unable to [provide] for themselves and their families."

The man, who by the force of his personality and distilling skill, had put the remote Highlands river valley of Glenlivet on the commercial map was buried beside his wife on a cold, misty morning in early December 1871. In terms of legacy, perhaps it was George Smith's unstinting bravery in the face of ruination in the mid-1820s that he was remembered for as much as his prototypical malt whisky. A dozen years after George's death, John Gordon recalled in a sworn affidavit taken during hearings on smuggling activities in the 1820s and 1830s, "For the first four or five years [my father] carried on his business . . . under great difficulties from the animosity shewn [shone] by the people in the Glen to the existence of a legal distillery. He had to carry firearms for his protection. I have no doubt that if my father had not been a man of great courage and determination, as well as a powerful and active man physically, he would have succumbed to the opposition which he encountered."

In 1887, Alfred Barnard, writing in his delightful memoir, titled *The Whisky Distilleries of the United Kingdom*, described George's early tribulations, "So great was the opposition of the smugglers to his settlement in the district that for a long time until they were dispersed . . . but his indomitable perseverance overcame all obstacles in the end, and his efforts were crowned with such success that 'Smith's Glenlivet' has become a household word, and the whisky is appreciated in every country."

In 1871, the King of Whisky had perished.

The Infamous "Glenlivet Suffix"

In the aftermath of his parents' deaths, John Gordon acutely missed the astute, razor-edged counsel and reassuring presence of his father. As his father had done after William's death and his mother's death, John

Gordon rolled up his shirt sleeves and delved back into the work both at the distillery and on the farms. He looked especially to his bright and enterprising nephew, George Smith Grant, and his sturdy and dependable distillery manager, John McConnachie, to assume more responsibilities in the distillery operation.

Though the Smiths' whisky business was hale and hearty, false prophets using the name Glenlivet lined up outside the door. All through the 1870s, word reached the second-floor offices of The Glenlivet that yet more malt whiskies were appearing in Edinburgh, Glasgow, Aberdeen, and London touting the name made famous by the patriarch of the Smith family. The cachet of the term *Glenlivet* proved to be irresistible to competing distillers. The word had, in the minds of the public, come to signify instantaneous affirmation of quality, no matter the actual contents of the bottle. John Gordon was offended and outraged by the opportunism of other Highland distillers who freely traded on the good name of Glenlivet.

In 1875, when the new, more definitive Trade Mark Registration Act was ratified by Parliament, John Gordon, unsure about the convoluted wording of the new law, instructed his solicitor [attorney], E. D. Jameson of Elgin, Scotland, to reapply in London for trademark protection. Ill-advisedly and without consulting anyone at George & J.G. Smith, Jameson submitted the name "Glenlivet" set against a decorative background of double circles and the plaid tartan of Gordon when he should have simply submitted the word Glenlivet without any graphic image. By some interpretations of the law, a loophole in the legislation appeared to allow other distilleries the use of the word Glenlivet because of Jameson's erroneous application. Livid at hearing this news, John Gordon chided Jameson and nearly fired him as the family counsel.

As more distilleries and brands continued to appropriate the name Glenlivet in the late 1870s and early 1880s, John Gordon's fury at both his inept Scottish solicitor and his competitors grew more crystallized and purposeful. The cases that enraged John Gordon the most were whiskies whose names had incorporated Glenlivet but were of inferior quality or, just as bad, were selling for much cheaper prices. John Gordon justifiably believed that the whiskies which did not uphold his father's standard of quality severely damaged the image so carefully cultivated by George Smith for over 47 years.

By 1881, John Gordon had endured enough. He informed his nephew, his staff, and his solicitors that he was preparing—despite the cost—to do battle in court if necessary, to strike down, or at least restrict, the improper use of the name Glenlivet. It is believed in many quarters that he had the financial support of his longtime allies and merchants/agents, Andrew Usher & Co. John Gordon, who was a former lawyer, set the wheels in motion by proffering a statement of his position prior to the commencement of court proceedings.

In his carefully presented statement, John Gordon said not without a little passion: "They [the offending parties] are attempting to appropriate to themselves the name of a place in which distilleries are not situated but in which a whisky [John Gordon's very own The Glenlivet] is manufactured which always has commanded a higher price than that obtained from their [the offenders] whiskies and to injure me and my trade. I should have commenced proceedings before this but I was most unwilling to enter upon legal proceedings and I did not feel able to incur the great expense which I knew such proceedings would involve as I should have to fight single-handed the whole of the Distillers who would combine . . . to deprive me of my property [the name Glenlivet] and to make the word a common term . . ."

John Gordon continued, ". . . it was not until it was brought prominently under my notice that in the large towns in Scotland and England dealers were beginning to sell as Glenlivet Whisky lower priced Whiskies of a different character bought by them as Glenfarclas Glenlivet or Cragganmore Glenlivet or some similar combination of words calculated to deceive any one not having local knowledge and to cause such person, by tacking on the word Glenlivet to the name of a particular distillery, to buy a different class of whisky at a higher price than it would have borne in the market if left to find a purchaser under its own name. I determined at whatever cost to myself to protect my right."

If Andrew Usher & Company did indeed lend financial backing to the legal effort, which rumors cast as highly probable, it was with their own interest in mind since they had for half a century been closely associated with The Glenlivet. Andrew Usher & Company had, in fact, with John Gordon's approval registered the trademark of "Old Vatted Glenlivet" in 1879. If the court's decision went against John Gordon, Andrew Usher & Company would feel the pain as well. But with the name Glenlivet being brandished on, what to the plaintiffs seemed to be, a new whisky every other week, there was no choice but to fight it out in the courts.

John Gordon's initial action involved correcting the error concerning his Glenlivet trademark made in 1875 by the Elgin-based lawyer, E. D. Jameson. The London-based firm of Paddison Son & Company served the Register of Trade Marks with a formal request asking that the graphic images be discarded and the focus of the trademark be made solely on the word Glenlivet as had been rightly filed back in 1870 by John Gordon and his father. The Registrar agreed to this request and the trademark reverted back to just the word. That accomplished, the lawyers representing George & J.G. Smith Company and Andrew Usher & Company moved ahead with their legal filings in autumn 1882.

Early verdicts in December 1882 disallowing the trademark use of the word Glenlivet by two parties favored the cause of John Gordon and Usher. Yet, those decisions proved to be victories against just two of the tens of distilleries that were suddenly applying for trademark rights to the term Glenlivet. Paddison filed more suits. The defendants' ranks swelled in early 1883. John Gordon sued Charles Drewe Harris, the London agent for Benrinnes Distillery. Charles Haig, London agent for Glenburgie Distillery, was sued next. The rancor within Scotland's distillery industry was the highest it had been since the mid-1820s when smugglers wrangled against licensed distillers.

In 1883, John Gordon enlisted the support of local merchants who testified to the authentic origin of the one and only The Glenlivet. John McHardy, the proprietor of The Pole Inn, a popular rest stop in the village of Knockandhu, purchased 300 gallons of The Glenlivet each year to serve to his guests. In his sworn affidavit McHardy said, "I have been asked by strangers and visitors for a glass of the 'real Glenlivet' who thought that they were sure to get it genuine in this neighborhood. Glenlivet people themselves occasionally took from me a bottle of the 'real

Glenlivet' to take south to friends thinking that it would be more difficult to get it genuine there." That same year, Mary Turner, the innkeeper
at the Craighead Inn in Glenlivet, testified under oath that she considered the malt whisky produced by John Gordon Smith to be the "real
Glenlivet."

To John Gordon's dismay, countersuits alleging that he didn't have
exclusivity to the word Glenlivet began being filed in late spring 1883.
These countersuits challenged John Gordon's rights partly on the basis
of faulty trademark applications but also on the grounds that the word
Glenlivet had evolved during the smuggling era as a generic term depict-
ing high-quality illicit whisky. To characterize how common the word
Glenlivet had become by the 1880s, one witness against John Gordon,
David Danziel, testified that as a lithographer he had printed "many" labels for various whiskies over the previous decades that incorporated the
word Glenlivet. Another printer, John Brown from Glasgow, testified,
". . . on average I prepare not less than fifty different Glenlivet labels in
the course of the year." James Murdoch, another respected lithographer,
gave evidence along with his colleague John Brown that in his opinion
"Glenlivet" had evolved into a general term on the same level as "Islay"
(a Hebrides island known for its malt whiskies) or "Campbeltown" (a famous whisky region located on the Kintyre Peninsula).

Numerous other legal actions taken against John Gordon and
Andrew Usher revolved around creative and ludicrous strategies. One of
the more absurd approaches by opponents of John Gordon and Usher
claimed that distilleries, even those that weren't near the actual place of
Glenlivet, but had used the word Glenlivet as part of their post office
registry prior to the 1870s should have the sanctioned right of continued
usage. A group of distillers banded together and had their solicitors
present the case against George & J.G. Smith & Company, that both
John Gordon and his father had long acknowledged and accepted that
some distillers used the word Glenlivet to their benefit and had taken no
actions against them, so why now?

By autumn 1883, John Gordon found himself embroiled hip-deep
in legal battles on a daily basis, simultaneously attacking other distillers
and their merchants and defending his own legal rights of trademark

ownership. His able nephew George Smith Grant earned his spurs during this tumultuous period overseeing both the distillery and farming operations, a positive development that did not escape John Gordon's overburdened attention. Legal fees, depositions, affidavits, preliminary court appearances in London's High Court, Chancery Division, and legal motions mounted faster than John Gordon had ever imagined as multiple court cases crept along at a snail's pace. By the time that 400 affidavits had been filed and his and Usher's legal fees had topped £30,000, a king's ransom in the 1880s, John Gordon started to wither beneath the psychological and financial weight of it all. At last, a court date was set. The trial judge who was chosen to preside was Mr Justice North.

Observers lodged safely in the third millennium may ponder whether John Gordon regretted firing the first volley in 1882 for what that shot let loose. By 1884, with all sides including the courts feeling wrung out (except for the London lawyers, naturally, who continued to rake in huge fees), conciliatory words and phrases such as "compromise," "bridging the differences," and "mutually beneficial agreements" began to be heard. The coterie of distillers who struggled to maintain the right to use the word Glenlivet began discussing the possibility that all the nasty, broadly publicized legal maneuvering might, in truth, be causing more harm to the term than helping to clarify it, thereby undercutting all involved parties, including John Gordon Smith.

Talk of compromise and an end to the legal proceedings suddenly dominated the informal conversations held between the parties in February 1884. Representatives from all sides at last convened formally in March and consented to finalize the dispute by agreeing on a resolution that would spell out the guidelines for the use of Glenlivet by one and all. In May 1884, an indenture and deed of agreement was signed by the parties and ratified by the courts. In John Gordon's favor, the document stipulated that the trademark for Glenlivet, originally submitted by George and John Gordon in 1870, stood as applied for and that only they without qualification could legally identify their malt whisky as "The Glenlivet." Also to their benefit, all legal proceedings challenging that application were thereby dropped.

Andrew Usher & Company agreed to start labeling Old Vatted Glenlivet as "A Blend of Glenlivet and other whiskies," therefore capitulating to the argument made by other merchants that O.V.G. was not composed of only Glenlivet malt whiskies.

On the downside of the indenture for John Gordon and Usher, they agreed to drop all legal actions in progress against other distillers and merchants for use of the name Glenlivet. They likewise paid the legal fees of £3,000 incurred by the other distilleries. John Gordon also consented not to obstruct the use of the name for 10 specified distilleries: Aberlour, Benrinnes, Cragganmore, Linkwood, Glenlossie, Macallan, Glenrothes, Glen Grant, Mortlach, and Glenfarclas. This provision made clear that the term Glenlivet had to be preceded by the actual name of the distillery and that the names were to be separated by a hyphen. Thus, Glenlossie-Glenlivet, Glenrothes-Glenlivet, Macallan-Glenlivet, and so on became legal names.

So in the eyes of long-time observers who won? The exhausted and much poorer John Gordon Smith who, in essence, paid tens of thousands of pounds to purchase the definite article "The"? The usurpers who sowed and reaped lots of bad publicity? Sir Robert Bruce Lockhart, author of *Scotch: The Whisky of Scotland in Fact and Story* (p. 25) believed, "Mr Smith won a partial victory." Gavin D. Smith in his book *A to Z of Whisky* (p. 81) wrote tellingly, "At one time no fewer than twenty-eight distilleries used the Glenlivet suffix . . ." Writer Richard Grindal, author of *The Spirit of Whisky: An Affectionate Account of the Water of Life* (p. 33) took a much more realistic view of the agreement, saying, "In a judgment that now seems totally indefensible, although only his distillery was entitled to be called 'The Glenlivet,' others could still use the term if it were hyphenated with their own name. For almost a hundred years several distilleries did so, but recently most of them have discontinued the practice, preferring very rightly for their whiskies to stand on their own reputations."

Surely every time after 1884 that John Gordon Smith encountered the name of yet another usurper with the "Glenlivet suffix," either in the shop of a spirits merchant or in a print advertisement, he must have felt the pang of defeat. He may even have believed that he had failed to protect the memory of his father.

And so, for several years at least, the great and costly war over the term The Glenlivet was at an end.

A Final List of "The Suffix" Distilleries

While originally 10 distilleries were cited as being able to lawfully employ the suffixed version of Glenlivet, many more Highland distilleries took advantage of the opportunity over the ensuing years after the court case. Here is the complete list in alphabetical order, as compiled by writer David Daiches in his book *Scotch Whisky: Its Past and Present* (p. 138), of distilleries that have at one time or other used the suffix Glenlivet:

Aberlour-Glenlivet
Aultmore-Glenlivet
Balmenach-Glenlivet
Balvenie-Glenlivet
Benromach-Glenlivet
Coleburn-Glenlivet
Convalmore-Glenlivet
Cragganmore-Glenlivet
Craigellachie-Glenlivet
Dailuaine-Glenlivet
Dufftown-Glenlivet
Glenburgie-Glenlivet
Glendullan-Glenlivet

Glen Elgin-Glenlivet
Glenfarclas-Glenlivet
Glen Grant-Glenlivet
Glen Keith-Glenlivet
Glenlossie-Glenlivet
Glen Moray-Glenlivet
Glenrothes-Glenlivet
Imperial-Glenlivet
Longmorn-Glenlivet
Macallan-Glenlivet
Miltonduff-Glenlivet
Speyburn-Glenlivet
Tamdhu-Glenlivet

This practice is hardly ever applied today, except as an occasional marketing tool for independent merchant bottlings.

The Magic Words:
Chivas Regal

ALEXANDER JAMES CLAPPERTON CHIVAS, handsome, witty, and single, was 30 years old when the Chivas Brothers board of trustees directed that he take over the day-to-day running of the family business in the summer of 1886. In his last will and testament, James Chivas had ordered the firm's trustees to bestow within a reasonable amount of time one-quarter share of the value of the business to each of his four children. The total amount was £20,000 to be split among the four siblings. Additionally, the trustees made clear to the remaining Chivas family members that James had designated Alexander as the lone heir to the shops and that therefore he would disperse the four sums of £5,000 to each of James's children. The funds were to come straight from the business accounts. The assumption of responsibility and sole partnership of Chivas Brothers also meant that Alexander was to be bequeathed the Royal Warrants, which would be changed by the Court of Queen Victoria to name him as the warrant holder.

As Alexander was about to assume control from the trustees, thereby becoming the sole owner, he reviewed the Chivas Brothers books with his banker. He discovered to his astonishment that there was not enough cash available in the Chivas Brothers business accounts to simultaneously pay off himself and his brother and sisters and properly sustain the business. He met face-to-face with the trustees and his sisters, and sent a letter to his brother, who resided in America, informing him of the dicey cash-flow situation. He suggested to them all that he pay their shares in installments from the upcoming profits of the shops, since lump sums were out of the question. Business at both Chivas Brothers locations continued to boom and there appeared to be no end in sight to their growth. The sisters and the trustees readily agreed that Alexander's recommendation was for the best all around. James Chivas Jr. married resident of Milwaukee, Wisconsin, did not agree, however, and demanded of the trustees either that his share be paid immediately or that he be granted a full partnership with his brother.

James's brash and immoderate petition, launched safely like a missile from long distance, infuriated Alexander. His demand compelled Alexander to recall in a gray cloud of ire the many times he had rescued his irresponsible younger brother from the clutches of creditors to his own and their father's detriment; not to mention the times that James had surreptitiously raided his portion of the family business account to foolishly and capriciously fund ill-fated business ventures devised in taverns by ale-saturated scam artists. Alexander considered further the miscreants who had formed the inner circle of James's wanton Aberdeen existence. He was not willing to give James the benefit of the doubt that his life had dramatically changed in the United States, marriage or no marriage. In Alexander's mind, James remained an irredeemable scoundrel and a black stain on the Chivas name.

After advising his mother and sisters, Alexander informed the board of trustees in no uncertain terms that there was no way that he would agree to, one, pay his brother's share immediately or, two, share the family business in a partnership of any proportion with his feckless brother. If James continued to insist on either full immediate payment or partnership status, Alexander told the trustees, he would withdraw from the existing family business. He warned the trustees that if they acquiesced to either of James's unreasonable demands he could in short order start a competing business in Aberdeen under the name Chivas Brothers, taking with him his Royal Warrants, his keen and savvy retail expertise, his commercial contacts and key members of his staff, like Alexander James Smith.

Before the alarmed trustees could even render a final decision, James, stunned that his older brother had so forcefully called his bluff, backed down. James informed the board by letter that on further contemplation he accepted his brother's terms of payment and that he would not press for partnership status. James never again challenged his older brother on the matter of ownership. After this episode, the only correspondence between the two dealt with James's pleas for loans. Alexander handed over to the company lawyers one such request from James with a note saying, "Dear Sirs, I have received the enclosed wire from my brother, viz. 'Cable hundreds pounds'. If he is entitled to such a sum, kindly give effect to this in the usual manner."

From that time forward, Alexander dealt with his younger brother through his solicitor.

Chasing down Money, Markets, and Donkeys

With the inheritance bonfire skillfully extinguished, A.J.C. Chivas and A.J. Smith got on with the operation of the Chivas Brothers shops. Together, they operated the two locations in Aberdeen with the same legendary diligence and meticulousness of the late James Chivas. In the late 1880s, Aberdeen experienced another growth spurt as the textile, fishing, shipbuilding, banking, and granite quarry industries reached new heights of development, providing employment for thousands of Aberdonians. The city's population approached 125,000. Aberdeen continued to be the commercial heart of northeast Scotland. Despite the loss of James Chivas, the "two Alecs," as regular patrons affectionately called them, made certain that Chivas Brothers remained the city's and the district's leading food, wine, and spirits provisions purveyor.

Success had its snags and imperfections, though. The vibrant social life that Alexander Chivas had enjoyed prior to his father's passing came to an abrupt halt when he assumed the reins and weighty responsibilities of the family company. Working late into each workday evening, Alexander had little spare time for leisure pursuits. His once-regular rounds of golf at Balgownie Golf Course with old school cronies became as infrequent as his fishing or stalking expeditions in the wilds of rural Aberdeenshire.

Living still at 21 King Street with his widowed mother, Alexander longed for the days when he traveled unencumbered through Europe, visiting winemaking friends who had lovely daughters. He freely talked to friends and his sisters about wanting to get married. Rumor had it that Joyce Clapperton Chivas, his mother, was lonely and therefore urged her second oldest child not to rush headlong into marriage. In late summer 1887, Alexander mused to a friend about his lack of social interaction, writing somewhat bitterly, ". . . of late that I have not had time to think of the matrimonial market . . . but even were it so, the trouble is to find the correct 'tart.'"

A realist, Alexander accepted that it was necessary for him to first firmly establish himself as the head of Chivas Brothers before taking the time to troll Aberdeen's social waters for a spouse. Strapped for cash and therefore unable to expand until 1888 due to the Chivas siblings' inheritance payments, the two Alecs decided to chase down monies that were long owed to the business by vendors and customers. Alexander Smith pored over the account books, identifying the laggards. He tracked down accounts in arrears, some as hefty as £500, and recovered them, at least partially. Alexander Smith's skillful and polite, but persistent retrieval of tardy and unsettled account funds greatly assisted in the financial survival of Chivas Brothers through 1887.

Meanwhile, foot traffic in the shops and the mail-order segment of the business continued to accelerate in the late 1880s. The death of James Chivas, a man renowned for his ability to please just about any request, did not deter patrons from making unusual pleas of James's son. Doubtless, one of the most peculiar requests came from none other than the bestower of his Royal Warrant, Queen Victoria. At one of the queen's summertime stopovers at Balmoral Castle in the late 1880s, an urgent entreaty in the form of a note arrived from the queen's butler. In it, the butler asked if Alexander could locate, hire, and then deliver posthaste a young donkey to the castle. One could not blame the two Alecs if momentarily their imaginations scurrilously wandered, given the odd proclivities of some members of the royal household. But then, further word came that the queen needed the donkey to pull her invalid chair around the grounds of Balmoral. Chivas Brothers delivered a spry donkey to Balmoral the following day.

By 1889, the inheritance payments were fulfilled and the two Alecs set about expanding or adding new departments to the shops. While Alexander Smith managed the routine happenings at both locations, Alexander Chivas delved into expanding the Chivas Brothers whisky exports. Working with D.L. Shirres & Company, his late Uncle John's old company, he opened up the Australian marketplace for the Royal Glen Dee and Royal Strathythan whisky brands. A newspaper in Queensland glowingly noted in 1889, ". . . in every well-conducted hotel Messrs. Chivas' Whiskies are as well-known as Guinness [stout ale] or Pommery [champagne] . . ."

Wherever in the world Queen Victoria's British Empire planted the Union Jack, Alexander Chivas tried to make certain that Chivas Brothers whiskies were there. A tobacco fancier, he also significantly broadened the stores' tobacco departments by importing exotic cigars and cigarettes from Cuba and the Philippines.

The journal *Scotland of Today* reported on May 3, 1890, "Messrs Chivas Brothers possess what is undoubtedly the finest purveying business in the North of Scotland. . . . The stock, as is to be expected, is one of the most valuable, *recherché*, and extensive character, and includes almost everything that the most fastidious *chef* could desire. . . . The wine department is under the direct personal supervision of the principal [Alexander Chivas], who acquired a thorough practical knowledge of the department during a prolonged stay of several years in France, Spain, and Portugal."

After listing some of the wines, the article continued, ". . . the stock held by the firm . . . leaves nothing to be desired even by the most accomplished connoisseur. Some splendid blends are shown in north country Highland whiskies, which have been selected from the highest-class distilleries, matured in sherry casks. . . . A large number of assistants are actively engaged here [the stores and cellars], and if any competently qualified judge of such matters desires to see a business unique in its importance, faultless in its arrangement, perfect in its administration, and exceptional in its success, that business is undoubtedly the undertaking of Messrs. Chivas Brothers in Aberdeen."

From the early 1890s, the stores' official 20-page catalog, titled "List of the Wines of Chivas Brothers," offered consumers scores of amazing libations and that, it should be pointed out, was just a fraction of what was available in the shops. Sherries from Gonzalez, Wisdom & Warter, and Sanchez Romate appeared on pages 7, 8, and 9 along with Madeiras from Cossart Gordon. Ports and vintage ports from Taylor Fladgate, Ferreira, Dow, Sandeman, and Kopke occupied page 10. Clarets from Chateau Mouton Rothschild, Chateau Margaux, Chateau Latour, and Chateau Leoville were on page 11. Chianti from Italy, red and white Burgundies from Bouchard, Hungarian wines from Max Greger plus Mosels, Hockheimers, Sparkling Hocks, and Niersteins from the vineyards of Germany adorned pages 12 and 13. Australian reds and whites appeared on page 14, and champagnes from Bollinger, Moet & Chandon, Pommery, Ruinart, Perrier Jouet, and Krug were on page 15. Brandies from Otard and Martell, liqueurs with still familiar names such as Benedictine, Pernod Absinthe, and Chartreuse filled page 18. Cigars from Partagas, Upmann, Murias, and Flor de Cuba were listed on page 19, and cigarettes with names like Muratti, Hedges Nessim, and Nestor on page 20.

Pages 16 and 17 were reserved for the biggest prizes of all—Chivas Brothers whiskies. Identified were Magna Charta, 5 years old and selling for 17 shillings, sixpence; Royal Glen Dee, 6 years old for 18 shillings, sixpence; Royal Glen Dee Reserve, 8 years old for 20 shillings, sixpence; Royal Strathythan, 10 years old for 21 shillings, sixpence; and Royal Loch Nevis, Select Liqueur for 26 shillings, sixpence. Beneath the Royal Loch Nevis, printed in italics, was the unintentionally comic line, "*20 years old, recommended for invalids.*" The two Alecs also offered, "Single Whiskies from all the High-Class Distilleries in the North of Scotland" as well as "Cheaper Whiskies Supplied at from 15/- per Gallon."

To say that the Chivas Brothers shops on King Street and Union Street flourished under the dynamic leadership of the two Alecs is a flagrant understatement. What James and John Chivas founded in terms of retail excellence and inventory depth was taken to the next level by the succeeding generation. The two Alecs took Chivas Brothers to the world.

Ally and Dotty

Though little documentation exists, the few remaining scraps of information suggest that Alexander Chivas met Alyce Macaulay in the winter or spring of 1890. Ally (Alexander) and Dotty (Alyce), as the couple came to be known among their circle of friends, announced their surprise engagement on August 9, 1890. Joyce Chivas, Alexander's mother, was staggered by the news and wasted no time in voicing her deep dismay to her elder son. The outwardly projected reason for Joyce's disenchantment lay in her contention that, although he was 34, Alexander was too young to marry. Speculation filtered around the social circles of Aberdeen that, in truth, Joyce, a difficult woman who was wracked by severe bouts of anxiety and depression, simply couldn't bear to let go of him. Alexander robustly rebuked her censure, thereby instigating a major falling out between mother and son. With his sisters, Julia and Williamina and family friends, acting as conciliators, Alexander and Joyce arrived at a fragile truce following an apology from Alexander for his outburst.

One could sympathize with Alexander's difficult position. Thinking that a cooling-off period would be good for everyone, Alexander wrote to Alyce, explaining his precarious standing and imploring her to help, saying, "You know, sweetheart, that ever since my father's death I have been all to her, and that now you are going to have her all in all, trifling that all in all may be. That now she has no one to look to for the rest of her life except strangers, which, for her, is a very hard trial for a woman of her age, weak health and nervous, very nervous, temperament. And remember, also Dotty, that she had no conception that I should dream of marrying at least for some years to come. That view, of course, did not

Whisky room in Chivas Brothers shop, King Street. Recreation.

hold, but she held it and the announcement was a most complete surprise to her, tho' it was to no one else."

Having consciously or unconsciously set up the premise for capitulation by his fiancée, Alexander went on in his letter to lower the as-you-yourself-have-stated boom, writing, "Now, my dearest I want you, as proof of your love for me and as a proof that you really meant what you have so often said to me that you would do anything I wish, to write to my mother such a letter as you would write to your own mother, expressing your happiness to become her daughter and promising to be a daughter to her and to do your utmost to make up to her for taking me from her."

Painted into a corner by Alexander and Joyce, Alyce had little choice but to relent and compose a letter to Joyce Chivas or quash the engagement. In a display of her deep love for Alexander, she wrote an appeasing letter to the embittered and sulking Joyce that effectively sealed the deal of their marriage. On April 2, 1891, Alexander, 35, and Alyce, age unknown, were married in Aberdeen.

Because of the brittle veneer of tension connecting Alexander, Alyce, and Joyce, he decided to leave 21 King Street. He and Alyce moved to 2a Albyn Place, a residence situated near the Union Street branch of Chivas Brothers. Joyce, unable emotionally to remain in the large and empty King Street flat, was relocated, at Alexander's expense, to a home on Holborn Street Road in Aberdeen. To meet the financial demands of his mother's move, Alexander was forced to put up a portion of his interest in Chivas Brothers as security for a loan of £300. Interestingly, Alyce paid for the house on Albyn Place out of her own resources.

Little was reported about their union. Sadly, the childless marriage of Ally and Dotty lasted for a mere 25 months. In late April 1893, Alexander left the King Street shop early one afternoon, complaining to Alexander Smith of having a severe cold and a raw throat. By the first week of May, his illness had evolved into a throat infection, referred to at the time as *quinsy throat*. Antibiotics, a reliable cure for such a malady in today's world, were still unknown in 1893. The same illness from which George Washington died, quinsy throat was actually a peritonsillar abscess, a complication of strep throat that affects the throat, upper palate, neck, and lungs.

To the shock of the citizens of Aberdeen, the northeast Scotland business community, and the Chivas family, Alexander James Clapperton Chivas died at the age of 37 on May 9, 1893. His passing marked the last time that a family member would be involved with the firm of Chivas Brothers. Adding to the horror, Alyce died three days later. Friends, perhaps overcome with grief and the romantic notion of the tragedy, claimed that Alyce perished from a broken heart. If Alyce had nursed her husband, and by all the accounts of their closeness she very likely did, it is reasonable to conclude that she also had become infected. The lethal coupling of quinsy throat and the devastation of her personal loss most probably caused her death.

Chivas Brothers, the smooth-running retail machine that had been lubricated and fine-tuned first by James and next by Alexander Chivas, was left without an heir and was suddenly threatened by turmoil.

The Second Alexander and Mr. Howard

The board of trustees of Chivas Brothers was once again called into action in the middle of May 1893. With Joyce Chivas and her two daughters deeply distraught over the deaths of Alexander and Alyce, decisions concerning the thriving business nonetheless had to be made. Should Alexander's younger brother, James Jr., an untested, disagreeable, and unreliable man, who had built a life for himself in America, be asked to return to Scotland and take command of the family business? The board rejected that idea outright, believing that Alexander Chivas would never have wanted that to occur. On meeting with Alexander James Smith to seek his counsel, the trustees decided to name the second Alexander—the faithful lieutenant, friend, and confidante of Alexander Chivas—as a trustee. They likewise named him general manager of Chivas Brothers for the time being. Joyce and her daughters, who all liked the gentlemanly Smith, agreed with the board's decisions.

Over the ensuing months, Alexander Smith proved unequivocally to be equal to the task as everyday business at both Chivas Brothers shops ran smoothly and efficiently under his direction. He wisely promoted from within the Chivas Brothers ranks, naming a new manager for each location. Revenues continued to climb, and under the board's supervision, Alexander made certain that the standards of customer service and top-quality inventory were maintained at levels that would have pleased both James Chivas and his son Alexander. Whisky sales, in particular, were strong as Chivas Brothers brands won over new audiences throughout the world.

The one key area of responsibility in which Alexander Smith felt neither strong affinity nor a natural ability was in the blending of whiskies. A straightforward, self-effacing man, Alexander expressed his concern about the whisky-blending situation candidly to the board. He informed them that the whisky stocks from various Highland distilleries that Alexander Chivas had accumulated during his tenure were of superb quality. The varied and deep nature of the inventory, he went on to say, might well inspire a skilled blender to develop new and different blends. The board promptly consented that he make every attempt to find a competent blender who could not only continue producing the established Chivas Brothers blended whiskies but create new ones within the context of James and Alexander's vision.

In either late 1893 or early 1894, Alexander met Charles Stewart Howard, a well-regarded master blender based in Edinburgh. Charles assured Alexander that he greatly respected the accomplishments of Chivas Brothers, in that their whiskies represented the upper echelon of native spirits. Alexander told Charles that if he entered into Chivas Brothers he would be responsible for the whisky department. Charles agreed to come on board and move to Aberdeen. The relationship between Alexander and Charles rapidly advanced as their similar philosophies of providing uncompromising quality of provisions, integrity in all business matters, and peerless service propelled forward the business of Chivas Brothers.

By 1895, Alexander notified the board and Joyce Chivas that he and Charles had decided to form a partnership and make a bid to obtain the company of Chivas Brothers. The board of trustees and the remaining members of the Chivas family accepted their offer, providing that the business retained the name "Chivas Brothers" and that they did their best to operate the shops under the guiding principles set down by James Chivas back in 1841. Alexander and Charles pledged to do so, stating that James's tenets were so sound and the firm name so revered, why should they alter them now? The business name remained Chivas Brothers.

Queen Victoria, so pivotal a patron of Chivas Brothers, passed away to great national distress in 1901. Joyce Chivas died in 1904 in Aberdeen, and four years later her second son, James, passed away in Milwaukee, Wisconsin, his home for the last half of his life. Records of the life spans of Julia and Williamina, James and Joyce Chivas's daughters, have yet to be unearthed.

By the few remaining accounts of their stewardship, Alexander as partner and general manager and Charles as partner and master blender kept their promise to the board and the Chivas family. It was reported that in 1904 Alexander and Charles exhorted their staff to honor the name Chivas Brothers at all times, claiming that the company name should forever be regarded by employees as ". . . the equivalent of a hallmark of excellence." For the next decade and a half, Chivas Brothers flourished and remained the foremost purveyors of provisions retailing in all of Scotland. Alexander arranged for new markets to be opened, while Charles maintained the level of excellence of the Chivas Brothers Scotch whiskies.

Shortly after Charles joined the firm, he created a new blended whisky, Royal Glen Gaudie. Thus by 1900, the year in which over 82.5 million liters of grain spirits were distilled in Scotland (*Scotch Whisky Industry Record*, p. 560), the Chivas Brothers blended whisky roster totaled six: Magna Charta 5 years old, Royal Glen Dee 6 years old, Royal Glen Dee Reserve 8 years old, Royal Strathythan 10 years old, Royal Loch Nevis 20 years old, and Royal Glen Gaudie, age unknown.

News of the economic boom in the United States and Canada during the first decade of the twentieth century was regularly reaching Aberdeen. Alexander asked Charles to comb the warehouses for exceptional whiskies, old fine malt and grain whiskies, with which to make the ultimate, long-aged, deluxe blended Scotch whisky. After weeks of marathon blending sessions, Charles approached Alexander one afternoon and offered him a taste of what he thought was the finest whisky he had ever blended. Alexander took a sip, then took another, and greedily gulped down a third. Charles's new creation was a sublime blend of whiskies that were at least 25 years old. The resultant whisky was balanced and satin smooth, yet mature, hearty, and slightly woody. Most of all, Alexander agreed with his partner that it was the new benchmark whisky for Chivas Brothers. One can imagine the flow of their conversation.

"Let's offer it to Canada and the United States as Scotland's first authentic luxury blended whisky," probably suggested Alexander, wanting to capitalize on the North American economic miracle.

"What do we call it, though, Alec?" maybe wondered Charles.

Peering off into the afternoon bustle of the King Street shop, Alexander perhaps pondered for a moment. *Chivas Brothers. Royal Warrants.* "Royal" had already been used. Looking at Charles, Alexander uttered the magic words, "How about 'Chivas Regal'? How does that sound?"

Steam lorries delivered barrels of The Glenlivet.

The Gallant Major's Whisky, O!

IN THE AFTERMATH of the bitter legal actions that occurred from 1882 to 1884, John Gordon Smith and his nephew George Smith Grant got back to serious business at The Glenlivet. Although other Highland malt whiskies were then legitimately using the hyphenated "-Glenlivet," sales of George & J.G. Smith's The Glenlivet continued to skyrocket through the mid-1880s. By 1887, the weekly volume of malt whisky at The Glenlivet Distillery was up to 4,000 gallons. Production was so vibrant in the late 1880s, in fact, that the number of excise officers stationed at Minmore had to be increased from one to four, just to monitor the heavy output.

Unlike most other Highland malt distilleries that shut down for four weeks in the late summer months for repairs and maintenance, there was no temporary suspension of distillery activities at The Glenlivet. John Gordon then employed approximately 50 men, distributed both at the distillery and around on the family farms. Sales of The Glenlivet whisky surged forward in 1888, and in 1889 the distillery's weekly production of virgin malt whisky stood at nearly 4,800 gallons, an astonishing increase of 20 percent in only two years. So much for the rumors that floated around the whisky industry after the litigation fiasco suggesting the popularity of The Glenlivet had peaked. If the much reported, at times acrimonious, court case had diminished the name of The Glenlivet at all, it was hardly evident in the broad-scale acceptance of consumers, who appeared to all but ignore the legal proceedings.

The Glenlivet's popularity was such in the 1880s that it even became the object of songwriters. After the court case had ended, John Gordon took amused notice of a Highland song by Scottish composer James Scott Skinner that had become the rage of the district's inns and pubs. Skinner dedicated his pianoforte and violin ditty, titled *Glenlivet Whisky, O!* to "Major Smith, Minmore." It sang the praises of The Glenlivet, saying in two of the verses:

> The landlord o' the moon, quoth he.
> Auld bricks, let's ha'e a glorious spree,—
> Hooch! Lunar blades, why sudna we,
> Like earth-born things, be frisky, O!
> We'll drink Professor Blackie's health,
> An' wish him muckle Gaelic wealth,
> An' always get by groat or stealth
> The gallant Major's Whisky, O!
>
> Freemasons! To the Major drink—
> We daurna speak, but we can wink,
> An' heaven be thankit, we can think,
> An' thinkin', feel richt frisky, O!
> Lang may they thrive in stock an' store,
> Balmenach, Craggan, an' Minmore.
> An' I'll be up to ha'e a spoire
> In gran' Glenlivet Whisky, O!

With his nephew firmly in control of the distilling side of the family business, John Gordon focused on two of his other passions: cattle breeding and the Volunteers, a military group formed in 1867 by the 4th Duke of Gordon. Becoming a lieutenant colonel in 1890 of the Upper Banffshire Company of the 6th Battalion Gordon Highlanders, John Gordon retired in December 1891 with the rank of honorary colonel. In July

1890, George Smith Grant was named a major in the Upper Banffshire Company. Though neither John Gordon nor his nephew ever participated in actual hostilities, the Gordon Highlanders fought with distinction a decade later in the Boer War in South Africa.

John Gordon's commitment to his community went far beyond his deep involvement with the Gordon Highlanders. He was also at one time a Banff County justice of the peace and, during another period, a deputy lieutenant of the Banff County sheriff's office. He served as a director of the North of Scotland Railway. Many Banffshire residents, impressed with John Gordon's quiet reserve, intelligence, strapping physicality, and kind nature, encouraged him in the early 1890s to run for Parliament as the representative of their county. He repeatedly declined their entreaties, saying that he harbored no political ambitions nor did he want to leave Glenlivet or his family for London.

In the spring of 1890, a publication known as the *Illustrated London News* produced a four-page article on Scotch whisky, complete with drawings of The Glenlivet and Andrew Usher & Company (*Scotch Whisky Industry Record*, p. 153). The theme was the spread in popularity of Scotland's native alcoholic beverage. Reported the article, "The extent to which the consumption of Scotch whisky has increased during the past few years is truly marvelous. Thirty or forty years ago it was hardly heard of as a beverage south of the Tweed [River]; now it is the usual drink of a large part of the community, not only in England but all over that Great Britain which lies across the seas. . . . There are at present no fewer than 126 distilleries in Scotland, employing a small army of men . . . 113 of these distilleries use malt in the manufacture of their spirits . . ."

The remaining 13 distilleries produced grain whisky that went into making blended Scotch whisky, which as mentioned was the biggest whisky innovation in the half-century from 1850 to 1900.

In June 1890, a late night fire, always a potential hazard in a distillery, destroyed 200,000 gallons of low wines and 1,800 bushels of malted barley at The Glenlivet. A quick-thinking night watchman and other roused distillery workers struggled to put out the fire in the middle of the night, but not before £2,000 worth of damage had been done to the plant. To everyone's relief, no injuries to the staff were sustained. George was forced to halt whisky production for several weeks while repairs were made.

The next month, good news arrived when the Duke of Richmond and Gordon gave his prized and world-famous tenant, John Gordon Smith, a land charter that conveyed to Smith the 10 acres on which the distillery stood as well as the land situated around the subterranean spring that fed Josie's Well. That same month, George Smith Grant hired Peter MacKenzie, who eventually rose to the post of distillery manager.

In January of the following year, 1891, John Gordon and George formalized an agreement with Andrew Usher & Company. The terms called for The Glenlivet to annually supply 2,500 to 3,000 gallons of malt whisky per week for 40 weeks, or a total of 138,000 gallons per year, to Andrew Usher. The price was to be fixed by John Gordon every October. If Andrew Usher did not agree with the price, an arbiter would be called in to set a fair price. The contract likewise cited Andrew Usher & Company as The Glenlivet's sole executors on all orders placed south of the River Tay. The only exception was private customers of The Glenlivet. The formal pact was an excellent deal for George & J.G. Smith because it ensured that a large portion of their annual production was spoken for a year in advance.

John Gordon, who like his late father George Smith was an unrepentant workaholic, wanted to enjoy his wealth by putting his personal stamp on the family estate. With no major business crisis to dominate his time, he seized one opportunity to make his mark in 1891 when the owner of Delnabo, one of the farms that John Gordon leased, decided to put the property on the market. He bought the Delnabo estate from the Countess Dowager of Seafield. In short order, he renovated and extended the main house. John Gordon moved from Minmore, which was always noisy and crowded due to the proximity of the distillery, to the more bucolic Delnabo a year later.

The National Guardian described the renovated Delnabo estate in its February 22, 1893, edition: "This beautiful Highland farm of Delnabo, and two adjoining farms, Colonel Smith purchased two years ago. . . . Along with the arable land goes the fishing in the Aven and the Alnick, as well as an immense range of hill ground, which is mostly enclosed with a wire fence above sixteen miles long, for a sheep farm, and forms besides one of the finest grouse moors in the Highlands. . . . The house of Delnabo, by recent additions, has been made quite a mansion, and the hospitalities in it are as bounteous as they are bright, easy, and elegant."

On March 19, 1893, John Gordon was delighted to hear that he could add one more title to his already impressively long and colorful résumé: great uncle. His great-nephew, John Gordon Cheetham Hill Smith Grant, the first son and child of George Smith Grant then 48 years old, was even named after him. After the bumpy ride of the early 1880s and several years of regret and self-doubt, life was very good and comfortably settled in 1893 for the 71-year-old son of the founder of The Glenlivet.

Long Live the Colonel

The 1890s witnessed an explosion of technology throughout North America, Great Britain, and continental Europe. Newfangled gadgets could even be found in parts of Scotland's remote Highlands. New inventions and scientific breakthroughs fascinated the always-curious John Gordon, who fortunately could afford the luxury of possessing odd gizmos. He convinced his nephew in 1895 that a telephone, the landmark invention of Scottish-born American inventor Alexander Graham Bell, should be installed at Minmore for the distillery business. The device, reasoned John Gordon, would save George time by allowing him to make instantaneous contact with vendors and patrons, providing that they also had telephones. John Gordon's instinct was right. A telephone did help George.

Happy with the success of the telephone, John Gordon next in 1896 had electricity hooked up at the distillery, as well as at the main houses at Minmore and Delnabo, for lighting. The distillery boasted 180 new lamps. Each unit generated light of from 8 to 32 candlepower. The electric power was produced by a fitting attached to the distillery's steam engine, which had been installed several years earlier. The steam engine also ran some of the other machinery at the plant. In the house at Minmore, situated just down the hill from the distillery, 70 electric lamps shone brightly, all powered by the steam engine at The Glenlivet. The Delnabo source of power for electricity was a specially built dynamo run by waterpower.

Being open to fresh concepts and mechanical modernizations, John Gordon Smith, as well as a handful of other Highland distillers, was ahead of his time. In the more populated and industrialized south of Scotland, institutions like Glasgow University, for example, didn't enjoy the conveniences of electric lighting until the start of the twentieth century. Further, until the 1920s many towns in England still employed gas as the main source of lighting.

As cited by writers John R. Hume and Michael S. Moss in *The Making of Scotch Whisky: A History of the Scotch Whisky Distilling Industry* (p. 148), John Gordon Smith's The Glenlivet wasn't the only malt distillery embracing technology. Moreover, attaining powered mechanization and light was more than a dalliance for most distillers; it was smart business. Wrote Hume and Moss, ". . . The malt distilleries of the 1880s and '90s were laid out in a logical fashion, with the aim of reducing labour and energy costs. Power-driven machinery became a commonplace with waterwheels, steam engines, and water turbines used as motive power where appropriate. Glen Grant and Teaninich pioneered the use of electric light and telephones were quickly adopted by many of the larger distilleries . . ."

The year 1896 marked the welcome appearance of John Gordon's second great nephew and George's second son, named William Henry Smith Grant, and also of a second set of wash and spirits stills at the distillery. The extra pair of stills was installed to keep up with the increasing demand of whisky from private clients and from Andrew Usher & Company. The impact of the stills was immediate. The impact at The Glenlivet of John Gordon's second great nephew, however, would not be felt until a quarter century later in 1921.

But John Gordon was hardly finished introducing new modes of conducting distillery business to the glen. In February 1898, the *National Guardian* wrote, "Col Smith of Glenlivet, it is said, has fallen in with a motor cart, which is likely to enable him to work his traffic to and from the railway station independent of the new Glenlivet railway, which has been dangling in the air for years. It [the cart] weighs about three tons, and carries about three tons of load. . . . It may be driven by steam or oil. The best power for it is said to be steam, generated by oil instead of coals."

The carts, or *lorries* as they were referred to, moved large stores of barley to the distillery from the train station and then carried barrels of whisky back to the station from the distillery warehouses for railway transport to Aberdeen and the south of Scotland. With the transportation of goods and people so simple and automatic today, The Glenlivet steam-powered lorries [trucks] may seem like a minor improvement. But like the installation of a telephone and electric lighting, the lorries were a major advancement for the period, a significant step forward that saved George & J.G. Smith time and money.

Along with the growth in sales and production came expansion of the distillery complex as more warehouses were added for the maturing malt whisky. On June 23, 1900, the Wine and Spirit Gazette page of the *Harper's Weekly* wrote of the enlarged distillery facility and its little-changed home district, reporting, "Glenlivet is known the whole world over for its whisky, and the valley of the Livet cannot be traversed without thinking of the fame attached to the wild Highland Glen. The Glenlivet Distillery occupies a commanding position, and the large mass of buildings cover an extensive area. The Glen is meantime looking its best. All the trees are in foliage, the birches especially are particularly pretty at this season while the hills are beginning to assume their summer colour. It will be autumn before the heather is in full bloom, and by that time the silence will be disturbed by the sportsman."

That same year, John Gordon, like his father a lifelong contributor to local charities of all sorts, donated £1,500 to the 6th Volunteers Battalion Gordon Highlanders. He was determined to see the Volunteers' drab gray uniforms replaced with bright tartan kilts. He also received a note of appreciation from the 2nd Battalion Gordon Highlanders for sending them a cask of The Glenlivet while they were on duty at Ladysmith in South Africa during the Boer War. The note read, "The cask of whisky . . . arrived here yesterday in perfect condition. I am directed by Colonel Scott to convey to you the hearty thanks of the battalion for your most handsome and welcome present, and to assure you that your kind thought will be long remembered in the 2nd Battalion Gordon Highlanders."

In failing health and largely confined to his house at Delnabo during much of the following year, John Gordon Smith passed away at the age of 79, on September 13, 1901. Following the funeral ceremony and interment, George Smith Grant stood at his uncle's gravesite with his two young sons, fully aware that the welfare of The Glenlivet now lay solely with them.

Faithfully Carrying on to the Death

In the same manner that his great-uncle George and uncle John Gordon gracefully absorbed personal loss and bravely moved forward, George Smith Grant assumed the mantle of the proprietorship of Scotland's most famous malt whisky distillery, The Glenlivet. As the sole son of William Grant and Margaret Smith Grant, the original George Smith's daughter, George Smith Grant was, therefore, the lone direct male heir. The wishes of his uncle, as clearly spelled out in his last will and testament, specified that George inherit and operate the family businesses and the owned and leased properties not merely because of bloodline, but because of George's proven earnestness, dedication, and ability.

Described by author Sir Robert Bruce Lockhart in *Scotch: The Whisky of Scotland in Fact and Story* (p. 26) as "A tall and commanding man with a military presence . . ." George Smith Grant, who had been educated at Chapeltown of Glenlivet and then at Milne's Institution at Fochabers, immediately became a rich man upon the reading of John Gordon's will. Continued Lockhart in his depiction of George, ". . . Colonel Smith Grant carried on faithfully the family tradition of distilling, farming, public work, private generosity, and, not least, volunteering."

John Gordon Smith's personal estate was valued by the family attorney, E. D. Jameson, precisely at £200,455, 12 shillings and ninepence, an enormous sum for the time. This sum provides a telling glimpse into how successful The Glenlivet Distillery and the family farms had become over the course of the 77-year span starting from 1824, the momentous year in which The Glenlivet became a fully licensed distillery. The designated amount of operating capital left for The Glenlivet Distillery totaled £7,000. A key element of the estate, aside from the distillery, was the family holdings in prize-winning Aberdeen-Angus and Shorthorn cattle. George had shown a particular interest in the cattle-breeding side of the family empire, even when his uncle was alive. Soon after he assumed control of the family businesses, George leased Auchorachan, a 240-acre farm property that had been within the family decades before. He used Auchorachan as yet another cattle-breeding outpost.

Business at the distillery at Minmore remained brisk up until the year of John Gordon Smith's demise. Nevertheless, George preferred spending his days engaged in the cattle business with his two small boys rather than at Minmore, home site of the distillery. He named his dependable lieutenant, Peter MacKenzie, to be distillery manager. From late 1901 on, MacKenzie was viewed by the distillery staff as being the roast beef in the sandwich at The Glenlivet Distillery.

Sales of The Glenlivet stayed steady in 1901 and 1902. The craze in blended Scotch whisky started in 1853 when family business associate and friend Andrew Usher introduced Old Vatted Glenlivet to Edinburgh. From the early 1860s to 1900, the popularity of blended whisky careened past that of other libations, most notably, French brandy. Master blenders and their brands became almost as famous as George and John Gordon Smith and The Glenlivet. Men inextricably linked with the blended Scotch brand that they created—Thomas R. Dewar and Dewar's White Label, Arthur Bell and Bell's, Matthew Gloag and The Famous Grouse, James Chivas and Royal Strathythan (forerunner of Chivas Regal), James Buchanan and Black & White, Alexander Walker and Walker's Kilmarnock Whisky (forerunner of Johnnie Walker blends)—were known by a large portion of the drinking public.

Investors, who wanted to cash in on the sharply heightened demand for blended whisky, provided financial backing to open more malt distilleries in the Highlands. Too many opened. By 1904, the whisky trade faced serious problems, and *The Scotsman* newspaper cited, "In the comparatively short period between 1892 and 1899 the number of distilleries in Scotland had increased from 130 to 161. The production for the year

1891–2 was 20,287,115 gallons, while in 1898–9 it was 35,769,113 gallons, an increase of fully 75%."

The potent commercial combination of scores of malt whiskies and blended Scotch whiskies and vigorous drinking habits, particularly in England, kept Scotland's whisky industry rolling at fever pitch until about 1901 and 1902 when production finally began to drop. By then, the damage had been done. With so many malt and grain whisky distillers believing that the bubble would keep inflating deep into the twentieth century, whisky kept getting produced in enormous volumes all through the 1880s and 1890s.

Not until the final years of the nineteenth century did whisky industry leaders at last began to realize that the huge surpluses of whisky inhabiting hundreds of warehouses scattered throughout the nation would lead them en masse to disaster. Recounted the same 1904 article in *The Scotsman*, "The increase in the stocks in bonded warehouse was even more startling. In 1891–2 they amounted to 56,186,000 gallons, and in 1898–9 they had risen to 103,290,000 gallons. . . . The inevitable collapse came towards the end of 1898 . . . soon the trade was flooded with whisky thrown on to the market for realization."

By the 1902–1903 distilling season, the dreaded terms "whisky glut" and "slump" were uttered as prices headed south on all types of Scotch whisky, save a fortunate few. Because of its cachet, The Glenlivet still fetched 24 shillings per gallon in 1902–1903, well above the majority of other brands. But that situation would not last. On top of that, George's hands-off philosophy with the distillery operations and his all-consuming interest in cattle breeding and management concerned distillery manager Peter MacKenzie, who believed that tough times were fast approaching even for the handful of blue chip malt distillers. MacKenzie implored his distracted employer to become more engaged and aware of the situation. By late 1903, George took heed and once again became a familiar presence at Minmore.

Multiple problems were mounting, however. Because vast oceans of malt and grain whiskies were available, merchants began selling blended and malt whiskies for the lowest retail prices ever seen. By the spring of 1904, even The Glenlivet's retail price had dropped. A repercussion of the sell-off was a lowering of malt whisky orders from merchants and, thus, a marked decrease in production at the Highland malt distilleries. With some estimates indicating that there was enough maturing whisky in warehouses to meet demand for four to five years, malt distilleries began to close down in the Highlands in 1904, hurting local economies.

Since The Glenlivet's average costs were higher than most other distilleries, MacKenzie and family counsel E. D. Jameson recommended to George that they trim production costs at the distillery by two to three pence per gallon. Every cost-cutting scheme that they implemented, it seemed, was never enough to offset the decreasing monthly revenues.

To make matters worse, Andrew Usher & Company started to order less malt whisky from The Glenlivet than their 1891 formal agreement had stipulated. In the 1901–1902 and 1902–1903 seasons, years in which the total distillery output was slightly more than 250,000 gallons, Andrew Usher had ordered and paid for 240,000 gallons. By the 1906–1907 season, that annual amount had plummeted to 160,037 gallons. To Peter MacKenzie's surprise and disappointment, George had not once brought up the terms of the 1891 agreement to Andrew Usher. By the 1909–1910 season, sales to Andrew Usher had fallen to less than a paltry 60,000 gallons as The Glenlivet's annual production tumbled to 62,992 gallons. In early 1911, the representatives of Andrew Usher informed George and Peter that they wanted to lower their wholesale purchase price of The Glenlivet to 3 shillings, sixpence per gallon less their customary commission of 2 pence per gallon. George argued for 4 shillings, 1 pence per gallon and won, though not without a fight.

The acrimony between the two old business associates and the bleak outlook for the whisky industry in general took its toll on George. His health began to wane. On June 11, 1911, George Smith Grant died in an Aberdeen nursing home at the age of 65 while recuperating from an operation. According to the *Scotch Whisky Industry Record* (p. 196), "Probate was sought [on George's estate] in the sum of £77,178." Lacking an heir of legal age, the court appointed a board of trustees for the Smith Grant estate. The trustees charged Peter MacKenzie with overseeing all aspects of the distillery operation until George's elder son John Gordon Smith Grant turned 25 in 1918.

The dark rumblings of war on the European continent became manifest in August 1914, causing another seismic jolt to ripple through Scotland's already weakened whisky industry. But other priorities in the lives of young men and women overshadowed the making of whisky. In the fall of 1914, John Gordon Smith Grant, 2nd Lieutenant in the Territorial Royal Scots and elder son of the late George Smith Grant, went off to war and his brother William Henry Smith Grant, younger son of the late George Smith Grant, obtained his commission in the 1st Battalion Gordon Highlanders.

One Smith Grant brother would in time return to take his rightful place as the head of The Glenlivet; the other would never return to the glen at all.

PART THREE

The Barons

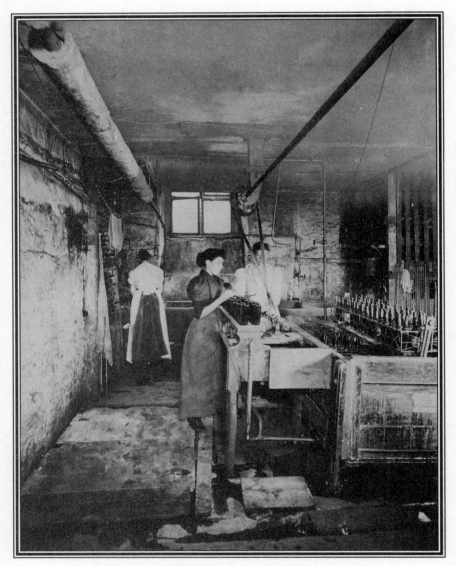
Whisky bottling line in Chivas Brothers shop.

A Spirit of No Common Rate

IN THE MIDDLE OF DECEMBER 1908, a half-year prior to the launch of
Chivas Regal, Alexander Smith and Charles Stewart Howard, copart-
ners and proprietors of the two Chivas Brothers' provisions shops in Aberdeen, received a letter from Julia Abercrombie Chivas Huxley. The
letter was postdated Birmingham, the English city where Julia and her
husband resided. The first child of the famous James Chivas Sr. co-
founder of Chivas Brothers, informed Alexander and Charles that her
brother James Joyce Chivas had passed away at the age of 49 in his
adopted home of Milwaukee, Wisconsin.

Though neither of them knew James Jr. well, Alexander and Charles
were aware of his stormy relationships with his older brother and father.
The late Alexander Chivas, from whom Alexander Smith had learned
the retail food and spirits business, had dealt with conflicted emotions
over his younger brother, who as an undisciplined youth had caused so
much familial strife in the 1870s and 1880s. Alexander and Charles respectfully expressed their condolences to Julia and her surviving sister
Williamina Joyce Shirres Chivas Stewart. With the demise of James Jr.,
the last male member of the Chivas family attached directly to the semi-
nal history of Chivas Brothers was gone.

The owners of Chivas Brothers were in 1909 poised to unveil to the world the crowning glory of the company's Scotch whisky blending heritage, a fabled legacy that James Chivas started in the 1840s when he began experimenting with combinations of malt whisky. In a pre-World War I store catalog titled "Chivas' Famous Whisky" and dated most likely between 1910 and 1913, "Chivas' Superb Liqueur Whisky *Regal*— 25 years old" was succinctly described on Page 7 as "This truly '**Regal**' Whisky is a superb example of all that is choicest and oldest in Scotch Whisky. It has an extreme delicacy and bouquet that age alone can confer, combined with the rare characteristics of the choicest Whiskies Scotland can produce." The retail price was a lofty 38 shillings per gallon, eight shillings more per gallon than its closest Chivas Brothers bottling, the well thought of Royal Loch Nevis. (*Author's note:* The term "Liqueur" in this sense did not intimate a sweet digestif. It was merely part of the name.)

As master blender with total control over the firm's enormous whisky inventory, Charles Stewart Howard replaced Magna Charta with a newly blended 5-year-old whisky named Chivas' Old Vat. To conserve and manage whisky stocks, he discontinued the Chivas' Royal Glen Dee 6-year-old, but maintained the 8-year-old version, a popular brand in Great Britain and other parts of the British Empire. Alexander and Charles also changed the spelling of the whisky from "Glen Dee" to "Glendee." Chivas' Royal Strathythan 10 years old, a favorite of customers in North America since 1895, and Chivas' Royal Loch Nevis 20 years old likewise remained unchanged and bottled in tall, high-shouldered glass bottles. Chivas Brothers Scotch whiskies were successful at home and abroad because, as much as any blended Scotches and more than most, they were models of consistency and quality, bottle after bottle.

Chivas Regal was created and targeted for the fast-expanding North American markets. The age of their new top-drawer blend, however, meant that there were limited quantities of Chivas Regal Superb Liqueur Whisky 25 years old. Cultivating whisky of such an advanced stage of maturity was costly and stocks were hard to maintain. Nonetheless, Alexander and Charles agreed that with the Chivas Brothers name then widely accepted both in the Canadian provinces and in the United

States, the release of what today would be termed an "ultra-premium whisky" seemed an appropriate step.

To distinguish it physically for easier identification, Alexander and Charles packaged Chivas Regal differently from its Chivas whisky stablemates. Presented in a squat, deep green-tinted glass bottle, the first generation of Chivas Regal was plugged with the best Portuguese cork in the warehouse off King Street. Next, the neck was dipped in bright red sealing wax, which was then imprinted with the customary Chivas Brothers stamp. The Royal Warrant, which in 1909 read "Purveyors to His Majesty King Edward VII and to Her Majesty Queen Alexandra," was prominently centered on the label along with the Chivas Brothers Gaelic motto *Treibhireas, Bunaiteachd, bho 1801* which means "Fidelity, Stability, since 1801."

Chivas Regal entered the North American marketplaces by early fall 1909 like a comet streaking out of the night sky. By the first week of December, the Chivas Brothers U.S. agents were wiring Aberdeen, requesting more stock of Chivas Regal. By May 1910, the month when King Edward VII died from heart failure at 68, Chivas Regal had become one of the most talked about new imported consumer goods among the well-to-do stratum of society in the New World. Upper echelon hotels and restaurants up and down the Eastern seaboard and as far west as Chicago and St. Louis hounded Alexander and Charles's agents for a single bottle or two whose contents, they promised hand over heart, would be meted out solely to their best and wealthiest clientele. Citing the rarity of Chivas Regal because of its age, the agents tried to get clients to buy more Royal Strathythan and Royal Glendee, which many did if for no other reason than those whiskies had the words "Chivas Brothers" on their front labels. The pinnacle achievement of Chivas Brothers whisky blending had become a retail phenomenon.

Chivas Regal in name and form oozed distinction and eminence, qualities that were infrequently seen in consumer goods during the pre-World War I years. Alexander, who personally composed the copy of their shop catalogs, liked to connect their crown jewel whisky to a line that William Shakespeare wrote in *A Midsummer Night's Dream*, "I am a Spirit, of no common rate." Alexander and Charles knew by the spring of 1910 that what they had in their possession was such an exceptional Spirit.

Official Definitions and War

As Chivas Regal's renown spread throughout Great Britain and North America, Alexander and Charles kept a close watch on other developments that directly affected the whisky side of the Chivas Brothers provisions business and Scotland's whisky trade as a whole. The half-dozen years immediately preceding World War I were pivotal for the advancement and appropriate characterization of Scotland's whisky industry. Squabbling between the malt whisky distillers in Scotland's Highlands and column still producers and blenders in the Scottish Lowlands about which type of whisky, malt or grain, was more authentic led to the formation of a Royal Commission. The Commission's objective was to examine Scotland's whiskies and to render a clear, unbiased, and binding decision on what precisely constituted "Scotch whisky." The formulation of such a definition held huge implications for both sides.

The Royal Commission, headed by Lord James of Hereford, dutifully interviewed 116 witnesses over the course of 17 months. The witness list included Highland malt whisky producers like John Gordon Smith of The Glenlivet, who was a leading voice on behalf of the nation's malt whisky distillers. Scotland's malt distillers argued that the light spirits mass-produced in column stills were not genuine whisky "except when made in Scotland and blended or mixed with 50% of Scotch malt whisky." Lowland column still producers and merchants who employed master blenders, on the other hand, countered the malt whisky distillers' assertions by claiming that grain whisky had become so widely accepted by the drinking public, in particular when combined with malt whisky, that it deserved to be recognized as "real whisky" as much as spirits made from malted barley in pot stills.

Other issues, however, reflecting power, influence, and traditional prejudices between Lowlanders and Highlanders colored the arguments of both sides. Since the 1860s, the Lowland distillers had gained considerable sway within the industry as well as financial resources due directly to the broad popularity and profitability of blended Scotch. The power achieved by the Lowland distillers was epitomized by the Distillers Company Ltd. or DCL, a massive amalgamation of about a dozen grain whisky producers that since 1877 had become the most influential entity in the trade.

The Highland malt distillers, known collectively as the North of Scotland Malt Distillers' Association, were less wealthy and not as well organized as their Lowland rivals. Their primary concern was that the Lowland grain producers were infringing on their trademark whiskies, thereby costing them market share. The malt distillers hoped that the Royal Commission would find in their favor by officially citing malt whisky as the lone true Scotch whisky and grain whisky as a mere fundamental grain spirit employed in blending.

The eight Commissioners visited Highland malt (pot still) distilleries, bonded warehouses, and Lowland grain (column still) distilleries during their exhaustive investigation. In the end to the deep dismay of the North of Scotland Malt Distillers' Association, the Commission in their 27-page report sided largely with the Lowland/DCL grain whisky producers and blenders, citing, "We have received no evidence to show that the form of the still has any necessary relationship to the wholesomeness of the spirit produced." The Commission concluded, as reported on by author Michael Brander in *The Original Scotch* (p. 114): "Our general conclusion . . . is that 'whiskey' is a spirit obtained by distillation from a mash of cereal grains saccharified by the diastase of malt; the 'Scotch whiskey' is whiskey, as above defined, distilled in Scotland and that 'Irish whiskey' is whiskey, as above defined, distilled in Ireland."

(*Author's note:* The commission's spelling of the word "whiskey" is somewhat misleading. Today, "whiskey/whiskeys" with the *e* is employed when referring to the greater worldwide category of whiskey, as well as to the whiskeys of Ireland and the majority of those produced in the United States. "Whisky/whiskies," sans the *e*, now denotes the whiskies distilled in Canada and Scotland.)

The malt distillers balked at the Commission's decision. The Lowland distillers and blenders, who because of their cohesion and deep pockets were better prepared in their depositions than the malt distillers, lauded the ruling as a victory for consumers as well as every distiller in Scotland, not just the column still distillers. Another noteworthy result of the Commission was the defining of Scotch whisky as a natural, native product made only in Scotland.

For the Highland malt distillers, matters went from bad to worse with the declaration of war on August 4, 1914. The start of hostilities meant economic uncertainty and customer trepidation. A few malt distilleries were mothballed; most others drastically reduced distilling output. The mood in the Highlands was sour and fraught with worry about what the future might hold.

In 1915, Scotch whisky was defined even further by a clause in the Immature Spirits Act, which stated that all spirits intended for use as whisky had to be kept inside bonded warehouses for a minimum of two years. Later in the year, that was lengthened to three years. To this day, malt or grain spirits must, by law, remain in barrels in bonded warehouses for that same minimum period—three years—before it can legally be called "Scotch whisky."

The gory horror of World War I stretched from August 1914 to November 1918 and brought with it, predictably, a sizable slump in Scotch whisky consumption. In June 1917 with the war going poorly, Parliament banned all pot still distilling in the Highlands to conserve barley for the baking of bread. This decree adversely affected enterprising blenders like Alexander and Charles who relied on large purchases of malt whiskies. Whisky merchants like Chivas Brothers who had taken pains to develop overseas markets had an additional area of concern: decreased exports. During the war years, shipping lanes across the Atlantic had shriveled up under fear of damage, a lack of transport ships or, worse, loss of cargo. A few months before the beginning of the war, exports of Scotch whisky topped 10 million gallons. By the tail end of the fighting in 1918, exports of whisky had plummeted to less than a third of that total.

Throughout the difficult war years, Alexander and Charles shifted the focus of their two shops to food provisions and the regional consumption of Scotch whisky. They cheered, as everyone did, when the war ended, thinking that their export business would again turn vibrant.

They especially looked to the North American continent, a place whose infrastructure had not been physically harmed by the international conflict. As they were gearing up in 1918 to resume what they hoped would be a steady flow of Royal Strathythan, Royal Glendee, and Chivas Regal to port cities such as New York, Boston, Montreal, and Philadelphia, word came from their U.S. agents that the United States Congress had passed the Eighteenth Amendment to the U.S. Constitution declaring national Prohibition. The near-complete shutdown of beverage alcohol production, importation, and consumption was slated to begin at 12:01 A.M. on January 16, 1920. The rumors and snippets of news that had been circulating throughout Great Britain concerning the Americans shutting off the liquor spigot through misguided, ultraconservative legislation became harsh reality.

With the closure of one of its largest and most promising foreign markets, what now for Chivas Brothers and its flagship Scotch whisky Chivas Regal?

Fire in the Hole

When the United States Congress, which had been manipulated by the fanatics of the Temperance Movement, turned the nation into an off-limits zone for alcoholic beverage exports in the middle of January 1920, Alexander Smith and Charles Stewart Howard focused their attention on other key overseas markets. Canada, Mexico, the Far East, and the rebuilding European continent became prime target regions of further development for all Chivas Brothers Scotch whiskies. They likewise redoubled their efforts to service their core patrons, the affluent Aberdonians and visitors to Scotland's northeast who had long been loyal customers. Despite the loss of the U.S. market, revenues were hovering near their prewar levels by the summer of 1920.

Continuing the Chivas Brothers tradition of promoting from within, Alexander and Charles elevated William Mitchell to junior partner status in 1920. He had been hired by Alexander as a cashier in 1908, and over his 12-year tenure, "Willie M" had shown unusual diligence and ingenuity as an employee and manager at both Chivas Brothers shops. By convenient coincidence, he had been born in 1886, the year that James Chivas died; and Mitchell's birthplace was Ellon Parish, home of the Chivas clan since the 1300s.

On ascending to junior partnership, Willie M took on the task, long overdue, of modernizing the Chivas Brothers antiquated office procedures. Typewriters were purchased. Filing systems were created for firm correspondence, inventory records, customer purchase histories, and employee documents. Willie M also introduced modern accounting methods and bookkeeping procedures. Around the same time, Alexander was busy bringing the shops' local delivery systems into the twentieth century. A motorized Ford lorry (truck) and Berliot van were purchased. The Berliot van replaced the final horse cart at the Union Street shop.

Signs that Alexander and Charles were gradually backing away from the daily operation of the business were hinted at when in 1923 a Royal Warrant appointing Chivas Brothers as "Purveyors of Scotch Whisky to His Majesty King George V" was written in the name of junior partner William Mitchell. This Warrant marked the tenth such Crown appointment earned by Chivas Brothers since 1843. During the 15-year span from 1896 to 1911, Alexander and Charles had earned no less than five Royal Warrants, a remarkable accomplishment and affirmation that doubtless would have pleased James and Alexander Chivas. Labels of Chivas Regal and all other Chivas Brothers whiskies had to be changed to reflect the new appointment to the Court of George V.

Six years later on a cold, overcast January morning in Aberdeen, calamity struck when a fire erupted in the ground-floor offices at 13 King Street. To the relief of the three partners, no employees or firefighters were hurt in the blaze. The damage to the Chivas Brothers showplace, though, was hard to swallow. The *Aberdeen Press and Journal* reported on the extent of the destruction, saying, "The cigar room itself was gutted, and beautiful oak panels, doorways and roofing which were erected in commemoration of the Jubilee of Queen Victoria, were destroyed. The floor of the room near the fireplace where it is thought the fire had originated through defective woodwork, had fallen through to a cellar below in which stout was stored, while the woodwork in a whisky tasting room abutting was badly charred."

The devastation paralyzed operations at the primary location for two weeks. Despite the losses, the partners counted their blessings since no whisky stock was lost. Had the fire not been brought under control before reaching the whisky warehouse, with its highly flammable contents, the situation could have been significantly worse for the entire block of buildings. Alexander, Charles, and Willie M moved headquarters temporarily to the West End shop on 501 Union Street. By the first week of February 1929, the main Chivas Brothers shop at 13 King Street reopened to considerable local fanfare.

Lock, Stock, Barrel, and Warrants

North America and much of the industrialized world plunged headlong into the dark abyss of global depression as stock markets collapsed in late October 1929. The whisky industry in Scotland and by extension its retail merchants across Great Britain and beyond were deeply affected by the double whammy of severe economic strife and continued Prohibition in the United States. The early to mid-1930s were hardly years of fond remembrance for anyone connected with Chivas Brothers. Except for the repeal of Prohibition in the United States in 1933 after a change of presidential and congressional leadership, little mirth emanated from either 13 King Street or 501 Union Street. Sales of top-quality food provisions and whisky at Chivas Brothers were slow, money was tight for everyone, and company morale was at low ebb.

But even in the midst of gloomy times, Charles kept buying and storing away casks of fine Highland malt whiskies, all the time believing that they would prove to be important in the future. Alexander agreed fully and encouraged Charles in his quest to scour the Highland malt distilleries, searching for the most intriguing whiskies. Knowing that their predecessors James and Alexander Chivas had dearly held to the philosophy that high-quality whisky would always sell and that the firm should always stock plenty of reserves, Charles painstakingly built what many contemporaries thought to be the finest, most extensive inventory of Scotch whisky in northeast Scotland. The Chivas Brothers warehouse on King Street was a virtual library of malt whisky.

Bad events are occasionally like horny rabbits and have the distressing habit of multiplying faster than most people have the ability to corral them. The deaths in 1935 first of Charles Stewart Howard (age unknown) while undergoing surgery and then several months later of Alexander Smith (cause and age unknown) capped the company's most miserable 15-year period in its history to date. The loss of the company's beloved senior partners, who were the final links to the Chivas family and to the tradition that had been the firm's compass since the time of Napoleon Bonaparte, left Willie M stunned and despondent as well as the sole remaining partner of Chivas Brothers. Following the deaths of Alexander and Charles, Willie M brought his own son, also named William Mitchell, into the business to help him survive the remainder of the year.

In early January 1936, the Board of Green Cloth altered the Royal Warrant of 1910, erasing the names of Alexander Smith and Charles Stewart Howard and replacing them with that of William Mitchell. The sole proprietor of Chivas Brothers, though, found little joy in the company. That summer, Willie M, overwhelmed by the firm's responsibilities and dispirited by the passing of his two friends and mentors, sold Chivas Brothers lock, stock, barrel, and Warrants to whisky brokers Stanley P. Morrison and R. D. Lundie.

The price of the transaction was £155,000 and was to be paid to Willie M in three installments over the course of 18 months. In a move that, had he known, would have had Charles Stewart Howard gyrating at thousands of revolutions per minute in his grave, the new owners financed their purchase by selling off a majority of the firm's famed whisky inventory for £149,000. The sale effectively wiped out much of Charles's arduous work. Morrison and Lundie immediately changed the legal standing of the company to a limited liability company, the British equivalent of a corporation in the United States, and Chivas Brothers thus became Chivas Brothers, Limited, on August 6, 1936. They named John Meikle as a board director and appointed him managing director of Chivas Brothers Ltd. and its two prized shops.

Under Meikle's steady hand, activity in the shops returned, the staff stabilized, and revenues even grew during the first two years. With profits once again appearing, the partners agreed that it was time to review what they should do to capitalize on the upswing. Acknowledging that blended whiskies were key to the continued success of the Chivas Brothers Ltd. retail enterprise, Stanley Morrison began to restock the King Street warehouse with high-quality malt whiskies by the autumn of 1938. The legacies of Royal Glendee, Royal Strathythan, Royal Loch Nevis and, most crucial of all, Chivas Regal would, Morrison told his partners, be the primary source of rejuvenation for the shops, as well as the export and mail-order businesses.

By the time that war broke out once again in Europe in September 1939, the whisky stocks of Chivas Brothers Ltd. were largely replenished. That accomplished, the partners turned their attention to the illustrious Chivas blended whiskies. Because of the decimated stocks, Chivas Regal, the partners decided, would be changed from a 25-year-old blended whisky to a 12-year-old. Chivas Regal Blended Scotch Whisky was legitimately available in the U.S. marketplace in late 1939 for the first time since 1920, the year that Prohibition started.

Swimming in the Scotch Whisky Pond

During the same half-decade period leading up to the outbreak of World War II, a diminutive Canadian businessman, standing five feet five inches tall, quietly entered the Scotch whisky industry arena by acquiring a whisky brokerage and blending firm in Glasgow called Robert Brown Ltd. The small Canadian of Russian Jewish descent headed a large drinks company that was headquartered in Montreal. His family-owned company was the Seagram Company Ltd. The man's name was Samuel Bronfman. Everyone around him, however, automatically referred to him as "Mr. Sam." Sensing huge potential profits and, just as important to him, personal prestige by owning a Scotch whisky brand, Mr. Sam became dead set on swimming in the Scotch whisky pond.

The Glenlivet aging warehouse.

Young Men of
Conspicuous Gallantry

PETER MACKENZIE, AS instructed by the George & J.G. Smith Ltd. board of trustees, guided The Glenlivet Distillery as general manager through the tricky and restricted war years. Production for 1914, the first year of the war, was recorded as 137,000 gallons, down from the 166,000 gallons produced in 1913. The years 1915 and 1916 each showed volumes well below that of 1914. Shifts were shortened from twelve hours to eight, and workweeks were staggered at times. MacKenzie temporarily reassigned some distillery workers to tending the prize-winning Aberdeen-Angus cattle and blackface sheep on the family's farm properties. Through it all, the resourceful MacKenzie kept nearly everyone on the payroll. The employees voluntarily accepted less salary with the understanding that by doing so MacKenzie was able to retain their services.

While the longtime employees of the distillery and the farms toiled diligently under MacKenzie's skillful direction on the home front, the great-nephews of the late John Gordon Smith, the sons of the late George Smith Grant, acquitted themselves well in the teeth of battle against the German army and air force on the Western Front in France. John Gordon Cheetham Hill Smith Grant, the elder son and heir to The Glenlivet on his return from the war, fought bravely and continually in France through 1915 and 1916. After learning to pilot biplane aircraft such as BE2cs and Avro 504s, John Gordon Smith Grant advanced from the rank of 2nd Lieutenant to the rank of Captain in the 9th Battalion of the Territorial Royal Scots by summer 1917. The 9th Battalion was attached to Royal Air Force (RAF). Because of his natural leadership capabilities, John Gordon Smith Grant was named a Flight Commander of his Highlanders Battalion. The Highlanders flew regular low-altitude surveillance sorties to the Front and occasional bombing raids deep into enemy territory.

Meanwhile, William Henry Smith Grant, the younger son of George Smith Grant and brother of Captain John Gordon Smith Grant, graduated from the Royal Military Academy Sandhurst and was immediately assigned to the 1st Gordon Highlanders from February to September 1915. In July 1916, W. H. Smith Grant, or simply "Bill" as he preferred to be called, was wounded in battle. He rejoined his regiment in January of the following year and, like his older brother, ascended to Captain status. While engaged in battle at Arras, France, in March 1917, Bill Smith Grant was once again wounded. During his recovery in hospital, Bill was awarded the Military Cross, a decoration that cited his "conspicuous gallantry and devotion to duty when in the command of a raiding party."

As the war raged on, older brother John Gordon Smith Grant looked forward to returning home to peaceful Glenlivet to assume possession of his inheritance that included The Glenlivet Distillery, Minmore, and the other family-operated farms. In March 1918, John Gordon Smith Grant turned 25 and thus became eligible to take full and unfettered control of the family business as soon as his tour of duty ended.

In late May 1918, John Gordon Smith Grant was recovering at the Stationary Hospital at Doullens, France, from wounds he received on a surveillance mission flying over the Front in northwestern France. Robbed of enjoying even a single day of his inheritance in Glenlivet, Captain John Gordon C. H. Smith Grant perished along with other patients, doctors, nurses, and aides at Doullens when German aircraft bombed the hospital to oblivion on the afternoon of May 31, 1918. Notified of his older brother's death a few days later after returning from a mission, Bill Smith Grant accepted the terrible news as he had always led his men in battle, with stoical courage.

Several months after his older brother's death in late 1918, Captain Bill Smith Grant married Helen Gordon, a young war widow. No wall-flower herself, Helen valiantly served during the war first as an ambulance driver for the Red Cross in Aberdeen and then later in France as a member of the FANY Corps (First Aid Nursing Yeomanry), as a driver and a nurse. Together, Bill and Helen Smith Grant spent three years in Europe after the war. When they returned home to Glenlivet in May 1921, the year Bill Smith Grant turned 25 on March 21, Peter MacKenzie and all the assembled employees and staff of The Glenlivet and Minmore greeted the returning couple at a gala dinner held in the distillery's grain lofts. His job of general manager done well, Peter MacKenzie, in effect, handed over the keys of The Glenlivet kingdom to Bill and Helen Smith Grant, its new, young, and inexperienced proprietors.

The homecoming of the war heroes was reported on in the July 12, 1921 edition of the *Wine and Spirit Trade Record*. "Glenlivet recently celebrated the succession of Captain Smith Grant to the proprietorship of the distillery by making him and his wife the recipients of handsome gifts from the employees at the distillery and from friends in the districts of Tomintoul, Ballindalloch, and Kirkmichael . . ."

The article went on to paraphrase Peter MacKenzie's stirring welcome speech which turned out to be a sage and astute summon to the young Smith Grant never to forget the close relationship between employer and employees, a bond that had been so carefully fostered by Bill's father, great-uncle, and great-great-uncle. Said the account of MacKenzie's eloquence, "Mr. Peter MacKenzie (manager) said they had gathered under very happy circumstances. . . . It was unnecessary for him to go into details so far as Captain Smith Grant's ancestors were concerned. He was quite sure his grand-uncle, the late Col. John Gordon Smith, and his father, Col. Smith Grant, were much better known for their many kind acts and considerations towards their employees than any words could express. (Applause.) No better testimony to that fact could be had than looking round the table and seeing how many heads had grown grey in the service. There were some with 10, 15, 20, 25, and 30 years' service. There were some whose fathers served before them, some whose fathers were still serving, and one at least whose grandfather was a long and faithful servant. It seemed to him that no light responsibility was placed on the shoulders of Captain and Mrs. Smith. . . . He felt certain it would be their earnest endeavour to preserve and maintain those interested and good feelings between employer and employee . . ."

Then it was Bill Smith Grant's turn to speak. His enthusiasm, recognition of the company's traditions, and amiable, self-effacing manner instantly won over the gathered employees. The article continued, "Captain Smith Grant, in the course of his reply, said he felt he had come into a great inheritance in succeeding to the Glenlivet Distillery and Minmore Farm. Those two had a combined reputation for Whisky and cattle second to none in the north. . . . He did not know much about either the distillery or the farm, but he hoped that would come in time. He could not possibly have come to a better place to learn, as he would be among friends, and would soon pick up the threads . . ."

Bill Smith Grant likewise graciously paid tribute to the outstanding jobs done in his and his brother's absences by the board of trustees and the distillery's two senior employees George MacDonald, a 35-year veteran, and Peter MacKenzie, distillery manager. They had all pulled together to keep the distillery and the farms operating through the hardest of times. According to the published account, following several speakers and an unspecified number of toasts, the new proprietor of The Glenlivet and Minmore Farm stood once more and closed the evening by pledging, ". . . he would try his best to carry on the traditions of the farm and distillery as they should be carried on. He would be a helping hand to any in need as far as it was in his power to do so."

And with those vows, the term of the fourth-generation owner of The Glenlivet began.

Surviving Ghostly Memories and Tough Times

With the distilling restrictions imposed during wartime being lifted and whisky exports again rising to about the industry-wide 6,000,000-gallon level, the Glenlivet Distillery's 1922 to 1923 annual distilling volume rose again to 161,000 gallons as postwar demand in Great Britain and Europe for fine malt and blended Scotch whisky steadily increased. In 1924 to 1925, The Glenlivet's yearly spirits output ballooned to a huge 220,000 gallons.

Bill and Helen Smith Grant settled comfortably into Minmore in the minds of the staff as though they had always been there. Even so, the ghostly memory and tragic tale of Bill's older brother seemed always to be on people's lips those first few years. In the August 14, 1923, issue of the *Wine and Spirit Trade Record,* a reporter wrote of his recent visit to The Glenlivet, writing, "Glenlivet Distillery has remained in the family, and the present owner, Mr. William Smith Grant, is a great-nephew [actually Bill was the great-great-nephew] of the original proprietor. Many people in the Whisky trade will recollect the tragic death on active service of Mr. William Grant's elder brother, the late J.G.S. Grant, only two months after he had come into legal possession of the distillery."

Like other accounts published before this particular one, the mesmerizing ambiance of Minmore and Glenlivet did not go unnoticed to the journalist, "The Glenlivet premises cover ten acres of ground, and the site is some nine hundred feet above sea level. Owing to the enormous growth of the business the buildings were entirely rebuilt and remodeled in the year 1859, and although the modern apparatus has been installed in a large scale the place retains an indefinable air of antiquity."

Then, by the second half of 1925 a crippling economic downturn in Great Britain quelled the demand for malt whisky, even Bill Smith Grant's fabled The Glenlivet. Contributing factors to the whisky slowdown included postwar overproduction instigated by overenthusiasm and the eroding effects of America's five-year-long Prohibition. The volume difference between the 1925 to 1926 season (161,000 gallons) and that of the next season of 1926 to 1927 (109,000 gallons) depicted the serious impact of both national and world events on The Glenlivet. In 1927 to 1928, the bottom dropped out of the floor altogether as annual volume stumbled to 65,000 gallons. A large number of distilleries were shut down, while others changed hands or were gobbled up by larger companies.

John R. Hume and Michael S. Moss discussed the dire conditions of the mid-1920s in *The Making of Scotch Whisky: A History of the Scotch Whisky Distilling Industry* (p. 174), writing, "During 1925 the malt distillers heeded . . . stern warning(s) about the consequence of overproduction. In August the North of Scotland Malt Distillers Association [of which The Glenlivet was a leading member] decided to lower output by 25 percent. . . . In an atmosphere of dwindling sales and increasing losses, the rest of the malt distillers needed little convincing of the merits of joint action. . . . During 1926 only 113 distilleries were working in Scotland compared to 124 the previous year and in 1927 just 84 distilleries were licensed for production. Of the 50 distilleries that had been shut down since 1921, about 40 had been closed, to all intents permanently, often being converted to bonded warehouses . . ."

The already precarious situation in Scotland's whisky trade was made catastrophic in late 1929 with the coming of the worldwide depression. At The Glenlivet, Bill Smith Grant mourned the death of distillery manager Peter MacKenzie, then watched the 1929 to 1930 distilling season produce 88,000 gallons. In 1930 to 1931, the season in which the economic decline became palpable, they distilled a scant 47,000 gallons. In 1931 to 1932, the total dropped to 40,000 gallons as only eight men worked in the distillery. The worst season by far, however, was 1932 to 1933 when 31,000 gallons were produced, a mere trickle to a modern distillery like The Glenlivet. By late summer 1932, malt distilleries in the Highlands closed on a weekly basis. At The Glenlivet, shifts and workweeks were staggered and nonkey distillery laborers were either laid off or given tasks on the farms. Bill Smith Grant had little alternative.

In August 1932, the Distillers Company Ltd. (DCL), the consortium of many malt and grain distilleries, sent shock waves through Scotland with the announcement that all their malt distilleries would close down for the entire season of 1932 to 1933. Stunningly in 1933, only 2 malt distilleries in all of Scotland, The Glenlivet and Glen Grant, along with 13 Lowlands grain distilleries remained open. The total annual volume of malt whisky generated by the two Highland malt distilleries was 285,000 gallons, the lowest national amount since the 1820s. Gloom set into the Highlands like rain clouds as villages economically dependent on distilleries suffered. Young, unemployed men flooded into metropolitan areas like Aberdeen, Edinburgh, Glasgow, and Perth searching for jobs.

The mass closing of scores of malt distilleries rippled through the farming community of north Scotland as the demand for barley shriveled. Barley farmers replanted former barley fields in wheat to ride out the temporary shutdown. Shop owners opened every other day because there were few shoppers and little inventory. The only glimmer of hope that year came in the form of an American known for his crinkly smile accented by a cigarette holder. Franklin Delano Roosevelt loved to drink alcohol, especially martinis. The cocktail was a sign of civilization in his eyes. And, he would be damned if he would let Congress allow the legislative failure known as Prohibition to continue.

With the repeal of the Eighteenth Amendment to the Constitution, the Scots once again began to feel guardedly optimistic. The reopening of the export channels to the United States in 1934 led to the reopening of over 40 malt whisky distilleries that same year. The Glenlivet, of course, was in an excellent position because it had never closed for an entire season. In the 1935 to 1936 season, production at The Glenlivet jumped up to 139,000 gallons. It skyrocketed to 264,000 gallons in 1936 to 1937 and then exploded to a record 306,000 gallons in 1937 to 1938. Bill Smith Grant had the distillery operating on two shifts around the clock in 1937 to 1938, six to seven days a week. By 1939, the malt and grain distilleries in operation leaped to 92 mainly because of the lifting of Prohibition in the United States.

As Sod's Law would have it, though, just as the Scotch whisky industry and its key members were revving up and hitting stride after a decade of steady decline, Adolf Hitler and his Nazi followers defiantly turned their backs on the Versailles Treaty of 1919. War again erupted in

Europe when Hitler's army invaded Poland in September 1939. Once more for the Scotch whisky industry, all bets were off.

War, Its Aftermath, and Strange Requests

By the start of 1940, Great Britain began rationing food and drink commodities, including Scotch whisky. The duty on whisky was also raised from 15 shillings per gallon to a staggering 97 shillings, sixpence. This, of course, drastically affected the retail price of a bottle of standard blended Scotch in Great Britain, which rose to 16 shillings per bottle on average. Seven million gallons of Scotch whisky were shipped to the United States in 1940, up from 4.8 million gallons in 1939. The following year, with shipping lanes across the battle zone of the Atlantic Ocean in jeopardy because of attacks by German U-boats, exported Scotch whisky totals fell to 5 million gallons. Distilleries in the Highlands began closing once more as the British government imposed distilling restrictions to conserve grain inventories and monitor their usage. To Bill Smith Grant's deep dismay in midyear 1941, The Glenlivet like the majority of other distilleries, went into "mothball" status by government decree.

Bill Smith Grant, in his mid-40s and still slightly affected by the two wounds sustained in World War I, was no longer able to actively participate in the regular British army. Leaving George Watt in charge of The Glenlivet, he did, however, serve Great Britain by joining the Royal Navy Volunteer Reserve in 1939. He served until the war ended and departed the RNVR in September of 1945 with the rank of Lieutenant Commander. He immediately returned to The Glenlivet and Minmore. The war, Bill Smith Grant quickly discovered, had taken its toll on the Glenlivet district, his distillery, and farms. Several male employees were lost in the war. The glen seemed unnaturally quiet and vacant. The Glenlivet's stocks were low and inadequate to meet the postwar demand.

Worst of all, his beloved wife Helen, who had done her best to manage The Glenlivet and the family farms in Bill's absence, was gravely ill. In 1946, Helen Gordon Grant died at her Minmore residence.

Realizing how crucial Scotch whisky could be in terms of generating revenue for the struggling nation, Prime Minister Winston Churchill issued a strong statement in response to some asleep-at-the-wheel Members of Parliament who wanted to continue distilling restrictions imposed at the beginning of the war to allocate more barley for bread-making. As accounted in the *Scotch Whisky Industry Record* (p. 256), Churchill insisted, "On no account reduce the barley for whisky. This takes years to mature and is an invaluable export and dollar producer. Having regard to all our difficulties about export, it would be most improvident not to preserve this characteristic British element of ascendancy."

Hardly allowing himself enough time for grieving, Bill Smith Grant plunged into the business of the distillery and the farms, hiring new staff and upgrading equipment that had become unworkable by disuse. In the 1947 to 1948 distilling season, annual production at The Glenlivet surpassed 200,000 gallons (204,677 to be precise) for the first time since the 1938 to 1939 season. Demand was high from wine and spirits retailers in Scotland's south, from London's merchants, and from Bill's U.S. and Canadian agents. The Glenlivet had to be meted out in small allocations. Production in 1948 to 1949 eclipsed the previous year's total by more than 1,000 gallons. The Glenlivet was back on track as Scotland's most coveted malt whisky, even if its availability was spotty.

In 1948, Bill remarried. The second Mrs. William Henry Smith Grant was Margaret Stewart Grant of Edinburgh. Warm and amiable, she was known to all as "Peggy." With a new love and renewed vigor, Bill Smith Grant embraced the challenges brought on by the postwar era. The largest problem was the severe shortage of production and packaging materials. He knew instinctively that if he could make The Glenlivet a success in the United States, all other export markets would benefit and maybe eventually follow suit. The Pullman Company, a major Midwestern U.S. train service, started serving The Glenlivet in two-ounce miniature bottles as they had before the war. The small bottles became a sensation. By 1950, half of all the Scottish malt whisky sold in the United States was labeled "The Glenlivet, Distilled and Bottled by George & J.G. Smith Ltd., Glenlivet, Scotland."

The Glenlivet became the favorite whisky of the day for stateside celebrities. Actor Yul Brynner and singer-actor Frank Sinatra were avid devotees. Robert Taylor, a famous Hollywood actor of the period, went so far as to write directly to The Glenlivet in 1950, making an odd request of the proprietor. Said Taylor in his formally written letter, dated February 8, 1950, "Dear Sirs: This will undoubtedly strike you as a rather presumptuous request and I hasten to beg your pardon for intruding upon your time in this matter. However, I have no other way of obtaining the information I desire.

"In the very near future I shall be leaving for Italy, where I will be engaged in the making of a motion picture for a period of at least eight months. From the inquiries I've made thus far it seems extremely unlikely that I will find it convenient to obtain your Glenlivet Scotch Whisky in Rome; at least none of the sources from which I've sought the information believes it to be one of the brands available there.

"Over a period of time I've come to consider all other brands of Scotch whisky second rate and strenuously dislike the prospect of six months in Italy without your Glenlivet . . . the assurance that I'll have ample stocks of Glenlivet during my stay there is one of the most urgent elements of my present departure efforts. Any information you are able to give me will, I assure you, be greatly appreciated. Very truly yours, Robert Taylor."

It is unknown whether the international star's wishes were granted during the filming of Mervyn LeRoy's *Quo Vadis* (which also starred Deborah Kerr and Peter Ustinov). For anyone who has ever endured watching this tedious let's-feed-those-Christians-to-the-lions toga-epic produced by MGM, a few drams of The Glenlivet after the day's shooting—or viewing—seems completely understandable, if not a requirement.

The United States, more than any other nation, became smitten with Scotch whisky during the 1950s. Still feeling the bruising pinch of Prohibition, the wrath of the Great Depression, and the pain of World War II, Americans turned in droves to salve their wounds with the whiskeys of Kentucky, Canada, and Scotland. Drinking Scotch whisky became something of a badge of sophistication for many Americans. Scottish brands, mostly blended Scotches, flooded the thirsty marketplace: Dewar's White

Label, Black & White, J&B Rare, Johnnie Walker Red Label, Cutty Sark, Ballantine's Finest, Teacher's Highland Cream—and the hallowed deluxe brand known as Chivas Regal.

Though the competition from blended Scotches was at fever pitch, The Glenlivet simply remained The Glenlivet, Scotland's foremost malt whisky made from 100 percent barley malt at a single distillery. Bill Smith Grant knew intimately the legacy that he had inherited after the death of his brother in 1918. He acknowledged that he would stay the course set by his great-great-uncle, no matter the business atmosphere, and allow The Glenlivet to speak for itself.

To meet the trials of the postwar era, Bill Smith Grant reorganized the company, incorporating in 1951. The next year, George & J.G. Smith Ltd. joined forces with the company, J. & J. Grant Ltd. that owned nearby Glen Grant Distillery, to form a new corporation, The Glenlivet & Glen Grant Distillers Ltd. The two distilleries had worked in tandem for many years and were familiar with each other. By combining forces, they significantly cut their operating costs. In 1952, Bill Smith Grant named Robert N. Arthur as general manager of The Glenlivet, succeeding George Watt.

Through all of Bill's modifications and changes in staff, The Glenlivet's quality remained true to the original. Sir Robert Bruce Lockhart observed in his book *Scotch: The Whisky of Scotland in Fact and Story* (p. 26), written in 1951 and revised in 1959, "While slumps and depressions have caused the closing, temporary or permanent, of other distilleries, [The] Glenlivet has never stopped except under war restrictions. . . . In spite, too, of the changes in taste and in manufacture which blending has introduced, [The] Glenlivet remains, in the opinion of many connoisseurs, the premier whisky of the world."

Samuel Bronfman.

Mr. Sam and Scotland's Prince of Whiskies

GREAT BRITAIN WAS victorious, but its economy and infrastructure were fractured after World War II. The six long war years and their aftermath were rife with shortages in the kinds of foodstuffs and libations that had been the cornerstones of Aberdeen's two most famous provisions shops. Rationing remained in effect all over Scotland, England, and Wales long after the surrender of the Axis nations. The proprietors of Chivas Brothers had to reestablish the customary commercial alliances with French cheese, paté, wine, and truffle producers; Italian olive, wine, and olive oil makers; Swiss preserves and cheese producers; Spanish wine and sherry makers; and Portuguese port houses. Some suppliers were dead; others were out-of-business or had relocated. Even the whisky distillers in their own backyard, most of whom had been closed down by government decree from 1941 to 1944, had to rebuild their stocks before they could supply new whiskies.

By the end of the war, the luster had worn off Chivas Brothers Ltd., at least for its owners R. D. Lundie and Stanley P. Morrison. In 1947,

Lundie bought out Morrison's shares and Morrison moved on, opening another brokerage business a few years later. John Meikle, the stores' operations director, had left at the start of the war. Lower than average annual revenues from 1940 through 1948 had pushed the company's financial reserves to the brink of collapse. In Aberdeen's social circle, it was said that only sales of the whiskies had kept the stores afloat.

Although 12-year-old Chivas Regal was again available and selling in the United States, Chivas Brothers was floundering in the stagnant economy of northeast Scotland, which was still recovering from the ravages of war. Gossip that bemoaned the woes of Chivas Brothers coursed through Scotland's whisky industry as fast as rivulets of snow melt pulsed through Grampian Highland burns in early May. Times were bleak for Lundie. Yet, the circulating blather described a remarkable cache of mature malt and grain whiskies that inhabited the King Street warehouse. Though inaccurate to a large degree, some of the rumors depicted a virtual treasure trove of whisky gems that had been accumulated since 1937 when Morrison and Lundie set out to restore the core wealth of their company.

The radarlike ears of Scotsman and whisky man James Barclay picked up the tittle-tattle. Barclay, known as Jimmy, was the clever and savvy point man for Robert Brown Ltd. and Joseph E. Seagram & Sons Ltd., the incorporated Glasgow beverage concerns and subsidiaries of the Seagram Company of Canada. Barclay, who was aware of Samuel Bronfman's keen yearning to enter the Scotch whisky business, regularly heard the tantalizing whispers about the moribund condition of Lundie's shops. By early 1948, Barclay began to wonder whether it would be feasible to pair up a shaky Chivas Brothers Ltd. and the irascible Canadian whiskey baron through a buyout that Barclay would arrange on behalf of Seagram. To team the farseeing, if volatile Mr. Sam, with Chivas Regal, the acknowledged class act of mature blended Scotch whisky, was an intriguing, not to mention, entertaining concept to Barclay. The meeting he arranged with R. D. Lundie would prove to be the initial step in what would become one of the biggest coups in Scotch whisky history.

A Reign of Brilliant Terror

Samuel Bronfman was descended from Orthodox Jews who left the harsh life of Russia in 1889 and immigrated to the harsh plains of Manitoba, Canada. The fourth child and third son of Yechiel Moshe and Mindel Bronfman, young Sam (1891–1971) learned the value of hard work at an early age from his father. But more than being remarkably industrious, Sam eclipsed his older brothers Abraham and Harry in vision, uncommon stamina, and inner drive. Sam's inner drive, in fact, could best be described as "volcanic." Along with wind, fire, and rain, Sam was a veritable force of nature. The potency of his capricious, blistering personality was doubtless sculpted while he was selling firewood and frozen whitefish door-to-door as a youngster in Winnipeg—the icebox disguised as a Canadian prairie city. But it was the heat of competition that fueled Sam's fiery character and fathomless self-motivation. For him, the hotter the challenge, the greater the effort and the sweeter the triumph.

Sam freely characterized himself throughout his paperback novel-like life as a Canadian, not as a man born either in Bessarabia, Russia, or on a ship coming to North America in the late 1880s, as some accounts posit. Documents determining his place of birth as well as the year of his birth are as clear as swamp water. Whatever the reality, Sam and his brothers intentionally paid no heed to their ancestors' life in Czarist Russia. To the public, they were Canadians raised and reared on the expansive Manitoba prairie. Case closed.

Saying that Samuel Bronfman's mind and disposition didn't suffer fools, slowness, or inaccuracy gracefully is the height of understatement. Sam's daily and routinely violent displays of temper provided fodder for hundreds, probably thousands of "I remember when Mr. Sam threw his telephone at the head of . . ." and "Mr. Sam brutally belittled so-and-so in front of everyone . . ." tales over the 60 years of his reign of brilliant terror. His brothers and nephews, his own sons, his employees, his peers, and his competitors dreaded his fierce and unexpected cross-examinations, detailed interrogations typically laced with the foulest of language. Some of his management team became physically ill just hearing what they thought might be his footsteps approaching their office. One executive, Frank Marshall, an export manager, famously kept a suitcase permanently packed in his office so that he could make a lightning-quick getaway when he heard that Mr. Sam was on the prowl looking for him. Sam thought that Marshall traveled more than any man he had ever known.

Sam's scorch-and-burn management style was the same to virtually everyone: unfailingly confrontational, invasive, rapid-fire, and prodding. If he didn't receive the replies he wanted—and sometimes even when he did—torrents of disparaging remarks would come firing out of his mouth like the rat-tat-tat of a machine gun, leaving no one standing. Sam's unpredictable moods and withering vitriol became part of everyday life at the Seagram headquarters at 1430 Peel Street in Montreal.

In the book *Bronfman Dynasty: The Rothschilds of the New World* (McCelland and Stewart Limited, Toronto, Canada, 1978; pp. 27, 32) writer Peter C. Newman wrote evenhandedly of Sam's personality, "To some, he became a paternalistic father-confessor; to others, the unsympathetic reflection of his own inadequacies. His many probing queries were answered cautiously lest a reply rouse his legendary temper. . . . This was a rowdy, blasting fury that pushed an inner plunger in Sam's brain, detonating him. It could leave men physically shaking, mentally spent, and frequently ducking the objects that Sam would hurl at them . . .

"What set Sam off swearing most frequently were the inevitable lapses of memory among his staff. He had the gift of total recall, especially with balance-sheet tabulations, and became livid whenever lesser talents had to look things up. His capacity for retaining facts and trivia was phenomenal . . ."

In time, Sam's unquenchable drive, his flawless memory, his involvement with all facets of his company, his endless curiosity, and his innate business savvy would make him one of the twentieth century's two or three most successful liquor industry entrepreneurs and barons. Sam reportedly was once pressed about what he believed to be the most important asset of the human mind. He snapped back, "Interest."

With not a little bit of irony, the name *Bronf-man* translates in Yiddish to "liquor man," or as some people preferred to interpret it, "whiskey man." If Sam was anything throughout his 80 years, he was every inch of his 65 inches in height a legendary liquor and whiskey man. Sam's first foray into actual distilling occurred in 1925 when he and his brothers, who were already successful hoteliers and liquor salesmen in western Canada, opened their own distillery seven miles west of Montreal in the town of Ville LaSalle. They had incorporated the year before in 1924 as the Distillers Corporation Limited, a name that vaguely mimicked the title of Scotland's mighty Distillers Company Limited, or DCL, the long-prosperous Scottish company of malt and grain distilleries.

The name Sam gave his new firm proved to be an early telltale sign of his lifelong fascination with absolutely anything having to do with the traditions and the lifestyle of the British Isles. His son Edgar M. Bronfman, who eventually wrenched the reins of Seagram from the vicelike grip of his father in the 1960s, amplified this trait in his book *Good Spirits: The Making of a Businessman* (G.P. Putnam & Sons, 1998; p. 63), writing, ". . . Father was a real Anglophile, and he had enormous respect for the DCL. 'Distillers in America were indicted, while in England they were knighted,' he told me." Sam longed, to the point of desperation, for recognition as a respected whiskey man in the muffled wood-paneled offices of Great Britain's power elite.

By 1928, the eighth year of America's Prohibition, Sam's international ambitions propelled his Distillers Corporation Limited of Montreal to merge with an established distiller, the Waterloo, Ontario, company known as Joseph E. Seagram and Sons Ltd., a company that was founded in 1857 as a grain mill and distillery. Their brand of whiskey, Seagram's 83, was a popular tot across Canada. Sam wanted his company to grow, and therefore he reckoned that he needed more stills. Though his brothers Abe, Harry, and Allan were partners with him, for all intents and purposes, the thorny Sam called all the major shots at Distillers Corporation Limited. Sam decided to buy Joseph E. Seagram because in his Venus Flytrap mind it would be beneficial to Distillers Corporation Limited, and that was that. The family business of the Bronfmans then became Distillers Corporation-Seagrams Ltd. It was about this time that underlings began referring to him as "Mr. Sam." For the remainder of his life, he never dissuaded anyone—by the majority of eyewitness ac-counts—from mouthing this semiformal, obsequious salutation.

Prohibition was still restricting everyday life in the perturbed and thirsty population in the affluent country just to the south of Canada. In most people's minds, Sam and his brothers, despite being entirely legal Canadian distillers, almost certainly were involved with Prohibition bootlegging in the United States. Indirect and multilayered connections to notorious gangland figures such as admitted big-time bootleggers Meyer Lansky and Frank Costello were talked about for decades. No ironclad, irrefutable proof, however, was ever brought to public light di-rectly linking the Bronfmans with the illegal trafficking of alcoholic beverages across the U.S.-Canadian border from 1920 to 1933. Through trials in Canadian courts in which the Bronfmans were acquitted of charges brought by the Royal Canadian Mounted Police; through con-gressional investigations conducted in Washington, DC, that turned up only ambiguous circumstantial evidence against them, and through decades of adamant denial of bootleg activities by virtually all family members, many industry observers still believe that at least part of the tremendous wealth that the Bronfmans accumulated during the 1920s came from illicit dealings during the Prohibition years.

Michael R. Marrus, the author of *Samuel Bronfman: The Life and Times of Seagram's Mr. Sam* (Brandeis University Press, Hanover, New Hamp-shire, 1991; pp. 144–145) brushed off Bronfman-gangland connections, writing, "Sam, it has been said, had links with American gangsters during the rum-running era, and within the galaxy of U.S. crime two of the most brilliant figures have been mentioned—Meyer Lansky and Frank Costello. But the story rests far more on fantasy than fact . . . [U.S. Senator Estes] Kefauver's investigators certainly perked up at the mention of the Cana-dian millionaire Sam Bronfman, but they never uncovered more than Costello's vague ramblings and never even inquired about the possible con-tact with Lansky. As a result, Sam himself was never called to the stand."

Marrus, though, goes on to cite questionable relationships that Sam had with minor characters of dubious distinction, such as James Rutkin, a known gangster from New Jersey, and Joseph Reinfeld, a convicted bootlegger from the same state.

Yet, many people have felt far more certain of nefarious dealings between Sam and his brothers and American criminal kingpins all through Prohibition. Peter C. Newman, author of *Bronfman Dynasty: The Rothschilds of the New World* (p. 63) damningly wrote, ". . . Bronfman customers during Prohibition were an army (and navy) of bootleggers taking delivery in ships off the Atlantic and Pacific coasts, in small crafts at handy crossings along the St. Lawrence-Great Lakes system, in cars and trucks at dusty Prairie towns bordering on North Dakota and Montana. . . . The value of the legally produced Canadian product soared as contraband in the United States and the profits of the illegal trade gave birth to an underworld that meted out death as standard disciplinary action. It was on this brutish trade that the Bronfman family's fortune was squarely based."

During a rare 1966 interview conducted by *Fortune Magazine*, Sam admitted little, saying coyly, "We loaded a carload of goods, got our cash, and shipped it. We shipped a lot of goods. Of course, we knew where it went, but we had no legal proof. And I never went on the other side of the border to count the empty Seagram's bottles." The dark rumors and unsavory innuendos of mob connections and of vast illicit monetary gains haunted Sam his entire life.

Whatever the truth, Sam and his brothers were millionaires many times over by the time that Prohibition ended in 1933 and Distillers Corporation-Seagrams Ltd. was by then a major spoke in the North American liquor wheel. The main strength, the bread and butter of Distillers Corporation-Seagrams Ltd. was blended whiskey. With Prohibition over, Sam saw the opportunity to flood the U.S. market with his prized Canadian blends, most prominently, Seagram's V.O., a fabled blended whiskey launched in 1912 by Joseph E. Seagram himself.

Having gained a toehold in the United Kingdom in 1936 with the purchase of Robert Brown Ltd., Sam was poised to begin the search for a distillery in Scotland. The broker connected with Robert Brown Ltd. was James Barclay. In the book *Samuel Bronfman: The Life and Times of Seagram's Mr. Sam* (pp. 373–374), Michael R. Marrus wrote of the disarming Barclay, "[Sam's] principal broker was a legendary character named Jimmy Barclay—'one of the greatest whisky entrepreneurs ever to graduate into the respectable era from the bootlegging days' . . . a Scotsman who was literally raised in a distillery and who knew the history of the distilleries of Scotland like the back of his hand . . ." Jimmy Barclay became Sam's trusted emissary across the pond.

Throughout the remainder of the 1930s and into the 1940s, Sam and Barclay had been busy buying large lots of malt and grain Scotch whisky to have on hand whenever the circumstances proved fortuitous for Sam to make his move in the U.S. marketplace. Barclay warehoused their whisky holdings in Glasgow during the 1930s. In 1936, Distillers Corporation-Seagrams Ltd. racked up annual sales of $60 million in the United States alone and another $10 million in Canada. Flush with cash, Sam went on an acquisition rampage of North American distilleries and alcoholic beverage companies in 1937, scooping up Frankfort Distilleries, Carstairs Distillery, Dant & Dant, Old Lewis Hunter Distillery, and H. McKenna, Inc., to cite only 5 of the 14 that he bought.

Just 12 years after Sam's entry into Scotland, the total annual sales of Distillers Corporation-Seagrams Ltd. skyrocketed to a staggering $438 million, an astounding leap forward of 625 percent from 1936. Much of the sales advances were from three blended North American whiskeys, Seagram's 7 Crown from the United States and Crown Royal and Seagram's V.O., the company's hugely popular Canadian blended whiskeys. Sam knew of Americans' powerful preference for Scotch whisky after World War II, but he decided to wait for the right situation before entering the U.S. marketplace with a Scotch brand.

In 1949, continued author Michael R. Marrus in *Samuel Bronfman: The Life and Times of Seagram's Mr. Sam*, ". . . Barclay came to Sam with a remarkable prospect—Chivas Brothers, Ltd., an old and successful firm of grocers and whisky merchants of Aberdeen, with a distinguished name going back to the nineteenth century . . . thanks to Barclay, Sam finally purchased Chivas Brothers—essentially two grocery shops, their trade marks, plus a small inventory of high-class, well-aged Scotch—for a mere 85,000 pounds, and with these raw materials he set out to build what those in the trade came to see as his masterpiece, Chivas Regal."

Sam reasoned that if Distillers Corporation-Seagrams Ltd. had Chivas Regal, the benchmark of older blended Scotches, in its clutches, he could quite possibly trump the Distillers Company Limited in the huge American market. DCL was the post-World War II powerhouse for Scotch whisky in the States. Sam was privy to the fact that much of DCL's inventory consisted of immature whisky (because of the distillery shutdown during World War II), which was why they so heavily promoted their "lighter" blended Scotches to the massive Yank audience. Returning GIs brought back with them a burning desire for the whisky they had consumed while stationed in England, Wales, or Scotland, so the path had been cleared.

With a wealth of older whiskies resting silently in warehouses around Scotland and now in the possession of Chivas Brothers Ltd., Sam could introduce Chivas Regal as a classy 12-year-old, marketing it as a step up in quality and character from the skimpier DCL brands. Sam told his inner circle that if the sale went through he did not want to rush the Chivas Regal reintroduction. He would prefer to have word on the street whet the appetites of whisky drinkers. He knew that anticipation could drive robust early sales. In the process, Distillers Corporation-Seagrams Ltd. could potentially realize enormous profit margins because Chivas Regal would cost significantly more per bottle than its competitors like Johnnie Walker Red Label, Black & White, Cutty Sark, J&B Rare, and Dewar's White Label. Crown Royal, the pricey 10-year-old deluxe Canadian blend introduced in 1939 by Distillers Corporation-Seagrams Ltd. had already proven the upmarket/strong profit formula for Sam.

As Sam examined each aspect of the proposed acquisition, he had no doubt that Jimmy Barclay had located one of the sweetest deals he had ever seen. The upside for Sam and his company was enormous. For the exact, if relatively paltry sum of £85,070, of which £80,600 went directly into the woolen pockets of R. D. Lundie, Sam and Barclay bought Chivas Brothers Ltd. and its sparkling crown jewel Chivas Regal, "Scotland's Prince of Whiskies," outright in 1949. Sam had obtained an overlooked gem, a potential whopper of an international brand that he believed would catapult Distillers Corporation-Seagrams Ltd. further into the liquor industry stratosphere. In the deepest recesses of Sam's complex mind, he perhaps also contemplated that Chivas Regal might just be the key that would unlock the doors to the labyrinthine passages that led to the gilded place he badly desired to be—the British upper class.

Seeking Absolution

In addition to wanting to both best and vex his powerful British rivals at DCL, Sam had deep personal reasons for buying Chivas Brothers Ltd. and its superstar deluxe blended Scotch whisky. One strong incentive had much to do with his obsession with the British, whereas another key inducement involved his searing desire to finally hush the accusatory murmurs of bootlegging and corruption that he felt had badly and unjustifiably sullied his family's name and company's image. A pivotal element of the deal that had pricked Sam's interest lay in the Royal Warrants for food provisions and Scotch whisky that had been bestowed on Chivas Brothers Ltd. throughout its storied history. The Warrants were still in full effect at the time of the deal's consummation. Sam perceived the Warrants as a sort of ticket to respectability, a silver bullet that might once and for all slay the disapproving rumors and slights.

Immediately preceding the Chivas Brothers procurement, Sam had assigned his brother Allan and others in Canada, Europe, and Great Britain to assess the possibility of attaining a Royal Warrant for other Seagram whiskeys. Over the span of several years and through reams of letters, many of which are now part of the Seagram collection at the Hagley Museum and Library in Wilmington, Delaware, Sam, Allan, and their teams of agents, which included European nobles, military brass, and bankers friendly with the Bronfmans, applied tremendous pressure to members of the Royal Household for them to dispense through the proper channels a Royal Warrant.

Numerous letters addressing the Royal Warrant situation were written. Typical of the Bronfmans' failure to secure additional Royal Warrants is a missive sent to Allan Bronfman by Harvey D. Gibson, the president of New York's Manufacturers Trust Company, dated May 26, 1949: "I feel certain that everyone of the three who have been working on this are bitterly disappointed, as am I, to have our efforts end so dismally when at one time everything looked so hopeful. . . . Of one thing I am certain, and that is that our three friends in London have done their very best and . . . that it would be well worthwhile a couple of times each year to continue sending each one of them, in the same manner that we have in the past, a case of whiskey. . . . We should remember, I think, that changes often take place in the personnel of any organization and it might be that there would be some change in the person who has the upper hand at the Palace at the present time. Furthermore, if the King should retire and be succeeded by Princess Elizabeth, it is my understanding that her organization dealing with such matters as we are thinking about would be an entirely different one than now exists . . ."

Every attempt, every approach, every ploy conceived by the Bronfmans to obtain a Royal Warrant prior to the Chivas Brothers Ltd. sale was blocked by the Royal Court. Once the sale did become final, Sam at last had in his hands two of the things he had badly coveted since the mid-1930s: a white-glove Scotch whisky brand with an extraordinary history that made it the whisky equivalent of Rolls-Royce and, just as important, a Royal Warrant.

A vice-president of Seagram Overseas Corporation, Quintin Peter Jeremy Gwyn, said of Sam's decision making with Chivas Regal, ". . . it was Mr. Sam's intention to make Chivas Regal the greatest name in Scotch whisky. This involved a vast plan of buildings such as warehouses, distillery, offices, etc., and above all a period of maturing for at least twelve years before the brand was ready to be put on the market, I still recall an historic meeting with Mr. Sam when we discussed the eventual world-market possibilities for Chivas Regal. I submitted my modest estimates, which were immediately set aside by him as quite inadequate, and he gave his own, which were much greater. . . . This was not just a man marketing a new product—it was an artist producing his *chef-d'oeuvre*."

In the wake of founding, brick by brick, a Canadian beverage alcohol empire, Samuel Bronfman by 1950 had gained control of a Scotch whisky legacy that had first taken shape in 1801 when John Forrest opened a top-drawer grocery shop in downtown Aberdeen, Scotland, and then advanced further in 1841 when James Chivas took control of the retail provisions shop. Building on the foundation of that heritage, Sam would take Chivas Regal to the United States and the rest of the world. With the help of Jimmy Barclay, Sam would produce his career masterpiece.

William Henry Smith Grant and brewer Robbie Robertson.

Drams of America

In 1952, *I Love Lucy* and *Your Show of Shows* dominated black-and-white television screens in the United States. *High Noon*, *The Quiet Man*, and *The Greatest Show on Earth* were the favorite movies. American movie houses were still hallowed, multileveled places of dark escape that were vigorously promoted as being "Cooled by Air-Conditioning." The hottest tickets on Broadway were for the drama *The Four Poster* and the musical *The King and I*, which starred the electrifying Yul Brynner (who, incidentally, was a devoted admirer of The Glenlivet). Americans were reading James Jones's page-turning novel, *From Here to Eternity*, as well as their weekly issues of the *Saturday Evening Post* and *Life* magazine. American voters had just elected in a landslide former general Dwight David Eisenhower to be president as well as the nation's First Golfer. They consumed new-fangled meals called frozen dinners, as well as fruit-flavored Popsicles, Oscar Mayer hotdogs, and Pepsi-Cola. That same year, Americans likewise drank less than 300 cases, a paltry amount, of The Glenlivet 12 Year Old Scotch Malt Whisky.

With all wartime distilling sanctions finally lifted in Scotland by 1949, the producers of Scotch whisky acknowledged that they had no secret strategies for recovery in the early 1950s. There was only one screamingly obvious plan of attack. Once the remaining restrictions were

217

relaxed, the starting bell of a single industrywide dictum rang throughout the grain distilleries in the south and the malt distilleries in the Highlands and islands: Produce and legally age as much Scotch whisky as quickly as possible and then export it posthaste to the world's most vibrant and voracious economy, that of the United States of America.

By the summer of 1952, 97 distilleries were active again in Scotland, up from 57 in 1945. Twenty-seven million gallons of new malt and grain whiskies were produced, up from just less than 10 million gallons in 1945. "Once the inter-war peak output had been passed in 1954, more general expansion became necessary as exports steadily increased," wrote John R. Hume and Michael S. Moss in *The Making of Scotch Whisky: A History of the Scotch Whisky Distilling Industry* (p. 191).

The year 1953 saw Great Britain finally emerge from its postwar gloom. The country's renewed sense of optimism reached a crescendo on June 2, 1953, with the festive and ornately staged coronation of Queen Elizabeth II. In the Abbey Church of Saint Peter, Westminster, the young, composed queen spoke with conviction the ancient words that forever changed her life and the direction of her nation, "The things which I have here promised, I will perform, and keep. So help me God." As 20 million British subjects sat glued to their tellies, transfixed by the pageantry unfolding on the BBC, the flame of British spirit was rekindled to full candlepower. Among the invited guests at the Abbey Church were Canadians Sam and Saidye Bronfman.

(*Author's note:* Queen Elizabeth's coronation was celebrated by Sam Bronfman's Chivas Brothers in the form of Royal Salute Blended Scotch Whisky. This limited edition Chivas Brothers 21-year-old blend was specially formulated to honor the 21-gun salute to the new monarch performed by the Royal Navy. Royal Salute's core single malts included Strathisla, The Glenlivet, Longmorn, and Glen Grant. Recognized as a blended Scotch whisky classic, Royal Salute is available worldwide to this day.)

In still-bucolic Glenlivet, The Glenlivet Distillery manager Robert Arthur produced, to owner Bill Smith Grant's delight, 246,392 gallons of raw, immature whisky during the 1952 to 1953 distilling season. The distillery operated two 10-hour shifts, five days a week. The Glenlivet &

Glen Grant Distillers Ltd. partnership was working well for all concerned. Bill Smith Grant even had Arthur bottle a special 400-case lot in 1953 of what Bill called, "Coronation Glenlivet." The 3,600 bottles of the 16-year-old malt whisky came from 12 casks that had been distilled on May 12, 1937, the day of the coronation of George VI. To illustrate the crucial importance of the American marketplace at that time, Bill Smith Grant sent three-quarters of Coronation Glenlivet, 300 cases, west across the Atlantic to the United States. The Royal Yacht *HMS Britannia*, on the other hand, received but one 12-bottle case. Bill Smith Grant kept most of the balance, opening it for friends and visitors to the distillery all through the remainder of the 1950s, the 1960s, and up until 1975.

Even though production volumes at The Glenlivet rose through the 1950s (312,790 gallons in the season of 1959 to 1960), availability of The Glenlivet malt whisky continued to be tight the world over until 1960. The reasons were twofold. First, 98 percent of The Glenlivet total production during the period was sold off to whisky brokers, leaving a scant 2 percent to be bottled as single malt. With blended Scotch whiskies flying off the shelves of retailers in North America, it was more lucrative to Bill Smith Grant to sell his high-grade malt whisky directly to whisky brokers who would then turn around and sell it to the blenders in the south of Scotland. Blenders coveted The Glenlivet's impeccable malt whisky more than most others. Second, it took Bill and Arthur more than a decade to correct the inventory shortages caused by the shutdowns and restrictions imposed during World War II. By 1960 to 1961, a normal flow of The Glenlivet was restored.

The Glenlivet Distillery punched through the 400,000-gallon mark in the distilling season of 1962 to 1963. Meanwhile in the United States, sales of single malt Scotch whiskies as a category were moving not just at a snail's pace, but more like a dead snail's pace compared with the sales figures being posted by blended Scotches. The immense shadow cast by blended Scotches kept single malt Scotches in a state of perpetual darkness. Suspicions regarding the questionable activities and dubious motives of their stateside importer rose in the executive offices of The Glenlivet as case sales during 1962 and 1963 actually slid backward.

Bill Smith Grant's management team included his son-in-law, Major Ivan C. Straker, whom Bill had brought into the business as a company director in 1954. In a rancorous letter, dated November 12, 1963 (10 days before the assassination of John F. Kennedy), Straker bluntly questioned the willingness of their American agents, Leeds Imports Corporation of New York, to vigorously promote and sell The Glenlivet: "You may remember, after our meeting which your father attended in London, the [wholesale] price was materially reduced on the assurance of both yourself and him that this would enable you to get the distribution and sale of THE GLENLIVET really going. Since then, the business has gone from bad to worse. The total shipments to United States from 1963 to date are only 735 cases.

"I am at a complete loss to understand what is happening as, in all cases, we have tried to do our best to meet any of your requests, whether in regard to price or anything else. I might point out to you that, from our original programme and figures which we supplied to you, you should now be doing, this year, something in the region of 3,000 cases and, in my opinion, there really cannot be this falling off in business if your people were really exerting themselves. This is the considered opinion, too, of some of my friends both in the Trade and outside it, who have been in the States during the current year."

Straker's chastising letter improved sales, but not enough. In a letter to The Glenlivet from Leeds executive Robert Haas, dated October 28, 1964, nationwide case sale amounts for the top-five leading single malt Scotches were forecasted for the same year. Though the estimates were still well below what Bill Smith Grant and Straker thought they should be for The Glenlivet in the United States, case sales of The Glenlivet had more than doubled in a year's time. Cited Haas, ". . . I made the necessary inquiries of the different importers here and now have a complete picture of the amount of straight [meaning, single malt] Scotch Whiskies sold in the United States . . . The Glenlivet 1,600 cases. Glen Farclas 600 cases. Laphroaig 250 cases. Glen Grant 300 cases. Glenfiddich 200 cases. . . . From this you can see that the market is really quite limited. . . ."

The rationalizing tone of Haas's letter proved to be the final straw and ultimately sealed the fate of Leeds Imports. In 1965, Bill Smith

Grant and his board of directors ended their arrangement with the inept and indolent Leeds and replaced them with Barton Distilling Company of Chicago.

The half-million gallon mark was reached at The Glenlivet Distillery three seasons later (1965 to 1966). Still in the mid-1960s, The Glenlivet accounted for slightly over half of all single malt whisky sold in the United States in the 1960s. Bill Smith Grant and his agents opened other overseas markets in South Africa, Australia, Italy, France, and Germany. Odd, one-of requests for The Glenlivet came from many distant ports-of-call: Mexico, the Philippines, Burma, China, Japan, and Ethiopia. Like the whiskies maturing in their warehouses at Minmore, the mystique of The Glenlivet grew more tantalizing with age.

The Top Ten Selling Distilled Spirits in the United States—1967

1. Seagram's 7 Crown, Blended American Whiskey; 7,750,000 cases
2. Seagram's V.O., Blended Canadian Whisky; 3,975,000 cases
3. Canadian Club, Blended Canadian Whisky; 3,675,000 cases
4. Smirnoff, American Vodka; 3,600,000 cases
5. Jim Beam, Straight Bourbon; 2,650,000 cases
6. Gordon's, American Gin; 2,625,000 cases
7. Bacardi, Puerto Rican Rum; 2,550,000 cases
8. J & B Rare, Blended Scotch; 2,400,000 cases
9. Cutty Sark, Blended Scotch; 2,325,000 cases
10. Calvert Extra, Blended Canadian Whisky; 2,275,000 cases

Source: "Distilled Spirits Council of the United States," *BusinessWeek*, February 18, 1967.

No Place to Go but Up

By the late 1960s, demand for The Glenlivet as a single malt at last began to outpace its production. Bill Smith Grant's commitments to whisky brokers brought in large revenues that he invested back into the distillery in improvements, renovations, and extensions. Although the 1969 to 1970 season saw a record 774,442 gallons produced at Minmore, only a miniscule 11,000 cases of those gallons were sold as single malt whisky under The Glenlivet banner. Scotland's whisky industry as a whole produced over 136 million gallons of malt and grain whiskies that season, the second highest total since the conclusion of World War II.

In 1970, The Glenlivet was operating two pairs of overworked stills, two wash stills, and two spirits stills at full capacity. The distillery was running seven days a week on two shifts, over 168 man-hours per week. Bill Smith Grant began to plan for further expansion and the addition of another set of stills. Bill, Ivan Straker, and distillery manager Robert Arthur were now forced to allocate a larger percentage of whisky for bottling as single malt.

Around this time, David Daiches wrote about The Glenlivet in his book, *Scotch Whisky: Its Past and Present* (pp. 138–139), "Only 5 percent of [The] Glenlivet is today bottled as a single [malt] whisky: the rest goes to the blenders, and all the important blenders except Teacher's take some Glenlivet. The distillery itself bottles (though not at the distillery) only a twelve-year-old, which is splendid, though I have tasted older Glenlivets bottled by Berry Bros. & Rudd. Other bottlers bottle it at different ages: Gordon & MacPhail of Elgin bottle a variety of ages, each with a differently coloured label. If I had to single out one classic of malt whiskies it would be the twelve-year-old Glenlivet."

In the summer of 1970, The Glenlivet & Glen Grant Distillers Ltd. joined with two other whisky trade entities: Longmorn Distillers Ltd., whose two prize possessions were the Longmorn and Benriach distilleries located southeast of Elgin in Morayshire; and Hill, Thomson & Co. Ltd. of Edinburgh, producers of Queen Anne and Something Special blended Scotch whiskies. Queen Anne had been a popular brand of blended whisky in Scotland in the pre-World War I era, but after the war, its status had been eclipsed by other brands. The friendly amalgamation of the three whisky companies operated under the auspices of a parent company registered as The Glenlivet Distillers Ltd. Consolidation brought greater buying power in the materials arena as well as broader awareness in the consumer sector for all the brands involved.

At age 74, Bill Smith Grant's primary aim was to strengthen the financial base of his core concern, The Glenlivet Distillery, by making more funds available to it for further internal expansion and greater malt whisky production. The larger influx of revenue from the satellite companies helped Bill and his son-in-law enlarge the distilling capabilities at Minmore. Bill Smith Grant wanted passionately to grow The Glenlivet as an international Scotch whisky brand. The 11,951 cases of single malt whisky bottled and shipped for sale in 1970 were hardly enough to meet the growing demand from agents around the world.

Two years later in 1972, Bill Smith Grant and the board of The Glenlivet Distillers Ltd. named Ivan Straker chief executive officer of the company. Bill, who was always addressed by employees as "the Skipper," wanted to step back from the daily demands posed by running the company and began planning with Peggy, his wife, for the upcoming 150th anniversary of The Glenlivet. That same year, the distillery improvements began in earnest. Gas lines were installed to more efficiently heat the stills. In 1973, the pair of new copper stills added to the stillhouse almost doubled production. Production catapulted forward past 825,000 gallons in 1973 to 1974 and topped an astounding 1.3 million gallons in 1974 to 1975.

In August 1974, a public ceremony at Minmore marked the licensing of The Glenlivet in 1824 by George Smith, Bill Smith Grant's great-great-uncle. Later, on October 4, a private, invitation-only dinner was held at the Richmond Arms Hotel in the nearby village of Tomintoul to honor long-term employees as well as the Smith Grants. The keynote speaker was employee, Tommy Stuart, who traced the legacy of the Smith/Smith Grant family back to the time of the founder, George Smith. Said Stuart, ". . . it is a great privilege for me to speak on your behalf, to thank Capt. and Mrs. Smith Grant for their great generosity tonight. Indeed his family has been the main employers and the greatest benefactors of the Glen for generations. They have supported every good cause and no doubt their contributions led to the building of our beloved local hall.

"I have had long associations with the family as my grandfather worked for George Smith, the founder of the Distillery, my father worked for the Captain's father Colonel Smith Grant and I, the third generation, have worked for our worthy host Capt. [Smith] Grant."

Stuart's speech mixed the sweet with the bittersweet. He poignantly recounted the deaths of Bill's brother Captain John Gordon Smith Grant in 1918 and of his first wife in 1946. He addressed the joy that overcame the glen when Bill Smith Grant married Peggy in 1948. He likewise touched on her numerous kindnesses to the staff and to the Glenlivet community. After spinning several humorous anecdotes about Bill Smith Grant's father, his great-great-uncle, and the Skipper himself, Stuart closed by saying, "I had the pleasure of attending the Centenary Celebration in the Distillery loft 50 years ago, and thanks to our host and hostess, was again present at the 150th celebrations on 31st Aug. Captain [Smith] Grant says that we will meet again at the 200th and ha'e a wee dram thegither if by that time I have tasted whisky. The following few lines I have composed . . .

> 'Minmore Glenlivet is the best
> In bottle or in cask,
> Nae finer says St. Peter,
> Mak wey, get it in fast,
> O' a' the spirits coming up here,
> Rejected, Yes, believe it,
> Except what is so genuine. The Glenlivet.'"

Four-and-a-half months later on February 16, 1975, Captain William Henry Smith Grant, honored war hero, beloved husband of Margaret Smith Grant, worthy son of Colonel George Smith Grant, brother of Captain John Gordon Smith Grant, friend to all in Glenlivet, and fourth-generation proprietor of The Glenlivet, died at the age of 78. The Skipper's demise marked more than the end of an era in the glen. It propped open the door for the Barons at Seagram.

Mr. Sam's Historic
Scotch Whisky Gambit

SAMUEL BRONFMAN, BUSINESS WARRIOR, whiskey man, and elfin genius, was smitten with the concept of Chivas Regal 12-year-old blended Scotch whisky. He knew instinctively that Scotsman Jimmy Barclay had found the gem that he and Distillers Corporation-Seagrams Ltd. had long been waiting for. But Chivas Regal in conceptual form was far different from Chivas Regal, the reality. Though he and Jimmy Barclay had been buying large quantities of Scotch whiskies in barrel for a decade and a half, maturing them in warehouses as James Chivas, Alexander Chivas, Alexander Smith, and R. D. Lundie had done before them, Sam felt that one piece of the puzzle was missing.

Navigating the choppy waters in the narrow straits controlled by Scotland's whisky brokers, as all the previous owners of Chivas Regal had done, worried Sam. Scottish whisky companies, mostly the omnipotent DCL, were known to be making things hard for North American distillers to enter Scotland's whisky industry by scooping up prime whisky stocks and, thereby, keeping entry prices high. The head of Distillers Corporation-Seagrams Ltd. of Canada decided not to leave the fate of his crown jewel in the hands of strangers, even if his man on the ground, Jimmy Barclay, was a skilled and shrewd whisky veteran.

"His first need was a distillery," wrote Michael R. Marrus of Sam in *Samuel Bronfman: The Life and Times of Seagram's Mr. Sam* (p. 374). "The grocers, in the past, had not made their own whisky; operating on a modest scale, as was the custom in Scotland, they purchased whisky from brokers on the open market and produced their own blends. Breaking through the 'tartan curtain,' as one former broker put it, Sam scoured the Scottish Highlands for a base of operations, intending to integrate production on a North American model. What he found was a perfect match for the venerable Chivas Brothers in tradition and reputation, the Strathisla-Glenlivet Malt Distillery at Keith in Banffshire . . ."

Known in 1950 as the Milton Distillery, Strathisla, as it would later come to be called, was reportedly the oldest malt whisky distillery still operating in the Highlands. George Taylor and Alexander Milne founded the business in 1786 and dubbed it the Milltown Distillery. In addition to being a distiller, Taylor was also a banker, owner of a textile works, and a postmaster. The name that Sam wanted for it, Strathisla-Glenlivet, originated from the malt whisky for which the Milton Distillery had become famous in the 1800s, Strathisla Whisky, a whisky that ". . . has an enviable reputation at home and abroad . . ." according to the July 14, 1922, edition of the *Wine and Spirit Trade Record.*

Jimmy Barclay had approached the proprietor of Milton/Strathisla in 1948, but retreated when the erratic owner demanded an exorbitant price. The owner at the time was George (Jay) Pomeroy, a London-based financier known for dubious dealings in operatic productions. An infamous scoundrel who had a weakness for gambling and losing copious amounts of cash, Pomeroy had, very conveniently for Sam, been convicted of tax evasion in 1949. The distillery property was subsequently placed into liquidation status by the Inland Revenue department, Great Britain's equivalent of the U.S. Internal Revenue Service. Acting on behalf of Sam, Barclay, purchased Milton/Strathisla for £71,000 at a public auction in Aberdeen in April 1950. Barclay's purchase marked the second time that Milton/Strathisla had changed hands in a public auction.

The distillery was located in the Banffshire town of Keith, situated on Route A96 between the towns of Elgin to the northwest and Huntly to the southeast. The distillery was described in a Distillers Corporation-Seagrams Ltd. interoffice memo from 1950 as being ". . . a little, run-down operation producing a very small supply of malt whisky each year." It had been severely damaged in a fire in 1876, ninety years after its establishment. Three years later, it absorbed another calamity when an explosion in the malt mill caused structural weakening. In the 1880s and 1890s, the foundation and walls were strengthened, a cobblestone courtyard was added at the entry of the building, the waterwheel that supplied fresh water from the River Isla was replaced, and the kiln, with its two louvered pagodas, was refurbished. Today, the Strathisla Distillery is perceived as one of the most beautiful and distinctive malt distilleries in all of Scotland.

Keith is an ancient hamlet that dates back at least to the twelfth century A.D. Celebrated for its natural springs and crystal clear water, Keith is bisected by the River Isla (pronounced, EYE-lah). Milton/Strathisla sits in a shallow basin on the banks of the pristine river. The Keith area is traditionally known for textiles, milling, and distilling. Aside from the Milton/Strathisla Distillery, at the time of the purchase two other malt distilleries, Strathmill Distillery and Glentauchers Distillery, were located nearby.

The feature about the Milton/Strathisla distillery of greatest interest to Sam back in 1950 was the Strathisla Old Highland Malt Whisky. In his quest to maintain Chivas Regal as the international standard for deluxe blended Scotches, Sam realized that for the quantities that he wanted to produce he would require a reliable and steady stream of top-quality Highland malt whisky. But as a stickler for quality and as a master marketer, Sam decided to wait for a few years before releasing Chivas Regal to the American drinking public.

As Sam's son, Edgar Miles Bronfman, recalled in his book *Good Spirits: The Making of a Businessman* (pp. 106–107) about his father's risky decision to wait in releasing Chivas Regal, "I remember sitting in Father's office . . . with all sorts of nonsense going on involving the details of the package design, paper for labels, and even glass supplies. It all seemed a bit much, and I asked Father what this was all about. He sat me down and told me that the British authorities were eager, to put it mildly, for exports. Meanwhile, here we were with a potential brand and all that whiskey sitting in our warehouses. Swearing me to secrecy, he explained his delaying tactics: he wanted to introduce Chivas Regal as a twelve-year-old whiskey. No one else could possibly produce another twelve-year-old brand for years to come; they didn't have the inventory. In a few months' time, when his whiskeys reached the magic age, he would begin to ship, but not a moment before!"

A key element to the success of a revitalized Chivas Regal, Sam acknowledged, was to maintain the peerless quality of the recipe devised in the early 1900s by Charles Stewart Howard, who as the partner of Alexander Smith co-owned the Chivas Brothers shops. Sam frequently described whisky blending as being every bit an art as it was a science. Sam, thereby, held master blenders in high esteem. Determined to sign up the best blender, Sam sent his brother Allan to Britain to secure the services of one of the day's preeminent whisky blenders, Charles Julian. A wisecracking Cockney from London, Julian worked on a gun-for-hire basis and had had notable success with the firm of Justerini & Brooks, makers of J&B Rare Blended Whisky. Allan hired Julian for a large sum.

Employing the full power and breadth of Sam and Jimmy Barclay's vast stockpile of malt and grain whiskies warehoused in Glasgow, Julian was let loose among the stocks to replicate the whisky made famous by Chivas Brothers. The warehouse operated by Jimmy Barclay was located beneath the Glasgow railway yard and left a lot to be desired in terms of cleanliness. A Distillers Corporation-Seagrams Ltd. interoffice memo from 1952 described the setting as, ". . . a huge emporium . . . where different whiskies were put together under something definitely less than hygienic conditions." This depiction was not lost on Sam.

A story involving Charles Julian revolved around Sam's perception of the whisky blending process, an activity that he held almost on the same plane as a religious ceremony. An unnamed Seagram executive was visiting the Glasgow operation while Julian, who always liked to be left alone when practicing his craft, was in the middle of working on a blend.

The executive made the offhand remark that he personally thought that many people exaggerated the act of blending and that to describe the process as "art" seemed ludicrous. Snapped the irreverent Julian, "You're bloody right there ain't [art in it], mate, but for God's sake don't tell that to Mr. Sam or Mr. Allan."

In the spring of 1954 and after an absence of over five years in the marketplace, Distillers Corporation-Seagrams Ltd. rolled out Chivas Regal 12-year-old Blended Scotch Whisky in the United States. According to a letter, dated February 10, 1955 (Hagley Museum and Library, Wilmington, Delaware), from Philip J. Kelly, vice president of Chivas Brothers Import Company in New York City, to DC-SL headquarters in Montreal, the total allotment of Chivas Regal into the U.S. marketplace for 1954 was 77,500 12-bottle cases.

Meanwhile, in the muffled quiet of his castlelike Peel Street headquarters in Montreal, Sam sat in his office, scrutinizing the faces of his inner circle, as Chivas Regal was distributed around the 48 states. His top brass may have been worrying about how Chivas Regal would be accepted in the United States, but Sam was already pondering the unsanitary situation of Jimmy Barclay's Glasgow warehouse and plotting his next moves in Scotland. The first priority would be to get his master blender better facilities. Next would be to build another malt distillery in Keith near the renamed Strathisla Distillery. And third would be to establish a brand-new headquarters in Scotland, a showplace that would be representative of the greatness of Seagram and Chivas Brothers. Sam sat back in his enormous leather chair behind his Chippendale desk, offered his cronies a slight smile, and trusted that his instincts about Chivas Regal were right on the money.

With that, Mr. Sam's historic Scotch whisky gambit had been launched.

The Business Philosophy of Creating a Shortage

"Our problem was to introduce and sell Chivas Regal 12-year-old Scotch Whisky at a price of about $8 a fifth. . . . Many people said that to introduce a new Scotch at a high price was impossible. When most people buy

Scotch, they specify the brand they want and consumer custom has been particularly frozen for many years," spoke Philip J. Kelly in a speech he delivered at the Statler Hotel in Boston in late June 1954. The occasion was the annual convention of the Advertising Federation of America. Eight dollars for a bottle of blended Scotch whisky was indeed very expensive for the day. Most ordinary, younger blended Scotches fetched from $4.50 to $6 for a 750-milliliter bottle.

Kelly described the early advertising strategies devised by Sam Bronfman and his team for marketing and promoting Chivas Regal and, most importantly, how they created the illusion of an overwhelming demand for Chivas Regal. "What . . . assets did we have?" asked Kelly of his fellow conventioneers. "The [Chivas Regal] label . . . it was so bad . . . it was good . . . but it seemed genuine. It is practically the same label that has been used for over 100 years in Scotland. . . . Another thing we found we had was the Royal Warrant. . . . We had the advantage of owning one of the oldest operating distilleries in the Highlands . . . and a slogan [that we] inherited—'Scotland's Prince of Whiskies.' . . . We had all the elements to make a great advertisement."

So, Sam had his advertising agency, the Lynn Baker Agency, create and run two-page, full-color ads in a select few upmarket magazines. He also had them design and execute free-standing, four-page, full-color inserts that were placed into key trade publications. The flashy inserts heralded the coming of Chivas Regal. The agency likewise produced a full-color booklet that told the Chivas Regal story, from pedigree to creation. The free booklet was sent out to thousands of intrigued consumers across the country.

In a lightning flash of marketing brilliance, Sam instructed his sales staff to tease their distributors by selling them only small amounts of Chivas Regal, thereby instigating an instant "shortage" as soon as Chivas Regal hit the streets. Kelly stressed the savvy astuteness of Sam's unusual plan of action, "One point which deserves emphasis is the fact that we told our distributors and their salesmen and the retailers that there WOULD NEVER BE ENOUGH CHIVAS REGAL. We emphasized the point that we would only attempt to cover 80 percent of our market. . . . We sold limited quantities to our distributors when we originally stocked them. We wanted them to get a fast turnover and come back for more. . . . Remember, people always want what they can't get."

The "CR shortage" strategy worked better than expected. Distributors quickly ran out of Chivas Regal and immediately reordered, but were then only given another carefully meted out case amount. Retailers placed Chivas Regal on strict allocation exclusively to their best, most affluent clientele because as Kelly pointed out in his speech, ". . . the best people in town were talking about Chivas Regal. . . . Styles start at the top and percolate downward . . ." The perceived, if hollow scarcity snowballed into a minor feeding frenzy for Chivas Regal in the major U.S. markets throughout 1954 and 1955.

Sam took great pains to expose Chivas Regal to the upper economic echelons of American society. In *Samuel Bronfman: The Life and Times of Seagram's Mr. Sam* (pp. 375–376), Michael R. Marrus explained, "[Philip J.] Kelly did not neglect snob appeal. One of the most successful promotional ventures, he recalled, was a letter he wrote over the signature of Jimmy Barclay to some 200,000 officers in U.S. corporations rated over $100,000, including 50,000 in New York City. 'The recipient was urged to visit his pub or his spirit shop and to ask for a bottle of Chivas Regal, which would continue to be very limited in quantity and was to be sold only to those who appreciated the best in Scotch whisky. The recipient was reminded, of course, that he was a connoisseur in this class and therefore should insist upon getting his share . . . '"

The shortage ruse, to Sam's amusement, created an actual dearth of Chivas Regal by 1958. Wishing to cash in even further on the marketing ploy, the delighted Sam ordered Philip Kelly to instruct the Lynn Baker Agency to devise a series of "shortage crisis" print ads in which the copy decried the deficit situation of Chivas Regal. Consumers were asked in the ads' copy to show "patience" while more Chivas Regal was being produced and matured across the Atlantic. They were promised that their wait wouldn't be "overly long." Sales of Chivas Regal in 1958 and 1959 were steadily growing, decimating inventories.

Based on the early success of Chivas Regal and amid the Chivas Regal hurricane occurring in the United States, Sam had another revelation: Create another blended Scotch whisky that was less expensive and lighter than Chivas Regal. It would compete head-to-head against the cheaper, so-called light brands that dominated America—most notably, Cutty Sark and J&B Rare. Sam's singular and most pressing problem, though, was a serious lack of proper plant facilities in Scotland from which to initiate this next phase.

Sam returned often to Scotland from mid-1955 through 1957 to begin his next project, the planning and erecting of a brand-new malt distillery to assist Strathisla in supplying enough malt whisky for Chivas Regal and to make the malt whisky for his next blended Scotch creation, 100 Pipers. To this end, he returned to Keith to meet with John Chiene, the Chivas Brothers Ltd. director. One day, they stood on the banks of the River Isla as different experts proffered their opinions on the construction of a sister distillery to Strathisla. According to company records, an Aberdeen geologist told Sam and Chiene, that Keith was one of the best places in Scotland to make whisky because, ". . . Keith has the most glorious mixture of rock and soil than in any other place in Scotland [Reason: More limestone is found there than in any other area. Limestone produces very hard, but pure water, nearly 100 percent iron-free and ideal for distilling.] . . . Keith is noted for its damp cold climate which is conducive to making good whisky. . . . Water from melted snow seeps through the soil more slowly than rain and in doing so absorbs more essences . . ."

Sam was sold. He selected the site of a former corn mill, the Mill of Keith, across the River Isla from Strathisla. In late 1956, Sam took personal charge of the distillery design and construction. He broke ground in 1957 on the first new malt distillery built in Scotland since the time of Queen Victoria. Simultaneously, Sam was making plans for a massive plant to be built on a 14-acre plot of land in Paisley, west of Glasgow. The Paisley edifice would serve as the headquarters for all of Seagram's Scottish interests, as well as being the bottling, aging, and blending center for Chivas Brothers Ltd. Anyone in the late 1950s who doubted Sam's open-throttle and open-wallet dedication to making Chivas Brothers the premier whisky firm in Scotland wasn't paying close attention.

A Regal Move

In 1958, Chivas Brothers closed both the King Street and the Union Place shops. Managing director William Mitchell opened a new retail location at 387-391 Union Street. The new site included a restaurant, called Chivas Brothers. In the early summer of 1960, a bar called the Crusader Bar was opened. The restaurant turned into a popular meeting place for well-to-do Aberdonians throughout the 1960s and 1970s. On January 31, 1980, after 179 years, Chivas Brothers closed down for good and has never reopened.

The Birth of a Textbook Advertising Campaign

By 1960, Chivas Regal 12-year-old Blended Scotch Whisky was being sent in limited quantities to over 35 countries through Seagram's expanding global distribution network, the Seagram Overseas Corporation. Annual case sales of Chivas Regal in the United States broke through the 100,000 case mark, claiming slightly over 50 percent of the deluxe Scotch whisky market. But, to Sam's consternation, younger, lighter blended Scotch whiskies were advancing in even greater proportion to Chivas Regal, each one selling in the millions of cases. Feeling the heat from the competition, Sam urged the contractors who were building the new plant at Paisley to work faster.

Also in 1960, Sam's new malt distillery in Keith, christened as Glen Keith-Glenlivet Distillery, opened to small local fanfare. He was immensely proud of the new modern distillery that boasted three copper pot stills. The idea was to triple-distill the malt whiskies as was done in Ireland and in some Scottish Lowlands malt distilleries, like Rosebank and Auchentoshan. Triple distillation resulted in clean, very light malt whiskies, something that Sam was aiming for with his new brand, 100 Pipers.

One year later, in the face of Cutty Sark and J&B Rare steamrolling the Scotch whisky competition in the United States, sales of Chivas Regal suddenly stalled. The president of Seagram's U.S. operation was

Edgar M. Bronfman, Sam's oldest son. Edgar was concerned that his father's beloved crown jewel was losing some of its luster in its most crucially important market. This was confirmed when Edgar's executive vice-president of sales, Herbert Evanson, in Edgar's own words (2004 interview with the author), ". . . showed me the decline of Chivas. . . . I don't remember the date, but I went to my father and told him that we had to change the whisky, the package and the advertising."

Arguing for a complete product makeover, Edgar Bronfman suggested, first and foremost, that the whisky be made less heavy. Since its reintroduction nearly a decade before, Chivas Regal, as developed by master blender Charles Julian in the early 1950s, had been a marriage of 65 percent malt whiskies and 35 percent grain whiskies. A highly skilled blender himself, Edgar recommended to Sam that the ratio tip more in favor of grain whisky. Sam, at first, was unconvinced. The running-in-place sales figures, though, supported Edgar's points of contention.

"To his credit, Father agreed to all three [of my suggestions], and designed the present package himself with the help of Gordon Odell. . . . Above all else, what he wanted was a label that projected dignity. He was a Prohibition-influenced distiller, and dignity was necessary to wash away the stain of that era. It was also essential in his lifelong quest to 'be someone'" (from *Good Spirits: The Making of a Businessman*, p. 107).

Edgar Bronfman personally supervised the alterations to the composition of Chivas Regal by daringly shifting the ratio to 40 percent malt whiskies and 60 percent grain whiskies. The bottle was changed from dark green to clear glass to accentuate the striking tawny-amber color of Chivas Regal. The last thing to do was to refashion and redirect the advertising focus. Edgar felt that the Chivas Regal account should be put up for review and should ultimately be handed over to a house with more creativity than the Lynn Baker Agency. Sam consented and along with Edgar started talking to other agencies. One of them was Doyle Dane Bernbach (DDB).

In *Good Spirits: The Making of a Businessman* (p. 108) Edgar Bronfman described his initial contact with DDB: "Bill [Bernbach] agreed to meet at Father's apartment at the St. Regis Hotel and make a pitch, but said that he would do no speculative advertising. He would show us the agency's current work and let that speak for itself. I consented to these terms, and Father was taken with Bill and his work. DDB got the account.

"Father tried to convince Bill that the proper campaign for Chivas was 'On a pedestal in every land.' He wanted the bottle of Chivas actually on a pedestal with Rome, Athens, London, Paris, etc. as backgrounds. I guess he knew that Bill wasn't going to give him that campaign, because he had his Montreal flunky, Merle M. Schneckenburger, hire one of the Canadian advertising firms to create a few pedestal ads."

Undeterred, Bernbach proceeded with what he and his crew at DDB thought would be an appropriate theme for the "new" Chivas Regal. At last, Bernbach called Edgar Bronfman and arranged a meeting at the Seagram headquarters in Manhattan to show him the concepts and mockups.

Edgar Bronfman recalled the meeting in 1998: "Bernbach brought the DDB advertising to my office. The ads were very good, but he had one on the bottom which he kept hiding. . . . I finally asked him what he was concealing, Showman that he was, he told me that he had an introductory ad for the new package, but that he didn't think I would dare run it.

"And hence came the ad that literally turned a fading Chivas Regal into the shining star it is today. Bill's concept broke all the rules: it had a ton of copy, and it disparaged the company. The headline read: 'What Idiot Changed the Chivas Regal Package?' The copy explained the reasons (you could now see the whisky, etc, etc). Its conclusion: 'Maybe the Idiot Was a Genius.'"

Edgar Bronfman responded favorably to the sheer brashness and self-mocking tone of the "Idiot" concept and told Bernbach that Seagram would consider running the ads. Reluctantly, Sam agreed to let DDB further refine the ads, though he was clinging tenaciously to his "Pedestal" concept. In deference to his father and to avoid a row, Edgar suggested to Sam that they internally test examples of the two campaigns prior to making a final decision. The close results, with Idiot marginally outpointing Pedestal, surprised Edgar. Nevertheless, the showing was enough for Sam to concede and give the green light to Edgar for the Idiot campaign.

In *Good Spirits: The Making of a Businessman* (p. 109), Edgar Bronfman wrote of his father's decision, "Today, I cannot state categorically that the pedestal campaign would have failed. What is clear is that Father, despite his ego, decided not to stand in the way of an innovative ad strategy, and was richly rewarded for his tolerance."

Rewarded, indeed. For more than the next two decades, DDB created what many advertising executives and experts have viewed as one of the most effective advertising programs for distilled spirits ever designed for the American consumer. The team at Doyle, Dane, Bernbach repositioned Chivas Regal as the quintessential upscale, yet hip and supremely satisfying indulgence, a timeless extravagance that should be judiciously poured, jealously guarded, and even squirreled away in a hidey-hole when guests were expected.

What made the campaign sizzle? The DDB ads clicked because they had the audacity to challenge and even gently taunt consumers while never cajoling or pleading with them to try Chivas Regal. Maybe most important, the ads never talked down to anyone. The bone-dry, clever, frequently naughty, or even snotty humor made them memorable. The DDB copy always assumed that everyone with the means and the brains wanted Chivas Regal in the same way that they coveted Cadillacs, penthouses, diamonds, nightly meals at "21," a torrid affair, and the best fashions. In one of their finest series, the ads poked fun at the lengths that people would go to in safeguarding or hoarding their cache of Chivas Regal.

Many of the best ads simply showed a bottle of Chivas Regal positioned at dead center of the page and had headlines that evoked images from snob appeal to product quality to its lofty price to ultimate gift-giving.

The following are two of the most famous lines used for snob appeal with a photo of a single Chivas Regal bottle:

1. We've given First More Class. (Reference to flying in first class while sipping Chivas Regal)
2. Of course, you can live without Chivas Regal. The question is, How well?

Many ads stressed the quality and price of Chivas Regal with a snotty tone and a photo of a single Chivas Regal bottle:

- If you can't taste the difference in Chivas Regal, save the extra two dollars.
- If anybody tells you that you're paying for the label when you buy Chivas Regal, he's not completely wrong.
- Not all the best things in life are free.
- Why think of it as an expensive Scotch when you can think of it as an inexpensive luxury.
- Your cost of living may go up a little, but your standard of living will go up a lot.

Clever ad copy, along with a photo of a single Chivas Regal bottle in various stages of fullness, often addressed people stingily hoarding Chivas:

- It's a great Scotch. And one of these days I'm going to open it.
- When serving Chivas Regal, do you suddenly become exceedingly generous with your ice cubes?
- To the host it's half-empty. To the guest it's half-full.

Some ads with a photo of a single Chivas Regal bottle were geared to Father's Day and Christmas:

- You can never thank your father enough, but at least you can give him Chivas Regal.
- Our sympathy to all those who get a bottle of Chivas Regal only at Christmas time.
- It's better to give than receive, with certain possible exceptions.

A classic ad about class with a photo of a single Chivas Regal bottle:

- The Chivas Regal of Scotches.

Not satisfied with the initial campaign, DDB created a coexisting campaign that featured line drawings by some of the period's top cartoonists. The situations routinely implied jealousy, greed, snobbery, and envy to humorously drive home the peerless quality of Chivas Regal:

- Man and woman walking down the street arm-in-arm. Man says: "Your Chivas or mine?"

- Drawing of a shipyard dock with a huge ocean liner just pulling away. Dockworkers are looking at cases of Chivas Regal left behind and one says, "They'll be back. They forgot the Chivas."

- Drawing of a fortune-teller saying to an anxious male client, "I see her running away . . . with your savings . . . your bowling trophies . . . your best friend. And now for the bad news . . . they're taking your Chivas."

- Drawing of man sitting at a desk at home, looking up at his wife and asking, "I'm listing our assets . . . how much Chivas Regal is left in the bottle?"

- Drawing of two birds perched on the rim of a birdbath. One says to the other, "Just once I'd like to see some Chivas in this damned thing."

Sam finally got his "Chivas on a pedestal" in one DDB copy-free cartoon in the late 1960s: A well-dressed man is standing left arm across midsection, right hand placed at pursed lips in an art museum or art gallery studiously pondering a bottle of Chivas Regal that has been placed on a pedestal amid a whole host of paintings.

At a sales conference in Majorca, Spain, on February 28, 1980, Martin H. Kreston, a DDB executive who had been close to the Chivas Regal account, gave a speech in which he distilled the elements of the landmark campaign (Hagley Museum & Library). Kreston first pointed out what DDB thought Chivas Regal was lacking when they received the account, saying, "In 1962 Chivas Regal had everything—everything but a personality. Before this personality could take form, there were very specific points that Chivas Regal had to communicate to Scotch drinkers.

"Just once I'd like to see some
Chivas in this damned thing."

One of Doyle Dane Bernbach's most famous cartoons.

They were: age—12 years old; taste—lightness, smoothness; product quality—a blend of the best Scotches available; price—expensive."

Kreston reviewed the planning from the first days in 1962 up to 1980, "Chivas Regal's media plan must be both defensive and offensive. Like a fine-tuned army under the direction of a seasoned general, Chivas must secure its current customers; aggressively attach and attract new customers; and remain flexible enough to commit or withdraw its funds as new situations may dictate. Chivas has consistently done this. . . . Chivas dares to do what other brands do not—and gets away with it.

"Chivas cartoon ads are the antithesis of regular Chivas Regal advertising in terms of size and coloration. But they are consistent with the personality that has been created for Chivas—so nothing is lost and everything is gained from a media point of view."

But the big question was: Had the DDB ad campaigns improved sales of Chivas Regal in the United States? When the agency took over the Chivas Regal account in 1962, around 135,000 cases of Chivas Regal were being sold on an annual basis in the United States. By 1979, the annual case sale total (just in the United States) had risen to 1.125 million cases, a jump of over 733 percent, or an average of 40.7 percent a year. In 1979, Chivas Regal, a deluxe whisky then selling at retail for $16 per bottle ($5 more than the leading brands), was the fifth best-selling Scotch whisky in America behind Johnnie Walker Red (4th), Cutty Sark (3rd), Dewar's White Label (2nd), and J&B Rare (1st).

Chivas Regal, to the World

Sam's vision for his company was that of a global giant, not just a liquor supplier to North America. In 1965, Sam, in his 70s, formed the Seagram Overseas Sales Company to complement the Seagram Overseas Corporation. While Seagram Overseas Corporation, started in 1956, located sites and built plants in foreign locations, Seagram Overseas Sales Company aggressively signed on equally aggressive distributors throughout Europe, South America, Central America, Japan, and Australia.

The mid-1960s proved to be a benchmark era for the Seagram Company Ltd. as Sam and his management team elevated Chivas Regal,

Crown Royal, Seagram's V.O., Seagram's 7 Crown, and most of the company's portfolio to genuine global status. Scotch whisky remained a top priority. The Paisley headquarters, outside Glasgow, was up and running, and plans were being developed for another blending plant in Scotland to be built on a 55-acre site at Dalmuir.

In *Samuel Bronfman: The Life and Times of Seagram's Mr. Sam* (p. 371), Marrus wrote, "Straining for the long-term view, as always, Sam undertook to develop manufacturing facilities far afield. . . . His rationale, which he repeated often to his sons and others in his entourage, was that plants in each of these countries would manufacture for their own domestic market, and would be advantageously placed to export to the others as well. . . . Sam looked increasingly to a global organization, rather than contracting his vision as he grew older."

Doubtless it was Sam's biggest Scotch whisky gambit that had paid off, not only in handsome profits but in advancing the cachet of the entire company. Chivas Regal, his career masterpiece, was viewed not just in the United States but the world over as the foremost deluxe blended Scotch whisky. In the mid-1960s, *Forbes* adroitly pointed out that Chivas Regal was doing ". . . for Seagram's what the Cadillac does for General Motors." International sales of Chivas Regal soared through the late 1960s. By 1970, when Sam was 80 years old, Chivas Regal enjoyed annual case sales of 700,000 in the United States and an additional 500,000 elsewhere in the world marketplace.

Chivas was, indeed, the Chivas Regal of Scotches.

The Strathisla Distillery in Keith.

The Joining of Two Scotch Whisky Giants

WITHIN EIGHT YEARS and five months from 1963 to 1971, the international whisky community lost two of its most influential figures and, as it turned out, the two men most responsible for the broad globalization of Chivas Regal.

First in February 1963, James (Jimmy) Barclay, the flamboyant whisky "lifer" and the Scotsman who had first envisioned the extraordinary possibilities of bringing together Chivas Brothers and Sam Bronfman, died in Glasgow at the age of 77. Barclay was neither a master blender nor a master distiller, but was every bit a master whisky trade businessman. Because of his astute dealings, he left behind a personal fortune of £751,145. As chronicled in the *Scotch Whisky Industry Record* (p. 290), "At the time of his death he was still active on the whisky business, being chairman and managing director at T. & A. McClelland Ltd., a Glasgow firm of whisky blenders and exporters. His connection with the whisky trade began in 1902 when, aged 16, he joined Benrinnes distillery for 2s. [shillings] 6d. [sixpence] per week as a clerk . . ."

Then in July 1971, Samuel "Mr. Sam" Bronfman died in Montreal from prostate cancer, a disease that had plagued and weakened him the last few years of his remarkable life. Edgar M. Bronfman recalled the day of his father's death in *Good Spirits: The Making of a Businessman* (pp. 138–139), "On July, 10, 1971, Charles [Bronfman], Leo Kolber [family confidant and the chairman of the Bronfman family trust, Cemps Investments], and I went to eat dinner at Ruby Foo's, a famous Chinese restaurant in Montreal. We returned to Leo's house for a cognac, and when the telephone rang, I went directly to the car, knowing that the end had come. Charles and I raced home to find Mother sobbing and wailing."

According to Edgar Bronfman, even though Sam was gone, there was no familial turmoil or blood relation infighting about the line of succession for the family business. Sam had famously hot and cold relationships with his brothers and their sons and had schooled his own sons well in the arts of power and supremacy. "Charles and I told Uncle Allan [their uncle and Sam's brother] that I would become president and that Charles would become executive vice president of Distillers Corporation-Seagrams Ltd. He was very gracious about it." That, by all appearances, was as far as the discussion advanced.

As for what Edgar had learned, good and bad, from working closely with his father for two decades, he elucidated candidly in *Good Spirits* (pp. 139–143) in 1998, "For all his faults, he was a great businessman, and he passed on much of his knowledge by example. Perhaps the most important thing I learned from him was a global concept . . . he knew that quality was of paramount importance, and that it could never be compromised. He took enormous pride in Seagram's products. . . . He always strove to create or acquire top-of-the-line brands. . . . Though he had no formal business training, Father had great instincts, particularly in the areas of advertising and packaging. There was no such thing as 'marketing' when he was building the business, but he grasped the essence of it and singlehandedly turned Seagram into the dominant force in the industry."

The one mistake that Sam regretted late in his life was the blind eye he had turned to vodka all through the 1950s and 1960s. Said Sam of this rare, if glaring oversight, "Yeah, I've made mistakes. The biggest was vodka. I never believed the public would want to buy something with no taste to it. My whole life was built on blending flavors."

Like anyone who moves mountains through the raw vitality of their life's deeds, Sam's faults were as numerous and deeply rooted as his virtues and innate abilities. In *Good Spirits* (p. 141), Edgar Bronfman revealed, "Father let his ego dominate everything. He did things that pleased his vanity, whatever they were. . . . The insecurity so intrinsic to father's character kept him from ever fully trusting anyone. . . . Father's insecurity, coupled with his ego and horrible temper, also prevented anyone from offering constructive criticism. Even those closest to father were loath to contradict him, and were thus reduced to sycophants. . . . Father's wealth meant very little to him in the material sense; rather, it symbolized 'arriving'."

Yet Edgar missed Sam after his death. "Indeed, life without Father was not at all what I had imagined it would be . . . his absence left a huge void. For all my rebellion, I deeply missed the discipline he had brought to bear . . ."

In the early autumn of 1971, however, it was time for Edgar and Charles Bronfman to get back to running DC-SL as their father had wished and had so designated. In the months prior to Sam's demise, Edgar had begun exploring the possibility of becoming invested in another legendary Scotch whisky company, The Glenlivet Distillers Ltd., the Highland company of Captain William Henry Smith Grant, the great-great-nephew of founder George Smith. Sam had expressed his support for the idea. Aside from controlling and operating such respected malt distilleries as Glen Grant, Longmorn, Caperdonach, and Benriach, the firm was owner of the distillery whose malt whisky was an important part of the Chivas Regal recipe, the near-mythical malt whisky of The Glenlivet.

In a 2004 interview, Edgar Bronfman remembered his musings on The Glenlivet, "I don't know that Father had his eye on [The] Glenlivet. I knew that we used quite a lot of it in the Chivas Regal blend, and I thought that if there was a path beyond Chivas for those who wanted something more impressive, then a single malt with the name 'The Glenlivet' would be the brand."

Snaring the Next Piece of Seagram's
Scotch Whisky Puzzle

With annual sales exceeding well past $1 billion for Distillers Corporation-Seagrams Ltd. through the 1970s and with Sam's pet project Chivas Regal passing the two-million-cases-a-year mark in international sales in 1976, first son and Seagram leader Edgar M. Bronfman was poised to make another major move in Scotland the following year.

Like his father, Edgar had learned to follow his instincts in business deals, and to back up those impulses with thorough research. He charged a team of Seagram and Chivas Brothers executives, attorneys, and accountants to assess the soundness of The Glenlivet Distillers Ltd. and then to delineate the possible benefits and pitfalls of an eventual acquisition. The research team discovered that Seagram had an opportunity to acquire through private negotiations a 24.5 percent interest in The Glenlivet Distillers Ltd. Most interestingly, this block would be the largest single holding of the company and could likely be the first step in a general takeover. The joint-group findings went on to strongly suggest to Seagram upper management that they proceed with the stock purchase. Seven advantages of the deal, as the group saw them, far outweighed the negatives and were described as follows:

1. The additional malt whisky production from the five malt distilleries of The Glenlivet Distillers Ltd. would greatly benefit the predicted growth requirements of Chivas Regal sales through the 1980s.

2. The added annual production capacity of 5.8 million gallons from The Glenlivet Distillers Ltd. would likewise ease the stress on the overstretched Strathisla Distillery in Keith, and since Chivas Brothers already had a 12-year purchase contract in place, the rails had been greased. The Chivas Brothers people were used to working with The Glenlivet Distillers Ltd. people on a regular basis; therefore, there would be no need after a deal was struck for either side to endure an "acquaintance" period.

3. Seagram could expect additional revenues from the sale. The single malt whiskies of The Glenlivet, the best-selling single malt in the United States, and Glen Grant, a highly popular brand as a 5-year-old in Italy, were particularly profitable. These two malts especially would thereby strengthen Seagram's Scotch whisky portfolio. Plus, thanks in large measure to the astute management of Bill Smith Grant and Ivan Straker, The Glenlivet Distillers Ltd. had an excellent record of earnings growth.

4. The Glenlivet Distillers Ltd. had an existing inventory of 10 million gallons of malt whisky and 5 million gallons of grain whisky at their disposal. The Chivas Brothers personnel believed that up to 7 million gallons of the malt whisky inventory was from GDL's own distilleries. The group felt that the acquisition would be an inexpensive method of obtaining assets required for one of Seagram's most important and profitable businesses: Chivas Regal.

5. The group recognized the expanding status of single malt Scotch whiskies, especially in the United States in the late 1970s, recording 16 percent per annum growth. Within this category, The Glenlivet, which was then distributed by Seagram in the United States, was the premier brand. In 1977, the group told Edgar, sales of The Glenlivet were 44 percent greater than those of the previous year, and that performance was limited by restricted supply. The select group envisioned growth for single malt Scotches well beyond that seen in the United States. They likewise postulated that the potential for growth was not limited to the United States and by the early 1980s would be global.

6. Seagram was already The Glenlivet's distributor in the United States, so the deeper investment made sense.

7. The prestige and the subsequent press coverage that Seagram would receive by purchasing Scotland's most storied malt distillery could not be overestimated. It would have positive spillover to all Seagram Scotches, most importantly, Chivas Regal, the acknowledged global leader of deluxe blended Scotch whiskies.

The joint group concluded by specifying what they called "Other Considerations" that would likely occur in addition to the financial benefits. The first consideration was to protect the quality of Chivas Regal by improving supply and gaining more flexibility. The second consideration had everything to do with out-and-out industry dominance. Suntory, the Japanese drinks giant, owned 11 percent of GDL stock. The team believed that the stock acquisition by Seagram would block rival Suntory from gaining control of this important source of high-quality malt whisky.

For Edgar Bronfman, the team's findings spelled out everything and more that he had sensed to be true and intrinsically positive about the stock acquisition. In early 1978, Edgar flew to Scotland to meet with Ivan Straker, CEO of The Glenlivet Distillers Ltd. and Iain Tennant, the firm's board chairman. At an early stage of the negotiations, nerves became a little frayed around the edges on both sides. In *Good Spirits* (p. 160), Edgar recalled, ". . . I thought they were being a little greedy. But sometimes you lose perspective in the heat of battle. When I called Charles [Bronfman] in Montreal to ask his opinion, he told me to 'pay the two dollars,' and after a little more negotiating, we agreed on the price."

Edgar Bronfman paid £46 million (approximately $88 million at the time) for the controlling stake in The Glenlivet Distillers Ltd. He knew that he had made a superb arrangement, writing, "It was a good deal for Seagram. The Glenlivet company sold more than 300,000 cases a year of Glen Grant . . . in Italy. By combining the Glen Grant distribution with our brands, Italy became our most profitable subsidiary in Europe." In Japan, executives at Suntory were disappointed.

The details of the Seagram-Glenlivet deal, as hammered out personally by Edgar, fit all the criteria that Mr. Sam would have demanded had he been at the table: Increase the Seagram distribution network, long the centerpiece of Sam's global strategy and dominance; deal face-to-face fairly but aggressively and get the best deal possible; fill an open spot in the Seagram product portfolio to make the entire book stronger; create an obstacle for the competition; and, perhaps most vital of all, obtain control of the leading brand, the acknowledged icon in its category.

On assessing the transaction, corporate observers agreed that Edgar Bronfman had learned well from his father. There was indeed more than a little bit of Sam in Edgar. The Glenlivet transaction was beneficial for all parties.

Vodka Strikes with a Vengeance

The second half of the 1970s and the whole decade of the 1980s proved to be a disastrous period for whiskeys, brandies, or anything else considered "old-fashioned brown" distilled spirits as American consumers changed tack away from what they perceived as being heavy and outdated. Instead, they leaned heavily toward "white" spirits, especially vodka and rum. Sam's only serious misjudgment of his later years—his belief that vodka would never capture the beachhead in a blended whiskey world—haunted Edgar and Charles. They watched Bacardi Silver (clear) Rum and Smirnoff Vodka bolt to the top of the leader board in 1980, finishing one and two respectively in U.S. total case sales, according to *Business Week* statistics supplied by the Distilled Spirits Council of the United States (DISCUS).

The two brands that had enjoyed one-two status all through the 1960s—Seagram's 7 Crown and Seagram's V.O.—were bumped down the ladder to numbers three and four. Chivas Regal finished the year mired in 33rd place at 1.05 million cases sold, well behind Dewar's White Label (13th place), J&B Rare (14th), Cutty Sark (18th) and Johnnie Walker Red Label (24th).

An article in the *New York Times,* dated April 18, 1976, written by correspondent Peter T. Kilborn, depicted the American consumer movement away from Scotch whisky and all other whiskeys and brandies: "Scotch whisky has just come out of the worst year in memory, and the industry doubts that 1976 will be much better. Scotland's distillers, blenders and bottlers produced 152 million gallons of whisky last year, down 17 percent from the 1974 level.

"Americans are a part of the industry's overall problem. The world's leading consumers of Scotch, importing half of all that Britain sells abroad, Americans have been switching to vodka. Vodka sales now exceed not only those of Scotch in the United States market, but also of home-grown bourbon. . . . Nearly 85 percent of all the Scotch produced is sold abroad and because of an unaccountable surge in demand from Japan, exports actually rose last year, although by an uncharacteristically low 3 percent."

The rise in Scotch whisky interest in the Pacific Rim, especially in the booming economies of Taiwan, Australia, Hong Kong, and Japan during the 1980s, helped Scotch producers but was not enough to offset the freefall decline that was simultaneously happening in the U.S. marketplace. In 1980, blended Scotch accounted for 99 percent of all Scotch whisky produced.

Arthur Shapiro, a vice president of market research at Seagram in New York from 1986 to 1989, witnessed firsthand the deterioration of Chivas Regal in the United States. "Simply put, by the 1980s the brand had lost its relevance. What was once seen as a badge, a status symbol, a sign of connoisseurship no longer applied. Other more relevant lifestyle symbols replaced it. . . . Much of this change in attitude was a Scotch problem in general. America discovered vodka with its easy to drink and fun imagery, leaving the Scotch category and Chivas to 'my father's drink status.'"

Chivas Regal was hardly the only major brand of blended Scotch whisky struggling all throughout the 1980s in the United States. Cutty Sark and J&B Rare also plummeted in popularity. What were the machinations behind the severe declines? Shapiro attributes it in part to a natural changing of the guard in generational attitudes, postulating, "Among earlier generations, the rite of passage that centered on drinking involved working hard to acquire the taste. The silent shudder of the first sip was met with the comment, 'It's supposed to taste bad, you'll get used to it and it will be worth it when you finish the drink.' Among baby boomers, parental counsel on these matters waned and vodka, odorless, colorless, and whose taste was easily masked became the new easy-to-drink rite of passage."

To put it another way, the "Era of the Acquired Taste" had fallen out of favor for sensory experiences that demanded no gradual buildup. The "Instant Gratification" generation was beginning to flex its economic muscles in the marketplace by influencing the direction of the distilled spirits categories.

Some of the blame for the spiral downward of Chivas Regal in the United States during the late 1970s and early 1980s has been placed squarely on uninspired advertising. According to Arthur Shapiro, "The loss of cachet for Chivas was most visible in the advertising arena. In the 1960s, the brand's ads (think the landmark *New Yorker* cartoons) were the Absoluts [the Swedish vodka that exploded in popularity due primarily to a now-legendary print ad campaign] of its day. But, along came Absolut with more contemporary and relevant creative and Chivas was lost in the shuffle. In short, an important factor in the decline [of Chivas Regal] had to do with the lack of compelling creative to turn around the negative attitudes."

By 1985 and 1986, the quest for greater quality and product complexity began to stir in the breasts of affluent American consumers who had become accustomed to beverage alcohol subtleties mostly through their wine explorations. In an expanding economy and with more disposal income available, the movers and shakers in America's major metropolitan areas launched their fascination with single malt Scotch whisky. At a time when Chivas Regal was losing ground in the United States, sales of The Glenlivet, the top-selling single malt in America then and now, were revving up. Edgar Bronfman's decision to lay claim to The Glenlivet Distillers Ltd. looked sweeter and shrewder with each passing year.

Even though global case sales of Chivas Regal hit three million in 1988, Chivas Regal in the United States was another story. Whereas sales of Chivas Regal were strong in other markets, especially Germany, Holland, Mexico, Taiwan, Hong Kong, and Australia, by 1990 U.S. case sales had dipped to 675,000, down 375,000 cases from 1980 (*Jobson Liquor Handbook 1991*, p. 24). Chivas Regal, still the nation's and the world's foremost prestige blended Scotch brand, was in freefall in its most important consumer market.

During the early 1990s in the House of Seagram (the American branch of the company), strategic planners shifted advertising monies away from Chivas Regal and earmarked them for more contemporary brands, most notably Captain Morgan Spiced Rum, the hottest Seagram brand of the period. In the meantime, internal management changes at the top of the House of Seagram were occurring, such as the predestined emergence of Edgar Bronfman's son, Edgar Bronfman Jr., who had joined Seagram in 1982. Edgar Jr. was made president of the Seagram Company Ltd. in 1989 and by the early 1990s was in charge of day-to-day operations.

Edgar Jr. recognizing that his grandfather's favorite brand was languishing in the American market, decided to take decisive action. He created the Chivas Brand Company, whose dictum was to help revitalize the brand in the United States. The idea behind the formation of the company was to make the advertising global and to make pricing and marketing decisions out of a single office, headquartered in London. Edgar Jr. directed London to call all the marketing shots concerning Chivas Regal and The Glenlivet. The affiliate offices around the world were instructed to implement the London office's strategies.

What next occurred, to the further detriment of Chivas Regal in the United States, was a regrettable half decade of intramural guerrilla warfare between the U.S. managers of the brand, based in New York, and the brand decision makers headed by James Espey, based in London. Espey worked for Seagram/London in the Chivas Brand Company from 1992 until his departure in early 1998.

Arthur Shapiro, who had advanced to the position of executive vice president for U.S. marketing, liked the concept of the Chivas Brand Company, but had reservations about the awkward execution of the mission statement. "In my view, this was an intelligent move but it had two shortcomings. First, the people running the brand in the United Kingdom did not have a clue about the U.S. market and were too arrogant to listen. As a result, there were a series of ad campaigns, each worse than its predecessor and often irrelevant to the United States. This frequent change in direction signaled to all, especially distributors, that we didn't know what we were doing.

"Second, the brand was growing around the world but bleeding badly here [the U.S.] . . . the 'underground' strategy of milking the brand, meaning 'managing the decline,' went even further underground.

There should have been a candid confrontation between the Global Brand Group and the U.S. sales management and recognition that the 'fix' in the U.S. would take time. Instead, there was silent discord. 'I'll show them' thinking ruled the day on both sides of the Atlantic."

Robert Dubin, who had helped to shepherd Captain Morgan Spiced Rum to record heights by 1991, was selected by Shapiro to revitalize Chivas Regal and to take marketing command of The Glenlivet. Dubin took control of Chivas Regal and The Glenlivet's U.S. marketing programs in 1992 with the title "U.S. Marketing Director of Seagram Scotches." Shapiro, in Dubin's own words, charged him with "replenishing the aging franchise with a new generation of consumers. . . . The objective was to have the current consumer drink better and more." Dubin believed in appealing to younger drinkers and to different ethnic groups that had gained market share within the American population.

Placing his own all-powerful oar into the muddied waters, Edgar Jr. made the decision to stop the long-running and highly successful DDB advertising campaign and replace it with a more contemporary look. Over the remaining years of the decade, Chivas Regal was represented by no less than seven different print advertising campaigns. Said Robert Dubin of the ad campaign indecisiveness, "The result was catastrophic."

Consumers across the United States would just start getting used to one advertising approach for Chivas Regal when another theme would abruptly replace it. The tepid slogans ran from *What are you saving the Chivas for?* to *Either you have it, or you don't* to *There will always be a Chivas Regal* to *Chivas is !t* to *When you know.* Retail liquor stores owners and distributors complained to Seagram employees about the lack of brand direction. Sales of Chivas Regal were static.

Amid all the internal wrangling between Chivas Brand Company in London and Seagram in New York during the early to mid-1990s, the primary direct competitor of Chivas Regal, Johnnie Walker Black Label 12-year-old Blended Scotch from the United Distillers stable [now Diageo], swooped in. It snatched from the grasp of Seagram-New York a crucially important and fast-expanding American consumer segment, the middle-class Hispanic sector—a group that Dubin had wanted to attract to Chivas Regal. The icily brittle bitterness between London and

New York accelerated to the point where Dubin, Shapiro, and their peers felt that the London office failed to comprehend the complexities of the evolving U.S. market, an arena that despite its problems of size and diversity produced the majority of global sales of The Glenlivet and still contributed mightily to Chivas Regal. "As a result, there was a stalemate for over three years. Nothing was accomplished," recalled Dubin.

Overall worldwide sales, however, stayed strong as the well-managed international distribution network of the Seagram Overseas Corporation, under the supervision of Ed McDonell, made Chivas Regal available in over 135 markets by 1995. Sam Bronfman's global concept of Chivas Regal, using North America as his launching pad, had become reality four decades after its reintroduction.

Single Malt America

While the managerial tinkering with the Chivas Regal brand concept continued on both sides of the Atlantic, often at odds with one another, sales of The Glenlivet in the United States marched forward as American consumers gravitated to Scotch whiskies with greater complexity than most blends. In New York, Robert Dubin and Arthur Shapiro both pushed hard for older and rarer expressions of The Glenlivet to appear. Dubin and Shapiro believed that offering an entire lineup of The Glenlivet bottlings would give the brand a greater chance to capture the growing numbers of single malt drinkers who were hankering for more idiosyncratic malt whiskies. With the U.S. marketplace responsible for roughly 80 percent of global sales of The Glenlivet in the 1990s and the consuming public eager for more varied single malt experiences, the London office finally agreed and decided to implement a new program of line extension for The Glenlivet.

Said Dubin of the time, "The single malt consumer was more interested in substance. What was the brand about, its history." Added Shapiro about the public's perception of single malts, ". . . single malt Scotches were the closest spirit to the wine category with their emphasis on connoisseurship and knowledge. And, these attitudes appeared to me to be genuine and studied . . . analogous to port, wine, cigar and other aficionado interests."

Working closely with Chivas Brand Company and The Glenlivet's master distiller Jim Cryle, Dubin, and Shapiro developed other, more exotic malts, such as The Glenlivet 18 year old, The Glenlivet French Oak Finish 12 year old, and the Cellar Collection, a variety of vintage malts from the aging warehouses of The Glenlivet. To instill brand enthusiasm for both Chivas Regal and The Glenlivet, Dubin also instituted an education program designed specifically for the Seagram sales staff in the United States as well as the company's key U.S. distributors. Groups of people were transported by Seagram to Keith, Scotland, where they visited The Glenlivet, the Glen Keith, and Strathisla distilleries to learn about the histories of both brands from experts such as Jim Cryle of The Glenlivet and Colin Scott, the Chivas Regal master blender. To represent Chivas Regal in the United States, Dubin hired an engaging young Scotsman, Jeremy Bell, to travel to the major markets of the nation, hosting tasting seminars for trade and private sector audiences.

Simultaneously, part of the Seagram Chivas restaging program was the introduction of Chivas Regal 18, an older expression of Chivas Regal created by master blender Colin Scott. Edgar Jr. supported the Chivas Regal 18 project, but his father was dead against it. In *Good Spirits: The Making of a Businessman* (p. 159), Edgar Bronfman Sr. wrote, "Not too long ago, I was in London and was shown a package for Chivas Regal 18. *What?* I thought. *Chivas Regal 18?* We'd spent forty years convincing people that Chivas Regal, a twelve-year-old brand, is the best whisky they could possibly buy. Then someone decided to introduce Chivas Regal 18, undermining everything we'd done. . . . When the London people put up a big fuss, I relented and told them that they could try it in some duty-free market in Asia. But it's still a mistake—you don't screw around with a brand like Chivas Regal."

The project went ahead. The new Chivas brand was well received by American spirits critics and is still available in the United States.

But not all Chivas line extension ideas worked. A Chivas concept tried in the mid-1990s, the Century of Malts, a blend of single malts, or vatted malt, from exactly one hundred individual malt distilleries was not as warmly welcomed as Chivas Regal 18 and has since been discontinued. Maybe the worst Chivas experiment of the 1990s was dubbed "Chivas DeDanu," a specially concocted blend geared for younger drinkers in Italy. Recalled Robert Dubin, who was against the idea from the start, "Perhaps the craziest thing I have seen in all my years. . . . We invested $1.5 million for a micro-test market. We kicked off Chivas DeDanu in June and by September the sales were completely dead." Chivas DeDanu was pulled from the Italian marketplace, never to resurface.

A changing of the guard at Chivas Brand Company in London in 1998 occurred when James Espey departed and Mike Spurling took charge. Previously a manager for Heublein, Spurling had worked the U.S. market for three years. Spurling's inclusive and informal leadership style went a long way in repairing relations between the London and New York groups. A single advertising campaign, titled *When you know,* was finally given the chance to settle in and tell the story of Chivas Regal. Nonetheless, global case sales of Chivas Regal started to drop, slipping from 3.55 million cases worldwide in 1997 to 3.2 million cases in 2000 (*Drinks International*, Vol. 30, No. 6, 2002, p. 18). Meanwhile, The Glenlivet line extensions flourished in the United States in step with the growing demand for more single malt whiskies.

For all the noble intentions and hard work of the American and British managers, the Chivas Brand Company, the brainchild of Edgar Bronfman Jr. obviously had not provided the right solutions. It had failed to develop the right marketing and promotion for a revered brand that was still viewed by consumers worldwide as the pinnacle achievement of blended Scotch whisky. But even if the marketing plans had been given time to evolve, the stark reality was that Sam Bronfman's coolly cerebral grandson, affectionately called "Efer" by Edgar Miles Bronfman, was more interested in investing in movies, theme parks, and music than remaining in the alcoholic beverage industry.

The Liquor Industry Equivalent of the *Titanic* Disaster

Longtime Seagram employees described a major shift in focus in this fabled beverage alcohol company from about the same time that Edgar Jr. took charge of the helm as COO in June 1994. From the accounts given by veteran Seagram insiders such as Arthur Shapiro, Robert Dubin, Ralph Pagan, and others, Edgar Jr. largely ignored the spirits and wines divisions, and they were subsequently cast adrift. Marketing plans and promotional projects were scuttled or sent into limbo by indecision. Budgets were cut, or sat unapproved on Edgar Jr.'s desk. Consequently, even old and established brands languished without marketing direction.

The globetrotting scion of Seagram, while offering words of soothing encouragement to his nervous beverage alcohol managers, had his own agenda. Impatient with steady growth from established sources of income, Edgar Jr. wasted no time in dismantling his father's greatest business feat, the ownership by Seagram of 24 percent of the stock of Du Pont, the Delaware-based multinational chemical firm. Reliably profitable year after year, the Du Pont holding that Edgar Sr. had purchased in 1981 at a good price, was viewed as dull by Edgar Jr.

To the shock of old-time Seagram observers and money managers the world over, Edgar Jr. sold the entire Du Pont holding in 1995 at a price that was listed at 13 percent lower than the market rate. The managers of Du Pont were more than happy to buy back the holding at such an advantageous rate. Leo Kolber, old friend of Sam, Edgar Sr., and Charles and the Bronfman family financial manager for three decades, condemned the sale. Said Kolber on his Web site, "Buying Du Pont was the deal of the century; selling it was the dumbest deal of the century."

Edgar Jr.'s ineffectual explanation was that he needed the money to purchase MCA, Inc., the parent company of Universal Studios, which made movies and operated theme parks. It appeared that in Edgar Jr.'s mind, entertainment was "in" and booze was "out." He spent $5.6 billion on MCA. As depicted by journalist Brian Milner in *Cigar Aficionado* (April 2003, p. 68), ". . . Edgar Jr. had no desire to run what he viewed as an old-fashioned business stuck in a rut, whose best source of income was a passive stake in a boring chemical company. And his father agreed." Seagram stock immediately plummeted.

Edgar Jr. wanted a suitable partner with which to build an entertainment empire. In October 1999, he met with Jean-Marie Messier in Paris. As short and blocky as Edgar Jr. was tall and lithe, Messier was the blustery top manager at Vivendi, the French water and utility firm. He, like Edgar Jr., was a fixated entertainment hound. Their initial meeting fueled the formation of a dubious bond and the meeting of out-of-their-league minds that would on December 8, 2000, result in the ill-fated union of Seagram and Vivendi. With Edgar Jr. trading the family's controlling stake in Seagram for what amounted to less than 9 percent of Vivendi, the two giant companies evolved into a single corporate entity, the unholy marriage officially called Vivendi Universal.

Even before completing the deal with Seagram, Messier, an excitable, rash man who described himself as a "Master of the Universe," decided that the spirits and wines divisions, though profitable, would have to be spun off immediately so that Vivendi Universal could focus solely on creating the largest entertainment company the world had ever seen. In early 2001, those Seagram entities, once the prototypes of their industry, went on the sale block. The seemingly irrational strokes spearheaded by Edgar Bronfman Jr. and Jean-Marie Messier threw into chaos all that Sam Bronfman had carefully built with guile, sweat, and guts and all that Edgar Bronfman Sr. and Charles Bronfman had cautiously safeguarded.

Foundational cracks in Edgar Jr.'s deal soon appeared when Messier ran amok, impetuously running up outrageous debts in a furious series of billion-dollar acquisitions that placed the new Vivendi Universal deep in debt. Within two years of the merger, the Bronfman family drinks business was disbanded and dispersed and the family fortune had been devalued by approximately three-quarters of its worth just prior to the deal. In the business press, harsh criticism of Messier's reckless behavior and of Edgar Jr.'s judgment ran rampant. Since he didn't purposely set out to destroy his family's fortune, few questioned Edgar Jr.'s motives; but most observers skewered his questionable business acumen and staggering lack of common sense. As for Messier, the veneer of charm and positive energy failed to mask his deficit of financial engineering skills and management ability. In midsummer 2002, the Vivendi Universal board deposed the self-proclaimed Master of the Universe, Jean-Marie Messier; and Edgar Jr. was found sitting on the sidelines.

Sam Bronfman, a canny character who would never have fallen for the vaudevillian antics of a Jean-Marie Messier, once said about the legacy of Seagram, "Shirtsleeves to shirtsleeves in three generations. I'm worried about the third generation. Empires have come and gone." In the end, it was indeed the third generation that foolishly turned its fashionably dressed back on the very businesses and investment holdings that had formed the family heritage and had fed the Bronfmans' vast fortune.

But in business, the fatal mistakes of one can be turned into the sweet advantages of another. Chivas Regal and The Glenlivet would live to see another, far better day.

Epilogue

The World
of Opportunities

On December 19, 2000, Pernod Ricard S.A. of France and Diageo plc of the United Kingdom proposed a joint bid of $8.15 billion to purchase the wines and spirits portfolios of the Seagram Company Ltd. of Canada, a holding of Vivendi Universal S.A. of France. Vivendi anxiously wanted to divest itself of these holdings to offset debt brought about by its purchase of Seagram's entertainment and beverage alcohol companies. Pernod Ricard, at the time the world's fifth largest beverage alcohol company, pledged under the terms of the framework agreement to raise $3.15 billion while Diageo, the world's largest drinks company, promised to put up the balance of $5 billion.

The division of the Seagram portfolios between Diageo and Pernod Ricard was the crucial issue facing regulatory trade commissions on both sides of the Atlantic. Before the Canadian, American, and European commissions would sanction such a massive joint deal, assurances had to be meticulously spelled out and formally presented by each company stating that unfair advantages would not occur in any European, Canadian, or North American market for either company as a result of the joint purchase. As Pernod Ricard CEO Patrick Ricard recalled in a 2004 interview with the author, "Before the bid was made, Diageo and Pernod Ricard had agreed on the spread of the specific brands . . . so, there was no issue about which company wanted what brands."

The underlying reason for the joint purchase was as clear as grain spirit fresh off the still. Both companies wanted to "plug some of the gaps we couldn't otherwise have done," according to Paul Clinton, president and CEO of Diageo's North American division. It was likewise a "mass" matter of Diageo wanting to further distance itself from its closest beverage alcohol competitor, Allied Domecq. For Pernod Ricard, the deal would allow it to transform itself into a major player in the world's beverage alcohol ranks, becoming number three in size.

Even though Pernod Ricard already owned Scotland's respected Aberlour and Edradour malt distilleries and Ireland's Irish Distillers, producers of Bushmills, Jameson, Redbreast, Powers, and Midleton, it coveted the big-ticket Scotch whiskies of Chivas Regal, The Glenlivet, and Glen Grant and to lesser degrees the famed cognac house, Martell, as well as the popular American-made gin cash cow, Seagram's Gin. The Scotch whiskies, especially, Pernod Ricard reasoned, would elevate their global status manifold. Diageo, uninterested in Scotch because of their impressive existing holdings, wanted Crown Royal, the highly profitable blended Canadian whisky, and Captain Morgan Spiced Rum, one of the hottest brands in North America.

"We couldn't have done the deal without Diageo because we couldn't afford [to purchase] Seagram alone. Diageo, on the other hand, couldn't do the deal on their own because of competition issues. Together, we resolved both issues, money and competition, by doing it as a joint bid. And, I might add that we had wonderful cooperation with Diageo throughout the entire process," said Patrick Ricard on the motivations of his company and Diageo.

Without any doubt, the former Seagram brand that Pernod Picard desired more than anything else was Chivas Regal. Said Patrick Ricard of the chance to buy Chivas Regal, "This was exactly the opportunity that Pernod Ricard was waiting for. Our interest was very clear. We were committed right from the beginning [to acquire] Chivas Regal and The

Glenlivet. These are brands that had strong equity still with consumers, but had been given less focus by Seagram in recent years . . . Chivas Regal is our number one priority in our network around the world."

The regulatory commissions on both continents eventually granted Pernod Ricard and Diageo permission to proceed with the deal in late summer 2001. Global sales of Chivas Regal in 2001 hovered at around 3.03 million cases (*Drinks International* Vol. 32, No. 6, 2004). The next year was a delicate time of transition for the brand as Pernod Ricard reshuffled its new deck, now filled with aces. Sales of Chivas Regal in 2002, to no one's surprise, dipped further to 2.76 million cases, the first time since 1988 that yearly final figure had tumbled beneath the three-million-case mark.

But in Paris at the Pernod Ricard S.A. headquarters on Place des Etats-Unis, there was no sense of panic, no biting of polished corporate nails. There was, in fact, a particular glee and a determined satisfaction that with five venerable spirits gems—Chivas Regal, The Glenlivet, Glen Grant, Seagram's Gin, and Martell—a new era had dawned for the company. In December 2001, Michel Bord, president and CEO of Pernod Ricard's stateside operation, announced the formation of a new entity in the United States, Pernod Ricard USA, headquartered in White Plains, New York, north of New York City.

Chivas Brothers Anew

The management team at Pernod Ricard made the early decision in 2001 to maintain Chivas Brothers' autonomous status, keeping it as a company operating within a company. As Seagram had successfully done for a half-century, Pernod Ricard let the company run itself from its London and Paisley, Scotland, headquarters. Martin Riley, international marketing director for Chivas Regal and The Glenlivet, describes the situation, ". . . with Chivas Brothers, we have a fully integrated Scotch whisky company managing everything from production and purchasing of spirit right through manufacturing to global marketing and sales. This means that Chivas Regal and The Glenlivet have our undisputed attention and makes us a tight unit . . ."

But since Chivas Regal and The Glenlivet are authentic global brands, how does this setup work with the numerous Pernod Ricard offices scattered around North America, Asia, South America, and Europe? "Chivas Brothers is what is known in Pernod Ricard as a Brand Owner, and oversees their portfolio of Scotch whisky brands globally," explained Chris Willis, the vice president of marketing for Chivas Regal and The Glenlivet for Pernod Ricard USA. "Commercially, they agree [on] long range plans and annual budgets with each market around the world. . . . From a marketing point of view, they set global brand strategy and direction as well as also designing all packaging and global advertising. Pernod Ricard USA [for instance] adapts the global direction to the unique needs of the U.S. market, based on [our] local knowledge."

Through the difficulties that started around 1990 to 1991, including brand neglect, an ownership change and, subsequently, a brand sales slump, how well has Chivas Regal's international image held up going into the first decade of the third millennium? An independent survey on consumer perception about so-called prestige brands was conducted by Synovate, a global research firm, in the spring of 2003. Chivas Regal placed first in brand recognition in the United States, Brazil, France, Spain, Canada, and Singapore and was listed as "most prestigious" in Germany and Russia. Said Gary Williams, senior vice president of Synovate, "Although single malts and more esoteric brands are making inroads among wealthy Scotch lovers, this study found that their bars at home are still stocked with Chivas Regal, which still is a leader among brands when it comes to images of prestige and sophistication."

In October 2003, Pernod Ricard/Chivas Brothers launched the first step in its long-range marketing strategy by unleashing its new electronic media and print advertising campaign, themed "This Is the Chivas Life." The financial commitment was approximately £28 million. The "Chivas Life" campaign was running in 50 nations in 2004, including the pivotal markets of the United States, Puerto Rico, Mexico, Australia, South Africa, Brazil, Taiwan, China, Hong Kong, Germany, Holland, and Hungary. With the executive teams at Chivas Brothers and Pernod Ricard in place by 2002 and the new advertising campaign in place by late

2003, global sales of Chivas Regal in 2003 reflected the commitment of its parent company, by rising 6.5 percent. With Chivas Regal available in over 150 countries, the first half of 2004 worldwide sales of Chivas Regal were even better, jumping a solid 9 percent.

By June 30, 2004, the news was good on all fronts ringing through the corporate halls at Pernod Ricard. International sales of The Glenlivet rose by 11 percent in the first half of 2004, spurred by vigorous sales in the United States. In all, Pernod Ricard reported that sales in its 12 key brands leaped ahead by 4 percent in the first half of 2004, led by Jameson, a blended Irish whiskey, and Chivas Regal and The Glenlivet.

These tantalizing out-of-the-starting-gate results necessarily generate intriguing questions. Said Martin Riley about the early growth and the potential growth, "One major aspect is that Chivas Regal has the absolute focus of the entire organization, Chivas Brothers and Pernod Ricard, much like it received in days of old when it was the premium spirits leader in the late 1970s and early 1980s." Can Chivas Regal again burst through the three-million-case mark and perhaps go for four million? "Yes," answered Riley.

But the focus on Chivas Regal by Pernod Ricard and Chivas Brothers is only part of the story. The other part has to do with The Glenlivet. With archrival Glenfiddich the world's overall number one single malt Scotch whisky (775,000 cases sold globally in 2003), could The Glenlivet with slightly less than 400,000 cases sold in 2003—still number one in the United States but number three worldwide behind Glenfiddich and Glen Grant—ever realistically overtake Glenfiddich as the world leader? "Yes. . . . We have a great opportunity to cross-fertilize some of The Glenlivet's strengths in North America into Europe and in some Asian markets," said Riley in an interview for *A Double Scotch*.

Riley's boss is Christian Porta, the chairman and CEO of Chivas Brothers since January 2004. Porta told reporter Guy Dixon of the *Scotsman* newspaper in an article published on April 11, 2004, "The Glenlivet is a brand in which we are going to invest more and have ambitions in the United States, in Europe and also in Asia." In fact, the decision has been made to invest more internationally in The Glenlivet than in its better-selling sibling Glen Grant because of the heritage linked to The

Glenlivet. Porta makes no bones about wanting to make Chivas Brothers the world's foremost Scotch whisky group.

Chivas Brothers stayed true to their word, relaunching The Glenlivet in late summer of 2004 with the theme, "The Single Malt That Started It All." The campaign's primary focus is the heritage of The Glenlivet and its connection to its place of origin, the river valley known as Glenlivet in Speyside. Coincidentally, news in August 2004 from London's International Spirits Challenge, an annual wine and spirits competition, was encouraging; three The Glenlivets—21-Year-Old Archive, French Oak Finish 1983 Cellar Collection, and 12-Year-Old French Oak Finish—won Silver Medals in the Scotch Whisky Division (*Drinks International*, Vol. 32, No. 7, 2004).

The U.S. market remains a key marketplace, with an audience that responds favorably to whiskey. In early 2004, the Distilled Spirits Council of the United States reported that overall whiskey category sales rose 4 percent over 2002, racking up $11.3 billion in revenues. Scotch whisky accounted for 9.2 million cases of those sales, with one-third ending up being superpremium blended and malt whiskies. Said Kevin Fennessey, senior vice president of marketing for Pernod Ricard USA, "Heritage matters to consumers in the whisky category, which is why these two brands [Chivas Regal and The Glenlivet] have been successful in the past, and will continue to prosper in the future. We talk about The Glenlivet as being The Single Malt That Started It All in our new advertising campaign, and illustrate this with stories from the brand's history, such as the pioneering spirit of its founder, George Smith. . . . Chivas Regal also has a rich history, and it has always been seen as the ultimate luxury. This image remains today, and the secret to growing the brand in the future will be in making this luxury relevant in a stylish, contemporary way to new consumers in their twenties and thirties."

Last Call

One Scotch whisky was designed and born as a deluxe blend in the backroom of an Aberdeen grocery store; the other was conceived in a picturesque natural trough in the Grampian Highlands that was once

Scotland's most notorious hotbed of illicit distilling. One became the unrivaled darling of an irascible Canadian liquor industry baron who took his masterpiece to the world market through guile and organization; the other became the archetype of its class, yet remained within its founding family through four generations spanning a century and a half. One became the world's hallmark blended Scotch whisky extravagance; the other became the best-selling single malt in the twentieth century's largest marketplace. Both Scotch whiskies were and still are the most famous brands in their individual categories. Both are authentic global icons, popular from Tokyo to Hong Kong to Taipei to Sydney to New Delhi to Rome to Paris to Madrid to London to New York to Toronto to Chicago to Denver to San Francisco. Both, as this final page is written, remain unique and historically important works-in-progress.

Nevertheless, one can't help but wonder what James and Alexander Chivas and George and John Gordon Smith would make of all the incarnations and permutations that their two cornerstone Scotch whiskies, now joined under the banner of Chivas Brothers/Pernod Ricard, have withstood and weathered. If they were able to taste their creations now and while doing so gauge the staggering impact that each whisky has had for more than 170 years on the international stage, what might they say? Based on the profiles of all four industrious yet modest Scotsmen, maybe the best guess is that they would simply say to each other and to the millions of consumers who enjoy their Scotch whiskies across the world, "Slàinte mhath, slàinte mhor," meaning "Good health, great health."

Really, what more is there to say?

Appendix

Whisky Talk

Colin Scott, Master Blender, Chivas Brothers Ltd.

Question 1: Why are blended Scotches so vital to the welfare of the Scotch industry?

Answer 1: With malt Scotch whisky being the original whisky of Scotland, and with its origins shrouded in the mists of time, there was great excitement, and even perhaps concerns, when grain Scotch whisky was introduced in the early 1830s. However, this was the small beginning of blended Scotches created by the famous blending houses around Glasgow and Edinburgh. Soon the blenders were enjoying the success of their brands as they spread across the world. Today many of these brands, like Chivas Regal, Johnnie Walker, Ballantine's . . . are internationally known and enjoyed by consumers in all corners of the world.

However, the success of the blended Scotches is due to the skills and passions involved in selecting the finest malt and grain whiskies that make up and deliver the unique taste of each blend. Many of the malt whiskies used in blending are famous single malts in their own right, and this is the fascinating part, these single malts and the blended Scotches thrive together, not only preserving, but also growing the welfare of the Scotch whisky industry. Single malts in general are much more widely written and talked about than blends, and consumers can visit and actually see these romantic distilleries. This plays a significant role in the understanding and appreciation of Scotch whisky but the malts only represent a small percentage of total Scotch consumption globally; and in fact, it is the blended Scotches that are really vital to the welfare of the Scotch whisky industry.

269

Question 2: What is it that makes Chivas Regal *Chivas Regal?* Describe its personality.

Answer 2: Chivas Regal is a global brand and probably one of the most famous blended Scotch whiskies in the world, which partly makes Chivas Regal *Chivas Regal.* Chivas Brothers Ltd. has a reputation that stretches back over two hundred years of unrivaled quality from which Chivas Regal was born nearly 100 years ago. Chivas Regal 12 years old is a premium blended Scotch whisky that has a unique taste that is multifaceted with flavors without any single character in predominance and therefore appeals to and is appreciated by a wide range of consumers. These flavors and characters hide behind each other and have to be teased out—for example, your first sip may taste of orchard fruits and apples, but the second sip presents honey sweetness and vanilla notes, with the third being hazelnuts and a creamy smoothness—this is the pleasure of the Chivas Regal personality. Little discoveries that translate to a full mouthful. The Chivas Regal personality resembles a diamond with many different tastes, all in harmony, which in total delivers a rich, smooth, and generous taste that is a real jewel. But, more important, Chivas Regal was created as a luxury whisky without siblings. From its very beginnings, it was always a premium Scotch and this is what made Chivas Regal *Chivas Regal.*

Question 3: What is the process that master blenders employ to maintain consistency in batch after batch of a brand?

Answer 3: Every year we purchase and fill into oak casks the new spirit from many different malt and grain whiskies, plus the new malt whisky from our own distilleries, to support all our brands in future years. However, the volumes and makes of whiskies may change slightly from year to year due to closure of a distillery or the overall availability of the spirit from a distillery. This could result in the stocks of inventory available to the blender after 12 or more years for Chivas Regal to vary slightly, year on year. Therefore, year on year the number of whiskies and the percentages of these whiskies in Chivas Regal may change slightly within the recipe, which, of course, is a well-guarded secret. BUT, this is the Art of the Blender.

Although there are these small adjustments, the final taste of Chivas Regal will always be the same rich, smooth, and generous taste year after year after year. Blenders are like conductors of a fine orchestra, the musicians may change but the tune is always the same. This is the Art of Blending, ensuring that our products are always of the same high quality and consistency of taste, year on year.

Question 4: How best can average consumers enjoy Chivas Regal? Neat? On-the-rocks? At what serving temperature? In mixed drinks?

Answer 4: Anyway you decide to drink your Chivas Regal will always be a joy! I recommend, however, that when you pour Chivas Regal, you pour some for your friends as this is a great whisky for sharing the moment whether as an aperitif or a digestif or just because it is so good at anytime. How to drink your

Chivas Regal is a matter of personal choice, whether neat, on-the-rocks, with water, with water and ice, with soda, or perhaps as one of our specially designed cocktails. The best way is your way, whether to sip and intimately explore the flavors or to enjoy the unique taste as a long cool refreshing drink.

Personally, I drink my Chivas Regal with good still water at about a 50/50 ratio. The addition of water opens up the whisky and releases all the magnificent flavors that lie hidden behind the pepperiness of the alcohol. On the occasions when I am in warmer climates than Scotland's, I add no more than a couple of ice cubes as well as the water. The cubes soon melt, making the whisky cool but not cold. The addition of too much ice makes the whisky shy and can flatten its wonderful aromas and flavors.

Question 5: What, in your opinion, is the legacy of James and John Chivas?

Answer 5: After the introduction of grain Scotch whisky, James and John Chivas were presented with new challenges in the business. Because Chivas Brothers already had a tradition of maturing their whiskies in their cellars below the shop, James and John perfected the art of blending aged Scotch whiskies. They also created a style of blend that was universally appealing to the consumer. This "house" style featured smoothness, richness, and the perfect harmony of flavors and was passed down from Master Blender to Master Blender.

They also chose older whiskies with which to blend. Chivas Regal starts at 12 years old, which follows the tradition of the early Chivas blends to be aged more than the standard three years. The brothers aimed high and ensured that their whiskies were of the highest quality and consistency of flavor. They built their legacy on their unrivaled inventory of maturing whiskies in their cellars. In 1909, Chivas Regal was born under the legacy of this style. Today, nearly a century later, honoring the proud traditions of Chivas Brothers helps me and my team to preserve the legacy of James and John Chivas. That reputation is still reflected in all our blended Scotch whiskies.

Question 6: Why is there more than one expression of Chivas Regal?

Answer 6: Chivas Regal 12 years old is the most famous premium blended Scotch whisky in the world, and every second of every day a bottle of Chivas is being opened and enjoyed. Building on that success, it was decided that the loyal and discerning consumers of Chivas Regal should be able to enjoy a very special and indulgent whisky. From this decision, Chivas Regal 18 years old was created in 1997. I hasten to point out that Chivas Regal 18 is not Chivas Regal 12, aged for a further 6 years. Chivas Regal 18 is a unique blend of many malt and grain whiskies specially selected to produce a luxurious and rewarding taste that is very different from Chivas Regal 12.

Chivas Regal 18 was created in the house style of Chivas Brothers with two of Speyside's most famous single malts at the center of the blend, Strathisla and Longmorn. The customary house style of smoothness and richness is found in both Chivas Regal 12 and Chivas Regal 18. It is here that the similarities end, as their tastes are very different. Drinking Chivas Regal 18 is an indulgence that is rewarding, satisfying, and very relaxing, especially in the company of friends and a nice cigar in the most comfortable armchair.

Question 7: What makes Royal Salute so special?

Answer 7: Right from the day it was first produced on the 2nd of June 1953, Royal Salute 21 years old has been a very special whisky. Special, because when our King died in 1952, Chivas Brothers had the skills, expertise and, most important, the stocks of casks of whiskies to produce a magnificent 21-year-old blend less than a year later in 1953. This had never been done before and Chivas Brothers have been able to keep producing Royal Salute every year, and today Royal Salute is the ultimate tribute to Scotch whisky and reflects the legacy of James and John Chivas.

Question 8: How do you drink Chivas Regal when you are away from the office?

Answer 8: As Master Blender for Chivas Brothers, I have nosed, assessed, and tasted wonderful whiskies every day of work. When we taste, we do not swallow for obvious reasons. Therefore, when I am away from the office, that's when I can swallow and really enjoy our Scotch whiskies. Generally my preference is for a blend rather than a single malt. When assessing whiskies in the Blending Lab, we always cut the whisky to 20 percent alcohol by volume (40-proof U.S.) to eliminate the hot alcohol and to maximize the release of the characters. Therefore, it is in this way at approximately 20 percent alcohol that I drink, savor, and enjoy my whisky. I use good still water added in, more or less, equal parts to the whisky in my glass. As I stated earlier, should I be in warmer climates I may add no more than a couple of small ice cubes.

There are occasions however, when your mood demands a long and refreshing drink. This is when I really enjoy the Chivas Cooler, especially with friends before perhaps a BBQ though sadly the weather in Scotland doesn't allow for many! Finally, what is most important is to drink with friends, to drink well, and to drink responsibly and, of course, to drink your Scotch in the way you prefer. Slainte Mhath!!

Jim Cryle, Master Distiller, The Glenlivet

Question 1: Aside from its history, what makes The Glenlivet *The Glenlivet* as a single malt whisky? Describe its personality.

Answer 1: The Glenlivet personality is multifaceted and versatile. It's the definitive leader. It is inspirational, authoritative, and pioneering. The Glenlivet inspired a whole region, which today is Scotland's most important distilling region. The Glenlivet is very approachable, yet has great depth of character.

Quality, above all, has always been its hallmark. The Glenlivet is a whisky of subtlety and grace. It is the single malt that started it all.

Question 2: Is The Glenlivet better as a single malt on its own, or does it likewise make a good "component whisky" in blends?

Answer 2: When George Smith was granted the first of the "new" licenses in 1824, there was only malt whisky. So, Smith created a style of whisky that was to be enjoyed for its fine individual character, smooth and perfectly balanced, fruity and floral, with a honeyed sweetness and lingering finish. The Glenlivet is a whisky fit for a King! As a single malt, it is in a class of its own. It satisfies the most discerning of connoisseurs, yet it is the perfect introduction to malt whisky. Since the introduction of blending in the second half of the nineteenth century, its elegant and balanced character has been sought after for the contribution it makes to a quality blend.

Question 3: What has the global popularity in single malts done for the Scotch whisky industry over the last two decades?

Answer 3: Until around 1980 only a handful of malt whisky brands were known and available outside Scotland since most of the malt production was utilized for blending. However, over the past two decades malt whisky has generated a renewed interest and awareness in Scotch whisky around the world. Consumer interest has helped to maintain and enhance the international prestige of our noble spirit. While the single malt category is still small compared to that of blended Scotch, it is steadily growing and stirs consumer awareness way out of proportion to its size. In markets like North America, The Glenlivet was the pioneer single malt and has been the number one malt whisky for over half a century.

Question 4: How best can average consumers enjoy The Glenlivet? Neat? On-the-rocks? At what serving temperature? In mixed drinks?

Answer 4: How to enjoy The Glenlivet is, of course, a matter of personal choice. I recommend using good quality glass, not necessarily heavy crystal. Similar to the same way that tea tastes more flavorful when served in a fine china cup, I think good glassware enhances the pleasure of fine malt whisky. The Glenlivet is supremely versatile and is enjoyed just as much either as an aperitif or as a digestif. The Glenlivet is ideal as a warming, reviving drink on a winter's evening or as a long cool drink with ice on a hot summer day.

I always recommend the addition of good still water in order to open up the aroma and flavor. At 80-proof and above, the palate can be overpowered by the alcohol and thus some of the wonderful flavor will be obscured. How much water to add is, again, a matter of personal taste. Similarly, if too much ice is used and the whisky becomes overchilled, the aroma and flavor will be reduced. I recommend serving The Glenlivet at room temperature or slightly below, but never chilled.

Question 5: When consumers are confronted with so-called merchant bottlings of The Glenlivet (Cadenhead's, Gordon & MacPhail, and the like) should they be wary?

Answer 5: I have tasted some excellent expressions of The Glenlivet from reputable independent bottlers. That said, consumers need to be aware that most of these will have come from either a single cask or from a small number of casks and, therefore, the character may be slightly different from what is anticipated. The importance of cask type quality and selection cannot be overstated. Our own bottlings of the core range are always consistent in their individual style because of careful selection. Where there will be variation is in The Glenlivet's different "Cellar Collection" releases. This is so because each year is from different casks and ages. Nevertheless, my job as the distiller is to ensure that the new spirit is consistent day by day, year by year. The variation comes during maturation. It is also worth remembering that age alone is not a guarantee of quality.

Question 6: What is the significance of the older and different expressions of The Glenlivet, namely the 12 year old French Oak, 18 years old, 21 year old "Archive" and "Cellar Collections"? What do they add to an already great 12 year old?

Answer 6: There is currently consumer demand for different and older expressions. While the underlying character is unmistakably The Glenlivet, different ages and cask types add subtle nuances that give people the opportunity to experience and to choose an expression to suit the mood or the occasion. All the while, though, they may still be confident that it is The Glenlivet. In The Glenlivet's case, these various expressions likewise afford people the chance to taste a great 21-year-old whisky, instead of a great 12-year-old whisky. It still amazes me how The Glenlivet can play to different strengths at 12, 18, 21, and even 40 years old. Not many malt distilleries can do that.

Question 7: How do you drink The Glenlivet when you are away from the office?

Answer 7: My personal preference for savoring the standard 12, the French Oak, the 18, or the 21 is two parts whisky and one part good still water. If the whisky is a little warm, I add one ice cube instead of water and allow a few minutes for the ice to start to melt. For the older bottlings, especially those included in the Cellar Collection, the age has given them a mellowness that does not require so much water, even at 90- to 100-proof. For these malts, I add only a few drops of water. Just answering this question has given me a great desire to pour a dram right now!

Appendix

Personal
Tasting Evaluations

THESE TASTING NOTES were compiled from formal tasting evaluations conducted over the course of several years and have largely come from the quarterly newsletter *F. Paul Pacult's Spirit Journal.* The simple rating system uses one to five stars, with five stars denoting a status of Highest Recommendation. Three and four stars are respectively Recommended and Highly Recommended.

The Chivas Regal Blended and Vatted Malt Whiskies

Chivas Regal 12 Year Old Blended Scotch Whisky, 40% AbV

Appearance: Pretty, warm, harvest gold hue.

Bouquet: Delicate, mature, and brimming with ripe notes of heather, apricots, peaches.

Entry taste: Lightly smoked.

Midpalate taste: Toasty, peaty, vanilla, complex.

Finish: Coating, moderately sweet, grainy, soothing.

Rating: Four stars.

Chivas Regal 18 Year Old Blended Scotch Whisky, 40% AbV

Appearance: Deep honey brown.

Bouquet: Layered, peat smoke, bacon fat, butter, raisins; a voluptuous aromatic feast.

Entry taste: Powerful and elegant on tongue.

Midpalate taste: Resiny wood; hints of apricot, nuts; buttery and lip-smacking.

Finish: Seemingly infinite; yellow fruit, butterscotch, vanilla; a blended Scotch classic.

Rating: Five stars.

Chivas Brothers Royal Salute 21 Year Old Blended Scotch Whisky, 40% AbV

Appearance: Medium amber/dusty yellow.

Bouquet: Floral, perfumy, light background peat, heather, violets.

Entry taste: Ripe, fruity on tongue tip.

Midpalate taste: Old oak, dried fruit, candied sweetness, dry cereal; mesmerizingly luscious.

Finish: Luxurious, but neither ropy nor decadent; light smoke.

Rating: Five stars.

Chivas Brothers Royal Salute 50 Year Old Blended Scotch Whisky, 40% AbV

Appearance: Honey/amber.

Bouquet: Full, biscuity, light toffee, nutmeg, vanilla.

Entry taste: Cotton candy, marshmallow, honey.

Midpalate taste: Fruity elements include banana, guava, unsweetened coconut.

Finish: Warming.

Rating: Five stars.

Chivas Brothers Century of Malts Vatted Malts Scotch Whisky, 40% AbV

Appearance: Medium amber.

Bouquet: Gentle waves of mocha, cocoa, malt, keenly biscuity.

Entry taste: Nimble, dry cereal, ethereal peat.

Midpalate taste: Turns deeper/sweeter in the throat; moderate smoke; lightly floral.

Finish: Flashes of iodine, malt, smoke, caramel.

Note: No longer produced, but some is still available in the worldwide marketplace.

Rating: Four stars.

The Glenlivet Single Malt Whiskies

The Glenlivet 12-Year-Old Single Malt Whisky, 43% AbV

Appearance: Golden yellow color.

Bouquet: Aroma is like walking through a florist shop; evergreen, heather, sweet William, rose petal, caramel.

Entry taste: Cookie batter, sweetly grainy.

Midpalate taste: Deceptively complex, layered; apricots, white raisins, pears; the quintessential Speyside.

Finish: Layers of butter cream, dried fruit, honeysuckle; classy and elegant.

Rating: Four stars.

The Glenlivet 18-Year-Old Single Malt Whisky, 43% AbV

Appearance: Topaz/harvest gold.

Bouquet: Malt, sweet oak, mint, honey, estery-fruity, compelling and inviting.

Entry taste: Firmly structured, multilayered, bittersweet.

Midpalate taste: Candied almonds, vanilla, dried apricot, oloroso sherry.

Finish: Crammed with nutty, toffee flavors; silky in the throat.

Rating: Four stars.

The Glenlivet Archive 21-Year-Old Single Malt Whisky, 43% AbV

Appearance: Copper/russet/burnished orange.

Bouquet: Dry, resiny at first, then creamy and floral (orange blossom).

Entry taste: Oaky sweet.

Midpalate taste: Mature, light caramel, red fruit, oloroso sherry; moderately thick.

Finish: Textured, long in the throat and tastes of sweet old oak.

Rating: Four stars.

The Glenlivet French Oak Finish 12-Year-Old Single Malt Whisky, 40% AbV

Appearance: Honey brown.

Bouquet: Ripe, grainy, almost citrusy, floral.

Entry taste: Polite, mildly woody, dry.

Midpalate taste: Sweeter than the entry; some creaminess.

Finish: Long, medium sweet, very satiny.

Note: Replaced by the 15-year-old French Oak Reserve.

Rating: Four stars.

The Glenlivet French Oak Reserve 15-Year-Old Single Malt Whisky, 40% AbV

Appearance: Medium amber/soft orange highlights.

Bouquet: Off-dry to semisweet; scents of fresh pineapple, cedar, paraffin, black tea leaves.

Entry taste: Firm, moderately oily, texturally like velvet.

Midpalate taste: Integrated flavors of ripe peach, pear drops.

Finish: Extended, semisweet, coconut-like.

Note: Replaced 12-year-old French Oak Finish.

Rating: Four stars.

The Glenlivet Cellar Collection 1959 Limited Edition/Cask Strength Single Malt Whisky, 42.28% AbV

Appearance: Yellow/light honey.

Bouquet: Ripe fruit, wax, autumn leaves, dried violets, light smoke.

Entry taste: Peppery, malty sweet.

Midpalate taste: Caramelized onion, beeswax, honey.

Finish: Firm, smooth, sinewy in the throat.

Rating: Four stars.

The Glenlivet Cellar Collection 1964 Limited Edition Single Malt Whisky, 44.8% AbV

Appearance: Deep amber.

Bouquet: Light toffee, milk chocolate, cocoa bean, dried red fruit, walnuts, nougat.

Entry taste: Smoldering, warm, satiny.

Midpalate taste: Mature oaky spirit, cedar/resin, caramel, plum eau-de-vie.

Finish: Firm, velvety, warm.

Rating: Five stars.

The Glenlivet Cellar Collection 1983 French Oak Finish Single Malt Whisky, 46% AbV

Appearance: Topaz/wheat field in August dusty gold.

Bouquet: Grainy, biscuit/wafer-like, light peat, tea leaves, creamery butter.

Entry taste: Moderately oily, off-dry.

Midpalate taste: Pine nuts, vanilla, light caramel.

Finish: Burst of vanilla and oak; plumper than one would expect from The Glenlivet.

Rating: Four stars.

Note: The following five offerings were packaged as one unit in five 200ml size bottles in 1998.

The Glenlivet Vintage 1967 Cask Strength Single Malt Whisky, 53.2% AbV

Appearance: Honey/gold hue.

Bouquet: Closed at first, then it opens up with toasted walnuts, dried red fruit, oaky resin.

Entry taste: Delicate, lightly floral, malty.

Midpalate taste: Off-dry, almost tart, grainy, moderately fruity.

Finish: Lean, clean, medium long, and elegant.

Rating: Four stars.

The Glenlivet Vintage 1968 Cask Strength Single Malt Whisky, 52.38% AbV

Appearance: Bright amber.

Bouquet: Scents of tropical fruits, malt, toasted cereal, a hint of honey.

Entry taste: Butterscotch.

Midpalate taste: Rich, intensely nutty (chestnuts), mildly fruity.

Finish: Long, herbal, woodsy.

Rating: Four stars.

The Glenlivet Vintage 1969 Cask Strength Single Malt Whisky, 52.99% AbV

Appearance: Warm amber/harvest gold.

Bouquet: Rich, highly aromatic; rich malt, sweet cereal, cocoa butter, hard candy, lanolin, toasted almonds, bacon fat.

Entry taste: Satiny texture, layered, creamy.

Midpalate taste: Integrated, harmonious, honey sweet, mildly oaky, roasted/ toasty, concentrated.

Finish: Medium long, creamy/buttery. My all-time favorite The Glenlivet.

Rating: Five stars.

The Glenlivet Vintage 1970 Cask Strength Single Malt Whisky, 57.45% AbV

Appearance: Dusty gold/amber.

Bouquet: Powerful, heady, spirity initially; then double cream, sautéed butter, bacon fat/rancio, molasses.

Entry taste: Citrus, fino sherry, seductive.

Midpalate taste: Richly fatty, nutty, oily, malty, background yellow fruit.

Finish: Warming, extended, full-bodied. Grand.

Rating: Five stars.

The Glenlivet Vintage 1972 Cask Strength Single Malt Whisky, 54.55% AbV

Appearance: Tawny/topaz/amontillado sherry-like.

Bouquet: Hazelnuts, oak, spice, black pepper, truffles.

Entry taste: Toasty, warm, welcoming.

Midpalate taste: Tobacco leaf, rose petals, almonds, fino sherry.

Finish: Medium long, a bit too nutty.

Rating: Three stars.

Biblography

Books: General—Scotland, City of Aberdeen, and Great Britain

Brotherstone, Terry, and Donald J. Withrington. *The City and Its Worlds: Aspects of Aberdeen's History Since 1794.* Glasgow, Scotland: Cruithne Press, 1996.

Fodor's Great Britain 2004. New York: Fodor's Travel Publications, 2004.

Fraser, W. Hamish, and H. Clive Lee. *Aberdeen: 1800–2000: A New History.* East Lothian, Scotland: Tuckwell Press, 2000.

Fry, Peter, and Fiona Somerset. *The History of Scotland.* London: Routledge & Kegan Paul, Ltd., 1982.

Grant, Jamie. *Culture Shock! Scotland: A Guide to Customs and Etiquette.* Singapore: Times Media Private Limited, 2001.

Herman, Arthur. *How the Scots Invented the Modern World.* New York: Three Rivers Press, 2001.

Houston, R. A., and W. W. J. Knox *The New Penguin History of Scotland: From the Earliest Times to the Present Day.* London: Penguin Press, 2001.

Mackie, J. D. *A History of Scotland.* London: Penguin Books, 1991.

MacLean, Fitzroy. *A Concise History of Scotland.* London: Thames & Hudson, Ltd., 2002.

The New York Times Almanac 2004. New York: Penguin Group, 2004.

Porter, Darwin, and Prince Danforth. *Frommer's Great Britain,* 2nd ed. Hoboken, NJ: John Wiley & Sons, 2004.

Porter, Darwin, and Prince Danforth. *Frommer's Scotland,* 8th ed. Hoboken, NJ: John Wiley & Sons, 2004.

Wilson, Neil, Graeme Cornwallis, and Tom Smallman. *Lonely Planet Scotland.* Victoria, Australia: Lonely Planet Publications, 2002.

The World Almanac and Book of Facts 2004. New York: World Almanac Books, 2004.

Books: Scotch Whisky, Whiskey Industry, Distilled Spirits, and Distillation

Alcohol Distiller's Handbook. Cornville, AZ: Desert Publications, 1980.

Brander, Michael. *The Original Scotch: A History of Scotch Whisky from the Earliest Days*. New York: Clarkson Potter, 1975.

Craig, H. Charles. *The Scotch Whisky Industry Record*. Dumbarton, Scotland: Index Publishing, Ltd., 1994.

Cribb, Stephen, and Julie Cribb. *Whisky on the Rocks: Origins of the Water of Life*. Nottingham, England: Earthwise/British Geological Survey, 1998.

Daiches, David. *Scotch Whisky: Its Past and Present*. Edinburgh, Scotland: Birlinn Limited, 1995.

Gabányi, Stefan. *Whisk(e)y*. New York: Abbeville Press, 1997.

Grindal, Richard. *Return to the Glen: Adventures on the Scotch Whisky Trail*. Chevy Chase, MD: Alvin Rosenbaum Projects, 1989.

Grindal, Richard. *The Spirit of Whisky: An Affectionate Account of the Water of Life*. London: Warner Books, 1992.

Gunn, Neil M. *Whisky and Scotland*. London: Souvenir Press, 1977.

Hills, Phillip. *Scots on Scotch: The Scotch Malt Whisky Society Book of Whisky*. Edinburgh, Scotland: Mainstream Publishing, 1991.

Hume, John R., and Michael S. Moss. *The Making of Scotch Whisky: A History of the Scotch Whisky Distilling Industry*. Edinburgh, Scotland: Canongate Books, Ltd., 1981.

Lockhart, Sir Robert Bruce. *Scotch: The Whisky of Scotland in fact and story*. London: Putnam, 1966.

MacLean, Charles. *malt whisky*. London: Mitchell Beazley, 1997.

McDowall, R. J. S. *The Whiskies of Scotland*. Revised by William Waugh. New York: New Amsterdam Books, 1986.

Morrice, Philip. *The Schweppes Guide to Scotch*. Dorset, England: Alphabooks, 1983.

Murray, Jim. *Classic Irish Whiskey*. London: Prion Books Limited, 1997.

Piggott, J. R., R. Sharp, and R. E. B. Duncan. *The Science and Technology of Whiskies*. New York: Longman Scientific, 1989.

Poems of Robert Burns. New York: Gramercy Books, 1994.

Smith, Gavin D. *A to Z of Whisky.* Glasgow, Scotland: Neil Wilson Publishing, 1997.

Smith, Gavin D. *The Scottish Smuggler.* Edinburgh, Scotland: Birlinn Limited, 2003.

Smith, Gavin D. *The Secret Still: Scotland's Clandestine Whisky Makers.* Edinburgh, Scotland: Birlinn Limited, 2002.

Townsend, Brian. *Scotch Missed: The Lost Distilleries of Scotland.* Glasgow, Scotland: Neil Wilson Publishing, 1997.

Wilson, Ross. *Scotch: The Formative Years.* London: Constable & Company, Ltd., 1970.

Books: Seagram Company and Bronfman Family

Bronfman, Edgar M. *Good Spirits: The Making of a Businessman.* New York: G.P. Putnam & Sons, 1998.

Marrus, Michael R. *Samuel Bronfman: The Life and Times of Seagram's Mr. Sam.* Hanover, New Hampshire: Brandeis University Press, 1991.

Newman, Peter C. *Bronfman Dynasty: The Rothschilds of the New World.* Ontario, Canada: McClelland and Stewart, 1978.

Annual Report Supplements

Bronfman, Samuel. . . . *From Little Acorns* . . . : *The Story of Distillers Corporation-Seagrams, Ltd.* Annual Report, 1969–1970.

Magazines, Newspapers, and Trade Publications

"A Taste of Scotland." *Bon Appetit: America's Food and Entertaining Magazine,* Vol. 49, No. 5, 2004.

Broom, Dave. *Whisky Magazine,* Whisky from the Wild Side, No. 10, June/July 2000.

BusinessWeek. February 18, 1967.

Drinks International, Vol. 30, No. 6, 2002.

Drinks International, Vol. 32, No. 6, 2004.

Drinks International, Vol. 32, No. 7, 2004.

Kilborn, Peter T. *New York Times*. April 18, 1976. Dark Days for Scotland's Own.
Milner, Brian. *Cigar Aficionado*. March/April 2003. Sinking Seagram.
Jobson Liquor Handbook, 1991.

Corporate Archives

Seagram Archives. Hagley Museum and Library, Wilmington, DE.

Trade Organizations

Distilled Spirits Council of the United States. 1250 Eye Street, NW, Suite
400, Washington, DC 20005. www.discus.org.

Photographic Credits

All photographs courtesy of Chivas Brothers except for "Tussle for
the Keg."
John Pettie, "Tussle for the Keg," Aberdeen Art Gallery and Museums Collections. Aberdeen, Scotland.
Map: Frommer's Great Britain by Darwin Porter and Danforth Prince, © 2004
Wiley Publishing. Reprinted with permission of Wiley Publishing, Inc., a
subsidiary of John Wiley & Sons.

Index

285